AA004123

ICSNC 2019

The Fourteenth International Conference on Systems and Networks Communications

November 24 - 28, 2019

Valencia, Spain

ICSNC 2019 Editors

Eugen Borcoci, University Politehnica of Bucarest, Romania

Jorge Cobb, The University of Texas at Dallas, USA

Lina Alfantoukh, King Faisal Specialist Hospital and Research Center, Riyadh, Saudi Arabia

Printed from e-media with permission by:

Curran Associates, Inc.
57 Morehouse Lane
Red Hook, NY 12571

International Academy, Research, and Industry Association (IARIA)
412 Derby Way
Wilmington, DE 19810

Phone: (408) 893-6407
Fax: (408) 527-6351

petre@iaria.org

Additional copies of this publication are available from:

Curran Associates, Inc.
57 Morehouse Lane
Red Hook, NY 12571 USA
Phone: 845-758-0400
Fax: 845-758-2633
Email: curran@proceedings.com
Web: www.proceedings.com

Table of Contents

ICSNC 2019

Forward

The Fourteenth International Conference on Systems and Networks Communications (ICSNC 2019), held on November 24 - 28, 2019- Valencia, Spain, continued a series of events covering a broad spectrum of systems and networks related topics.

As a multi-track event, ICSNC 2019 served as a forum for researchers from the academia and the industry, professionals, standard developers, policy makers and practitioners to exchange ideas. The conference covered fundamentals on wireless, high-speed, mobile and Ad hoc networks, security, policy based systems and education systems. Topics targeted design, implementation, testing, use cases, tools, and lessons learnt for such networks and systems

The conference had the following tracks:

- TRENDS: Advanced features
- WINET: Wireless networks
- HSNET: High speed networks
- SENET: Sensor networks
- MHNET: Mobile and Ad hoc networks
- AP2PS: Advances in P2P Systems
- MESH: Advances in Mesh Networks
- VENET: Vehicular networks
- RFID: Radio-frequency identification systems
- SESYS: Security systems
- MCSYS: Multimedia communications systems
- POSYS: Policy-based systems
- PESYS: Pervasive education system

We welcomed technical papers presenting research and practical results, position papers addressing the pros and cons of specific proposals, such as those being discussed in the standard forums or in industry consortiums, survey papers addressing the key problems and solutions on any of the above topics, short papers on work in progress, and panel proposals.

We take here the opportunity to warmly thank all the members of the ICSNC 2019 technical program committee as well as the numerous reviewers. The creation of such a broad and high quality conference program would not have been possible without their involvement. We also kindly thank all the authors that dedicated much of their time and efforts to contribute to the ICSNC 2019. We truly believe that thanks to all these efforts, the final conference program consists of top quality contributions.

This event could also not have been a reality without the support of many individuals, organizations and sponsors. We also gratefully thank the members of the ICSNC 2019 organizing committee for their help in handling the logistics and for their work that is making this professional meeting a success. We gratefully appreciate to the technical program committee co-chairs that contributed to identify the appropriate groups to submit contributions.

We hope the ICSNC 2019 was a successful international forum for the exchange of ideas and results between academia and industry and to promote further progress in networking and systems communications research. We also hope Valencia provided a pleasant environment during the conference and everyone saved some time for exploring this beautiful city.

ICSNC 2019 General Chair

Jaime Lloret, Universitat Politecnica de Valencia, Spain

ICSNC 2019 Steering Committee

Eugen Borcoci, University "Politehnica"of Bucharest (UPB), Romania
Sathiamoorthy Manoharan, University of Auckland, New Zealand
Leon Reznik, Rochester Institute of Technology, USA
Zoubir Mammeri, IRIT - Paul Sabatier University, Toulouse, France
Maiga Chang, Athabasca University, Canada
David Navarro, Lyon Institute of Nanotechnology, France
Christos Bouras, University of Patras / Computer Technology Institute & Press 'Diophantus', Greece

ICSNC 2019 Industry/Research Advisory Committee

Yasushi Kambayashi, Nippon Institute of Technology, Japan
Christopher Nguyen, Intel Corp., USA

ICSNC Publicity Chair

Paulo Gondim, University of Brasilia, Brazil

ICSNC 2019

Committee

ICSNC General Chair
Jaime Lloret, Universitat Politecnica de Valencia, Spain

ICSNC Steering Committee
Eugen Borcoci, University "Politehnica"of Bucharest (UPB), Romania
Sathiamoorthy Manoharan, University of Auckland, New Zealand
Leon Reznik, Rochester Institute of Technology, USA
Zoubir Mammeri, IRIT - Paul Sabatier University, Toulouse, France
Maiga Chang, Athabasca University, Canada
David Navarro, Lyon Institute of Nanotechnology, France
Christos Bouras, University of Patras / Computer Technology Institute & Press 'Diophantus', Greece

ICSNC Industry/Research Advisory Committee
Yasushi Kambayashi, Nippon Institute of Technology, Japan
Christopher Nguyen, Intel Corp., USA

ICSNC Publicity Chair
Paulo Gondim, University of Brasilia, Brazil

ICSNC 2019 Technical Program Committee

Habtamu Abie, Norwegian Computing Center - Oslo, Norway
Alex Afanasyev, Florida International University, USA
Lina Alfantoukh, King Faisal Hospital and Research Center, Saudi Arabia
Talal Alharbi, University of Queensland, Australia
Samr Samir Ali, Abu Dhabi University, UAE
Abdallah Alshehri, EXPEC Advanced Research Center - Saudi Aramco. Saudi Arabia
Mourad Amad, Bouira University, Algeria
Mohammed A. Aseeri, King Abdulaziz City of Science and Technology (KACST), Kingdom of Saudi Arabia
Muhammad Sohaib Ayub, Lahore University of Management Sciences (LUMS), Pakistan
K. Hari Babu, Birla Institute of Technology & Science (BITS Pilani), India
Ilija Basicevic, University of Novi Sad, Serbia
Robert Bestak, Czech Technical University in Prague, Czech Republic
Ashutosh Bhatia, Birla Institute of Technology and Science, Pilani, India
Eugen Borcoci, University "Politehnica"of Bucharest (UPB), Romania
Christos Bouras, University of Patras / Computer Technology Institute & Press <Diophantus>, Greece
An Braeken, Vrije Universiteit Brussel, Belgium
Martin Brandl, Danube University Krems, Austria
Francesco Buccafurri, University of Reggio Calabria, Italy
Dumitru Dan Burdescu, University of Craiova, Romania
Vicente Casares Giner, Universitat Politècnica de València, Spain

Maiga Chang, Athabasca University, Canada
Hao Che, University of Texas at Arlington, USA
Jundong Chen, Dickinson State University, USA
Stefano Chessa, University of Pisa, Italy
Enrique Chirivella, University of the West of Scotland, UK
Jorge A. Cobb, The University of Texas at Dallas, USA
Bernard Cousin, Irisa | University of Rennes 1, France
Fisnik Dalipi, University College of Southeast Norway, Norway
Sima Das, MST, USA
Mehmet Demirci, Karadeniz Technical University, Turkey
Poonam Dharam, Saginaw Valley State University, USA
Mustapha Djeddou, National Polytechnic School (ENP), Algiers, Algeria
Gulustan Dogan, Yildiz Technical University, Istanbul, Turkey
Jawad Drissi, Cameron University, USA
Safwan El Assad, University of Nantes, France
Müge Erel-Özçevik, Istanbul Technical University, Turkey
Marcos Fagundes Caetano, University of Brasilia, Brazil
Mah-Rukh Fida, SimulaMet, Oslo, Norway
Bin Fu, University of Texas Rio Grande Valley, USA
Marco Furini, University of Modena and Reggio Emilia, Italy
Katja Gilly, Universidad Miguel Hernández, Spain
Hector Marco Gisbert, University of the West of Scotland, UK
Paulo Gondim, University of Brasilia, Brazil
Rich Groves, A10 Networks, USA
Anna Guerra, University of Bologna, Italy
Barbara Guidi, University of Pisa, Italy
Youcef Hammal, USTHB University Bab-Ezzouar, Algeria
Eman Hammad, University of Toronto, Canada
Najam UL Hasan, Dhofar University, Salalah, Oman
Peter Hillmann, Bundeswehr University Munich, Germany
Md Shafaeat Hossain, Southern Connecticut State University, USA
Chitra Javali, UNSW Sydney, Australia
Muhammad Javed, Cameron University, USA
Magnus Jonsson, Halmstad University, Sweden
Yasushi Kambayashi, Nippon Institute of Technology, Japan
Sarah Kamel, Télécom ParisTech, France
Sokratis K. Katsikas, Norwegian University of Science & Technology (NTNU), Norway
A. S. M. Kayes, La Trobe University, Australia
Jinoh Kim, Texas A&M University-Commerce, USA
Yagmur Kirkagac, Netas Telecommunication Inc., Turkey
Peng-Yong Kong, Khalifa University, United Arab Emirates
Arash Kosari, K. N. Toosi University of Technology, Iran
Michał Król, University College London, UK
Takashi Kurimoto, National Institute of Informatics, Japan
Francesco G. Lavacca, Sapienza University of Rome, Italy
Gyu Myoung Lee, Liverpool John Moores University, UK
Jin-Shyan Lee, National Taipei University of Technology (TAIPEI TECH), Taiwan
Shunbo Lei, University of Michigan-Ann Arbor, USA

Wolfgang Leister, Norsk Regnesentral (Norwegian Computing Center), Norway
Kiho Lim, University of South Dakota, USA
Yang Liu, Nanyang Technological University, Singapore
Shouxi Luo, Southwest Jiaotong University, China
Zoubir Mammeri, IRIT - Paul Sabatier University, Toulouse, France
Sathiamoorthy Manoharan, University of Auckland, New Zealand
Michael McGrath, Intel Labs, USA
Farouk Mezghani, Inria Lille - Nord Europe, France
Sudip Mittal, University of North Carolina Wilmington, USA
Shohreh Monshizadeh, University of South-Eastern Norway (USN), Norway
David Navarro, Lyon Institute of Nanotechnology, France
Christopher Nguyen, Intel Corp., USA
António Nogueira, University of Aveiro / Instituto de Telecomunicações, Portugal
Jun Peng, University of Texas - Rio Grande Valley, USA
Zeeshan Pervez, University of the West of Scotland, UK
Kandaraj Piamrat, LS2N | University of Nantes, France
Paulo Pinto, Universidade Nova de Lisboa, Portugal
Valentin Plenk, Hof University of Applied Sciences, Germany
Aneta Poniszewska, Lodz University of Technology, Poland
Victor Ramos, Metropolitan Autonomous University, Mexico
Piotr Remlein, Poznan University of Technology, Poland
Yongmao Ren, Chinese Academy of Sciences, China
Leon Reznik, Rochester Institute of Technology, USA
Mohsen Rezvani, Shahrood University of Technology, Iran
Sebastian Rieger, Fulda University of Applied Sciences, Germany
Laborde Romain, University Paul Sabatier (Toulouse 3), France
Imed Romdhani, Edinburgh Napier University, UK
Luis Enrique Sánchez Crespo, University of Castilla-la Mancha & Sicaman Nuevas Tecnologías Ciudad Real, Spain
Oliver Schneider, DIPF - Deutsches Institut für Internationale Pädagogische Forschung / Hochschule Darmstadt, Germany
Ahmed Shahin, Zagazig University, Egypt
Alireza Shahrabi, Glasgow Caledonian University, Scotland, UK
Nabin Sharma, University of Technology Sydney, Australia
Roman Shtykh, Yahoo Japan Corporation, Japan
Richa Siddavaatam, Ryerson University, Toronto, Canada
Mujdat Soyturk, Marmara University, Istanbul, Turkey
Marco Aurélio Spohn, Federal University of Fronteira Sul, Brazil
Agnis Stibe, MIT Media Lab, Cambridge, USA
Masashi Sugano, Osaka Prefecture University, Japan
Young-Joo Suh, POSTECH (Pohang University of Science and Technology), Korea
Heru Susanto, The Indonesian Institute of Sciences, Indonesia / Tunghai University, Taiwan
Ahmad Tajuddin bin Samsudin, Telekom Malaysia Research & Development, Malaysia
Do-Duy Tan, Ho Chi Minh City University of Technology and Education (HCMUTE), Vietnam
António Teixeira, Universidade de Aveiro, Portugal
Angelo Trotta, University of Bologna, Italy
Tzu-Chieh Tsai, National Chengchi University, Taiwan
Thrasyvoulos Tsiatsos, Aristotle University of Thessaloniki, Greece

Dalton C. G. Valadares, Federal Institute of Pernambuco (IFPE), Brazil
Amir Varasteh, Technical University of Munich (TUM), Germany
Costas Vassilakis, University of the Peloponnese, Greece
Juan José Vegas Olmos, Mellanox Technologies, Denmark
Washington Velasquez, Universidad Politécnica de Madrid, Spain
Jagannadh Vempati, Kettering University, USA
Jingjing Wang, Tsinghua University, Beijing, China
Yunsheng Wang, Kettering University, USA
Mingkui Wei, Sam Houston State University, USA
Jozef Wozniak, Gdansk University of Technology, Poland
Demir Yavas, Netas Telecommunication Corp. / Istanbul Technical University, Turkey
Quan Yuan, The University of Texas of the Permian Basin, USA
Daqing Yun, Harrisburg University, USA
Chuanji Zhang, Georgia Institution of Technology, USA
Gaoqiang Zhuo, State University of New York at Binghamton, USA

Copyright Information

From Modelling to Designing:
A Streaming Network for Multi-Tenant Digital Twin Platforms

Based on the Reference Architecture for Industry 4.0.
Designed for Cross-Domain Applications.

Christoph Schranz, Mathias Schmoigl, Felix Strohmeier
Internet of Things
Salzburg Research
Salzburg, Austria
[prename].[surname]@salzburgresearch.at

***Abstract*—Modern business models rely increasingly on the interoperability of various Cyber-Physical Systems (CPS) and software systems. Different tenants, like producers, operators, suppliers and maintainers, are interested in different aspects of the system and therefore require different data of an asset. As those tenants demand different subsets of data of a CPS, complex entangled data flows emerge that are difficult to depict efficiently using traditional peer-to-peer data streaming. Even though multiple generic streaming platforms exist, the actual problem of entangled data flows is often neglected. The purpose of this paper is to reduce the complexity of modern multi-tenant, cross-enterprise streaming networks. Methodically, the Reference Architecture Model for Industry 4.0 (RAMI 4.0) is exploited to conceptualize a streaming network architecture that enables the scalable sharing of data between multiple tenants independently of their domain. Based on this concept, a Digital Twin Platform will be designed which will help to realize smart city visions.**

Keywords-CPS; Digital Twin; RAMI4.0; Industry 4.0; multi-tenant; multi-stakeholder; data streaming; streaming networks; smart-city;

I. Introduction

The Reference Architecture Model for Industry 4.0 (RAMI 4.0) was introduced by the German organization "Plattform Industrie 4.0" and is illustrated in Fig. 1. The model spans a three-dimensional room that helps to categorize "Industry 4.0" – components.

With the official publication of its norm DIN SPEC 91345:2016-04 [2] in April 2016, the model has gained momentum in manufacturing, where it supports structuring components and getting a common understanding of a complex architecture. Additionally, RAMI 4.0 comes with the administration shell, which is a conceptual layer that abstracts physical components in order to interact digitally with others [3]. However, a detailed consideration of the administration shell itself is out of scope for this paper, but will be part of further investigations.

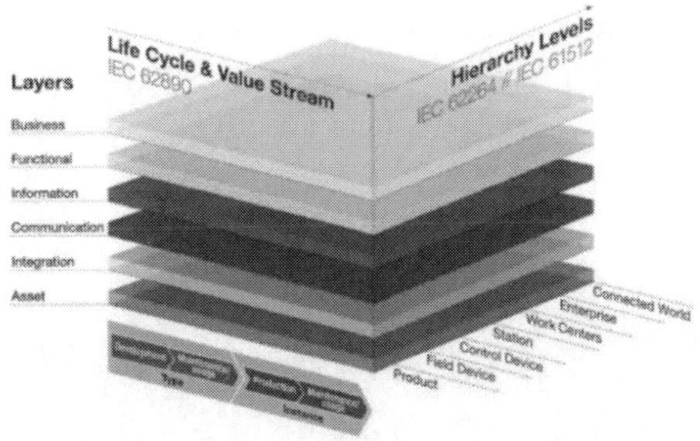

Figure 1. Reference Architecture Model for Industry 4.0 (RAMI 4.0). [1]

The manufacturing sector did not only establish a reference architecture, but also a de-facto-standard for the communication of devices. The Open Platform Communication – Unified Architecture (OPC-UA) is a protocol that is currently supported by a majority of "Industry 4.0" devices. In Fig. 2, OPC-UA and other protocols are mapped onto the ISO/OSI Layers. In this case they are orthogonal to the Life-Cycle/Value Stream and hierarchy levels of RAMI 4.0 to visualize potential protocol lacks in the industrial domain.

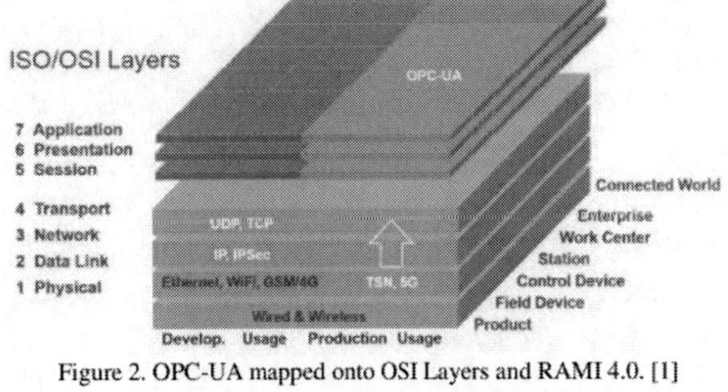

Figure 2. OPC-UA mapped onto OSI Layers and RAMI 4.0. [1]

The blocks marked in blue depict ISO/OSI Layers in the Development and Usage Life-Cycle, where an object only exists digitally, e.g., as a type design. The blocks in grey on the upper right, however, are associated with material instances in an "Enterprise" or "Connected World" hierarchy level. It indicates that OPC-UA fits for a "Work-Center" and levels below, but if data has to be shared across companies, it meets its limitations.

Moreover, the traditional concept of a stream of data from producers to consumers using a set of pipelines lacks when it comes to multi-tenancy, where tenants are interested in different compositions of subsets of multiple CPS. As an example, a single manufacturer of production machines delivers them to several customers. The manufacturer is interested in his/her machine's data. Additionally, the customers - including operators, maintainers and logistic partners - would like to utilize a subset of the machine's data to enhance their own production and maintenance process. Considering this scenario, each machine sends subsets of data to a tenant. However, as soon as additional machines are allowed, the 1:N relation between data producer and consumer expands to a M:N relation, because one machine sends its data to multiple tenants and one tenant can consume data from multiple producers.

As illustrated in Fig. 3, Arquimedes Canedo models data producers and tenants as nodes and subgraphs:

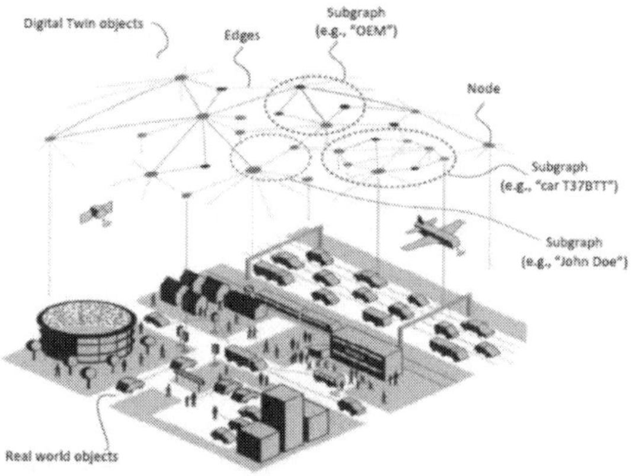

Figure 3. A. Canedo composes Nodes to Subgraphs in a Smart City. [4]

He describes his own scenario as follows:

„[…] real world objects such as cars, people, buildings, airplanes, highways, houses, transportation systems are represented digitally as Digital Twins. A real-world object is not represented by a single node, but by a subgraph of nodes and edges. For example, a car „T37BTT" is represented by multiple nodes and edges in a subgraph." – A. Canedo [4]

Hereby, the important term "Digital Twin" was mentioned, which can be regarded as an abstraction of a material or immaterial thing, which serves multiple purposes [5]. Therefore, a Digital Twin that refers to a real instance is often used as a synonym for CPS.

The representation of a real-world object also depends on its purpose. Different tenants that cope with the same "Subgraph" car during its usage, require different data to perform their job properly:

- The producer is interested in all kinds of feedback data to improve the production quality.
- The operator/driver is interested in data that enables or enhances the service "mobility".
- The infrastructure provider could be merely interested in the car's observation of the environment.
- The maintainer of the car is interested in data that supports his/her job, e.g., model numbers, operating distance/hours, detected anomalies, exhaust gas compositions, etc.
- The supplier of a component is interested in whether an updated version works as expected or not.
- The merchant is interested in parameters that determine the current value of the new or pre-owned car.
- Governments of countries where the car is used need to know, if it complies with national legal regulations.
- The automobile insurance may like to adjust its fee dynamically based on the individual driving style.

Hence, a single tenant requires only a subset of a CPS's data. As soon as the number of assets grows, the requirements on the data flows get more complex, as, e.g., a producer would like to receive data from all his/her assets, the operator of all assets in the plant, and so forth.

In addition to the number of interconnected producers and consumers, an inconsistent protocol, data format and data schema also increases the complexity of a multi-tenant communication network. Moreover, tenants have to be distinct about their privacy, safety and security policies of their assets. Finally, if different platforms for managing data streams are used, the same number of credentials has to be managed as well.

These considerations demonstrate that for multi-tenant and multi-asset scenarios (as they usually do exist in smart factory and smart city visions), peer-to-peer data streams have to evolve to streaming networks to handle the complexity of entangled interests. This paper helps to get a common understanding of cross-domain data streams. It shows how the RAMI 4.0 architecture can be used as a basis for the identification, communication and meta-data management of physical devices and data-streams, which involve implementation considerations of a Digital Twin platform that will overcome domain boundaries.

Therefore, in Section II, a use case is introduced that serves to comprehensibly explain the modelling and designing in the subsequent Sections III respectively IV. Finally, Section V contains our conclusion and shows an outlook on further work.

II. Use Case Introduction

In this section, an example use case is introduced to make the subsequent descriptions more comprehensive. We will start with the persona of Sue, who is a manager of a car rental company:

Sue is a manager of an Icelandic car rental company of connected cars. Iceland is known for continuously changing road conditions and therefore she is worried about the safety of her customers while driving. Slippages on icy roads or flooded pathways may lead to car crashes or other damages; however, if drivers are warned by nearby cars and sensor stations in real-time this risk would be reduced.

As a first step, Sue's company wants to implement a communication between cars to be able to warn the driver from nearby cold temperatures measured by her own car and other cars of her car fleet. Unfortunately, the density of cars owned by her company is too small to make useful statements. Therefore, she wants to buy temperature data from another car fleet and a weather service provider in order to increase the geospatial data density and therefore the safety of her customers. She also knows that her data can be of value for other car rental companies and others.

Briefly, Sue is interested in data exchange with other temperature data providers. For such data exchanges a digital online platform needs to be developed, which allows sharing data between its users. To provide her data on such platform, Sue has to go through the following workflow that can be generalized and adapted for similar use cases:

1. Register her company and users on the platform.
2. Register the connected cars with their available sensors.
3. Share selected temperature data of her cars securely and anonymized to others.
4. Request data from another car rental company and a local weather service provider.
5. Send and receive data securely to and from the connected cars.

III. MODELLING ACCORDING TO RAMI 4.0

In this section, the introduced scenario that can be associated with the transportation sector is modelled according the RAMI 4.. Although this model was originally designed for the industrial manufacturing domain, it is of special interest to demonstrate how such complete reference model can be applied across sectors, also because traditional manufacturing companies are increasingly interconnected with their customers, suppliers, logistics and other business partners, and cars can be considered as moving *assets.*

A. *Modelling Hierarchy Levels*

The first important consideration that has to be addressed is the logical unique identification of tenants, which relates to CPSs, client applications, meta-data management and data streaming. As RAMI 4.0 already defines hierarchy levels for contexts, these are utilized to construct unique namespace prefixes for tenants. RAMI 4.0 uses the following seven hierarchy levels:

Connected World → Enterprise → Work Center → Station → Control Device → Field Device → Product

1) *Abstraction of Real-World CPSs*

In order to map the first two levels, the already familiar and legally clarified domain categorization is utilized. The top-level and second-level domain are mapped to the "Connected World", respectively "Enterprise Level". Hence, the CPS identifiers in our example start with:

at.superrent

Synopsis: [top-level domain].[second-level domain]

As the mapping of "Work Center" and "Station" on real-world contexts is rather ambiguous [6], these levels will be investigated later and the modelling is continued with a bottom up approach where it is of interest which level of RAMI 4.0 can be associated as a CPS.

The term "product" refers to a tangible thing that has no direct digital interface [6] and therefore cannot communicate its own state by itself. Hence, a "product" represents either passive "thing" or a sub-component of an associated CPS like a smart asset, which could be depicted in the meta-data management of our designated Digital Twin platform.

A "field device" is a cyber-physical device that in general does not have a direct connection to the internet. Therefore, it does not abstract the physical world in the internet as a gateway. This step is rather examined by the "control device" level in the RAMI 4.0 [6]. As a result, the "control device" is the lowest level of RAMI 4.0 associated with a CPS. This implies that a CPS like a connected car must be connected both to the internet, as well as to underlying devices that sense or actuate the environment. In our use case, a car represent as CPS and the identifier can be expanded to:

at.superrent.*.*.car1

Synopsis: [top-level domain].[second-level domain].[…].[…].[CPS]
where '[…]' was not discussed yet.

The level "station" can be regarded as a set of CPSs and passive things that ensemble for a specific process or business service. In our case, the car fleet 1 constitutes a mobility service, which consists of multiple connected cars:

at.superrent.*.carfleet1.car1

Synopsis: [top-level domain].[second-level domain[…].[station].[CPS]

The final level of abstraction is the "work center", which organizes multiple stations, i.e., business services within a single company. As the organizational structures of companies vary significantly in their depth and labelling, this level must allow a broad spectrum of hierarchy depths. This is accomplished by allowing an arbitrary number of groups, which are separated with dashes in the global namespace.

Each level considered real world CPS can be identified in alignment of the RAMI 4.0 hierarchy levels as follows:

at.superrent.is-icecars.carfleet1.car1

Synopsis:
[top-level domain].[second-level domain].
[group('-' group)].[station].[CPS]*

2) Namespaces for Real-World Instances

As a further result, the derived namespaces are utilized to identify stations and CPSs globally, which were previously only unique within a specific context. The identifications are used as prefixes for the following types of instances:

a) Topic Identification in Data Streaming

The Internet of Things trend that appeared several years ago enabled CPSs to easily measure and send various system properties in near real-time with a suitable sample rate. This kind of data transfer is commonly known today as (real-time) data streaming.

Data streaming functionality requires an appropriate platform, on which a data stream has certain characteristics. For example, the unique identification of stream topics (similar to the concept of a table in a database; it refers to one single stream) is a fundament of every data-streaming platform. To guarantee, that data on a specific topic can be associated with its station of origin, the namespace for a station is used as a prefix for topics. The suffix of an associated topic is either "internal" or "external" and specifies its type.

Data Streaming topic identification, example: (Note that data are related to a topic.)

at.superrent.is-icecars.carfleet1.internal
at.superrent.is-icecars.carfleet1.external

Synopsis:
[top-level dom.].[second-level dom.].
[group('-' group)].[station].[internal | external]*

b) Instance Identification

The Management of Data about Instances varies significantly across and sometimes also within organizations. Our Digital Twin platform provides a unique namespace to identify basic instances of a semantic standard that distinguishes the CPS from its instances like "Sensors", "Actuators", "Observations" and "Datastreams". This CPS should have the capability to be augmented with arbitrary properties like core-data as well as meta-data.

B. Modelling Layers

As the identification along the RAMI 4.0 hierarchy levels has been described above, the next step is to map basic services of our Digital Twin platform onto the RAMI 4.0 Layers (z-axis).

A Digital Twin can be regarded as an abstraction of the real-world, which serves for multiple purposes [5]. Hence, this description of the term implies that a Digital Twin is neither part of an asset, nor of a business model. It can rather be associated with the functional-, information- and communication layer of RAMI 4.0, to which a data producer or consumer in the control device is connected to. Therefore, the primary goal of any Digital Twin platform is to organize data and data-flows in a way that facilitates decision-making. This process is often based on visualizations and analysis of an organized and cleaned dataset. Therefore, functionalities are mapped onto the functional layer in Fig. 4 should be provided by our Digital Twin platform.

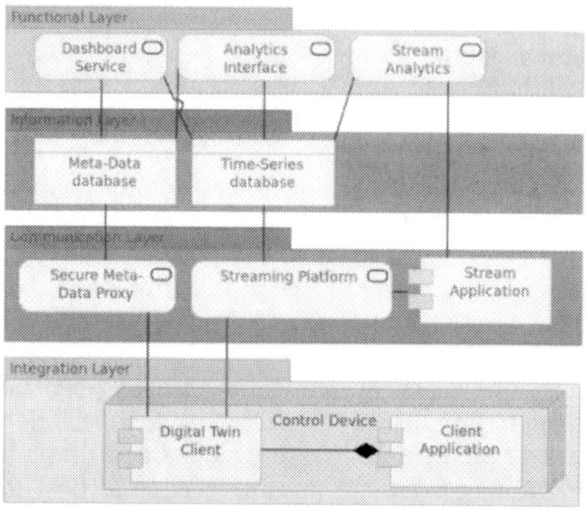

Figure 4. Mapping of Digital Twin services on RAMI 4.0 layers.

A next step is to separate the information from the communication layer, whereby the information-layer is used to store time-series and meta-data. The communication level, in contrast, should be context-free.

For reasons of security, proxies, firewalls or gateways are needed as a part of an extended security mechanism.

C. Modelling Life Cycle and Value Stream

The investigation of life cycle phases of a CPS helps to understand the discrepancies between PLCDM and time-series data better. There are phases in which a product is designed and exists non-materially like its early development. In comparison, a "smart product" in its usage phase produces usage data that varies significantly in schema, update frequency, validity period and so forth. Nonetheless, the rather static data from earlier life cycles can play an important role in subsequent phases, e.g., increased failure occurrences of some models, batch numbers, etc. Conversely, producers of an asset might be interested in some usage data in order to increase the product quality rapidly to a higher level. In conclusion, it is of importance to connect data of different lifecycle phases.

RAMI 4.0 splits the lifecycle axis into four phases, where the first two are immaterial and the last two material:

TYPE: DEVELOPMENT → TYPE: MAINTENANCE/USAGE → INSTANCE: PRODUCTION → INSTANCE: MAINTENANCE/USAGE

Type-related data are usually very purpose-specific and differs even in basic aspects like its schema and complexity. There already exist very sophisticated and implemented software concepts that handles theses phases, like CAD, Software-in-the-loop, Model-in-the-loop and Hardware-in-the-loop [7].

Consequently, the effort for establishing a general semantic for this data would be over-proportionally high. Therefore, domain- and company-specific data semantics likely will not be changed in the near future, which implies, that integration methods have to be developed to reconcile different data appearances.

In contrast to that, there are multiple semantic standards that can be applied on instance-related data, as it is sensed or actuated in most cases and therefore follow the similar patterns.

However, the linkage between data of the *instance:production-phase* and the *instance:maintenance/usage-phase*, as the taxonomy above shows, remains a non-trivial part of a Digital Twin platform. A solution could be again the development of a meta-description for external references.

IV. Designing a Multi-Tenant Digital Twin Platform Architecture

Based on the model described in Section 3, this section will now show how the Digital Twin Platform was designed for the cross-domain use-case including multiple tenants.

A. *High Level Component Architecture*

As the identification of CPS and tenants has been described in section III.A.2), the different interaction types of CPSs and users with the platform has to be considered. Different interfaces have to be provided for CPSs and users. While the communication of CPS narrows down to data streaming and meta-data usage, a user interaction is much broader, as it involves managing of organizations, platform users, meta-data for CPS and observations over an interface. In Fig. 5, multiple components for a Digital Twin platform are illustrated.

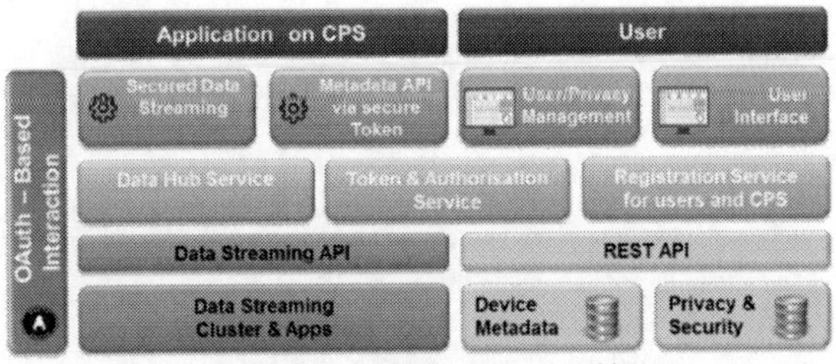

Figure 5. High Level Component Architecture.

The security component "OAuth-based Interaction" is present in each layer, which indicates the usage of security concepts in each service.

Components with blue background represent interfaces, implemented as plain APIs for CPSs, or graphically for users. The Data Hub service enables the scalable sharing of data between tenants, which are discussed in the next section. The Token & Authorization service will manage the access control on various topics for CPS clients. The Registration service connects the user interface with the backend that stores organizations, users and meta-data of CPS.

Finally, the orange components illustrate the secured internal data streaming API, as well as the actual cluster including with its deployed applications for data streaming and sharing.

B. *Multi-Tenant Dataflow*

Based on the high-level component diagram, the previously described use case is depicted in Fig. 6. On the very left, multiple CPSs are listed, grouped by their tenant. Referring to the RAMI 4.0, each CPS would be a "control device" in the hierarchy level and a tenant like the Car Fleet 1 represents a "station".

The second column gives an overview of services that provide security mechanisms and meta-data management through methods of indirection like proxies and advanced API.

In the third column, topics of the data-streaming cluster are listed. Each tenant is connected to exactly two topics that start with the tenant identifier and end with ".internal" respectively ".external". The unique identification of tenants within the platform is aligned on the RAMI 4.0 hierarchy levels.

The colorized arrows in Fig. 6 illustrate the dataflow between tenants, whereby the color represents the tenant of origin. The dataflow is kept clear, as each tenant can publish data only into its own "internal" topic and consume data both from "internal" and "external" topics.

As Fig. 6 implies, the distribution of data to other tenants is done by streaming applications in the stream hub on the right side, where each tenant is connected to one application that parses data sharing contracts into a distribution logic, which is then deployed by the stream hub service. The data sharing contracts will include temporal, as well as geospatial filtering criteria, in order to have more control over data flow to external tenants.

V. Conclusion and Further Work

In the presented work, the RAMI 4.0 was used as a starting point from which a cross-domain model was derived that handles several requirements to abstract real-world instances. The scenario of an Icelandic Car Fleet company was utilized to better illustrate data flows and to demonstrate the usage in a non-manufacturing domain. This approach lead to an architecture that facilitates managing even entangled data flows creating a data-streaming network.

In next steps, the conceptual architecture has to be sharped in regards to:

- Authentication and authorization mechanisms specialized for CPS
- Consideration of RAMI 4.0's administration shell for meta-data management

Additionally, an initial prototype of such a Digital Twin Platform will be implemented to validate and enhance the concept.

ACKNOWLEDGMENT

We would like to thank our project partners from the Digital Transfer Centre Salzburg ("DTZ", https://www.dtz-salzburg.at). DTZ is a collaboration by Fachhochschule Salzburg and Salzburg Research, funded by the regional government of Salzburg under the WISS2025 Knowledge Initiative.

REFERENCES

[1] S. W. Lin et al., IIConsortium and Plattform Industrie 4.0. [Online] Architecture Alignment and Interoperability, 05.12.2017. [retrieved: September 2019] https://www.iiconsortium.org/pdf/JTG2_Whitepaper_final_20171205.pdf.

[2] DIN Deutsches Institut für Normung e. V., DIN SPEC 91345:2016-04 Reference Architecture Model Industrie 4.0 [Online] Beuth, 04.2016. [retrieved: September 2019] https://www.beuth.de/en/technical-rule/din-spec-91345/250940128.

[3] Plattform Industrie 4.0, www.plattform-i40.de. [Online] Structure of the Administration Shell. [retrieved: September 2019] https://www.plattform-i40.de/PI40/Redaktion/EN/Downloads/Publikation/structure-of-the-administration-shell.pdf.

[4] A. Canedo, Industrial IoT Lifecycle via Digital Twins. International Conference on Hardware/Software Codesign and System Synthesis (CODES+ISSS). 2016.

[5] S. Grösser, wirtschaftslexikon.gabler.de. [Online] Springer Gabler, 19.02.2018. [retrieved: September 2019] https://wirtschaftslexikon.gabler.de/definition/digitaler-zwilling-54371/version-277410.

[6] R. Heidel, M. Hoffmeister, M. Hankel, and U. Döbrich, Basiswissen RAMI 4.0. Referenzarchitecturmodell mit Industrie 4.0-Komponente. s.l. : Beuth Verlag, 2017.

[7] S. Lescarret and S. Saliou, Acsystème. [Online] Model Based Design, 01.2015. [retrieved: September 2019] http://www.acsysteme.com/en/model-based-design-1.

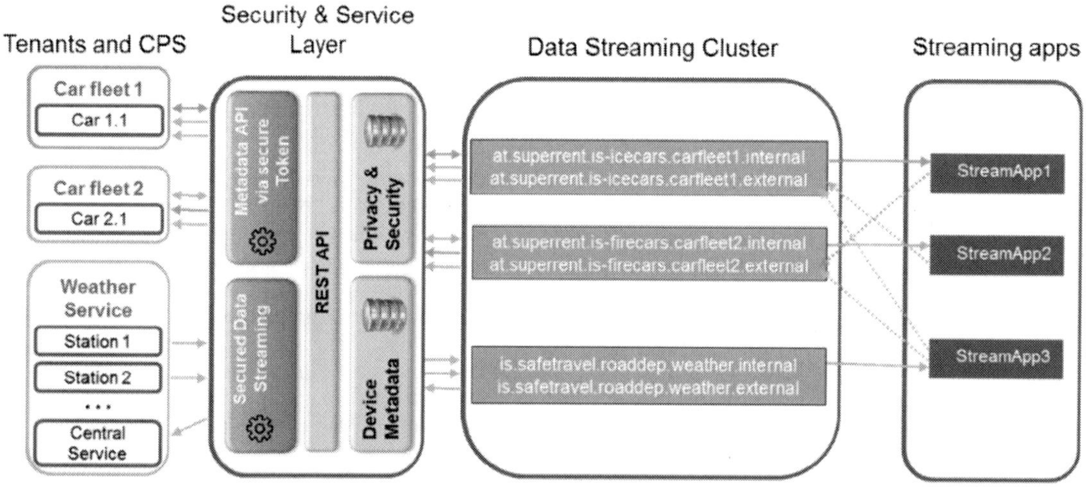

Figure 6. An exemplary Dataflow between multiple tenants.

Stabilizing Voronoi Diagrams for Sensor Networks

Jorge A. Cobb

Department of Computer Science
The University of Texas at Dallas
Richardson, Texas 75080
Email: cobb@utdallas.edu

***Abstract*—Wireless sensor networks are characterized by their lack of physical resources, such as memory, battery power, and communication bandwidth. For this reason, every protocol in the network should be as efficient as possible. For scalability, and given that many sensor networks are deployed to cover a large area, the paradigm of geographical routing has been proposed in the literature. In particular, the Voronoi diagram, where the sensor locations act as generator points in the two-dimensional plane, serve as the foundation of some of these routing protocols. Existing protocols for creating the Voronoi diagram are either not fault-tolerant or not fully distributed. In this paper, we present the first protocol that is fully distributed and resilient to a wide variety of faults. In particular, the protocol is *stabilizing*, i.e., it will converge to a normal operating state regardless of the initial value of its variables.**

Keywords–Stabilizing systems; Voronoi diagram; Delaunay triangulation; Sensor networks.

I. Introduction

Consider a wireless network consisting of a large number of sensor nodes distributed over a geographical area. Each sensor has limited resources, such as memory and battery lifetime, and is capable of sensing its surroundings up to a certain distance. Due to the limited resources, it is crucial that each task performed by the sensor nodes consumes the least possible amount of memory and energy [1].

Greedy routing protocols have been proposed as a scalable solution for routing in large-scale wireless networks, such as large deployments of sensor networks [2]–[5]. In greedy routing, the routing state needed per node is independent of network size. This makes greedy routing attractive for the resource-starved sensor networks. Greedy routing is also known as geographic routing because, for a packet with destination d, a node u selects as the next hop to d a neighbor that minimizes the physical distance from u to d.

For nearly a century, the Voronoi diagram, and its dual, the Delaunay triangulation [6], have had a strong impact on various fields of science and engineering. In the particular context of network routing, Delaunay triangulations are well suited for greedy routing [7]. In general, greedy routing on an arbitrary graph may become trapped at a local minimum and not reach the destination. However, on a Delaunay triangulation, greedy routing is guaranteed to reach the destination.

In this paper, we develop a distributed protocol where each node can compute its Voronoi region, and thus, is able to support greedy routing. Given that the objective is to support greedy routing, the protocol does not require an additional routing mechanism that can be used to aid in node communication. The only assumption is that each node can communicate with other nodes within its wireless transmission radius.

In addition to being distributed, our solution is *stabilizing* [8]–[11], i.e., starting from *any* state, a subsequent state is reached and maintained where the sensors become aware of their Voronoi region. A system that is stabilizing is resilient against transient faults, because the variables of the system can be corrupted in any way (that is, the system can be moved into an arbitrary configuration by a fault), and the system will naturally recover and progress towards a normal operating state. Thus, stabilizing systems are resilient against node failures, node additions, undetected corrupted messages, and improper initialization states.

Distributed protocols exist in the literature that allow each node to obtain its Voronoi region. However, they do not exhibit all our desired features. Algorithms such as those in [12] are fully distributed, but they are not fault tolerant, and they assume an underlying routing protocol exists. Works designed for wireless greedy routing make no such assumption [13] [14], but they have limited fault-tolerance, and in particular, are not stabilizing. Solutions that are distributed and stabilizing exist [15], but they also assume an underlying routing protocol, and are thus not suitable for greedy routing.

The paper is organized as follows. Section II presents a review of Voronoi diagrams and Delaunay triangulations. Section III discusses our approach to find paths between Voronoi neighbors. Section IV discusses the information that must be exchanged between nodes in order to find paths between Voronoi neighbors. Section V presents a more detailed specification of the basic protocol. This protocol is not fault-tolerant, and thus, Section VI presents enhancements to enforce stabilization, and argues their correctness. Conclusions and future work are presented in Section VII.

II. Voronoi Diagrams and Network Model

In this section, we review Voronoi diagrams and Delaunay triangulations. In addition, we present our network model and its relationship to Delaunay triangulations.

A. *Voronoi Diagrams and Delaunay Triangulations*

As shown in Figure 1(i), consider two points, a and x, in the two-dimensional Euclidean plane. The line segment from a to x is shown with dots, and the solid line corresponds to the perpendicular bisector of this line segment. Observe that any point below the bisector is closer to a than to x. Similarly, any point above the bisector will be closer to x than to a.

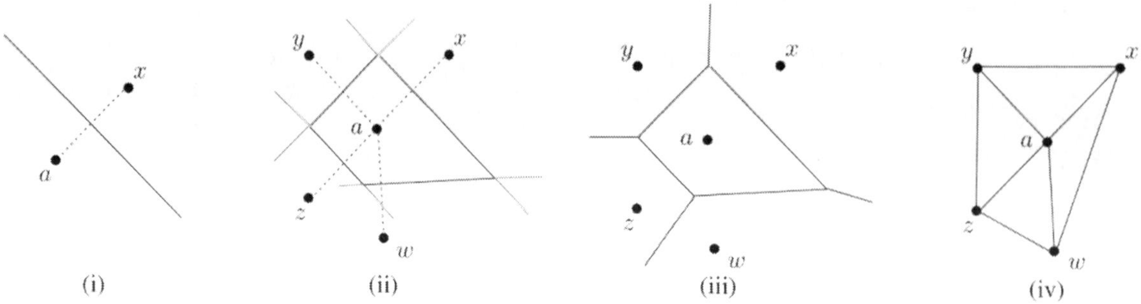

Figure 1. Voronoi diagram.

A *Voronoi diagram* (VD) consists of a set of *generator points* $P = p_1, p_2, \ldots, p_n$ and a set of regions $R = R_1, R_2, \ldots, R_n$. Each R_i consists of all points on the plane that are closer to p_i than to any other generator point in P. In Figure 1(i), $P = \{a, x\}$, R_a are all points below the bisector, and R_x are points above the bisector.

Figure 1(ii) shows the region R_a after a few more generator points are added. Region R_a becomes the convex hull obtained from the intersection of all the bisectors with all other generator points. Finally, Figure 1(iii) shows the regions of all five generator points.

An equivalent structure to the VD is the *Delanuay triangulation* (DT), shown in Figure 1(iv). Here, there is an edge between a pair of generator points p_i and p_j iff R_i and R_j share a face. E.g., point x has three edges: (x, y), (x, a), (x, w), because R_x shares a face with each of the regions R_a, R_y, and R_w. Thus, both the VD and the DT have the same information, but presented in different form.

B. Network Model and Connectivity

We consider a two-dimensional Euclidean space in which a total of n sensor nodes have been placed. Each sensor is assumed to have a transmission radius r. Thus, if the distance between any pair of sensors is less than r, then the pair is able to exchange data messages.

As discussed earlier, sensor nodes correspond to point generators, and each sensor node has the objective of identifying each of its neighbors in the DT (equivalently, the VD). I.e., each sensor node must learn the location of all other sensor nodes with whom it shares a DT edge. Throughout the paper, we use DT and VD interchangeably.

Let $T(u)$ be the set of nodes that are within transmission range of u, i.e., $distance(w, u) \le r$ iff $w \in T(u)$. Let $V(u)$ be the set of neighbors of u in the DT. These are referred to as the *Voronoi neighbors* of u. In Figure 1(iv), $V(x) = \{a, w, y\}$. Some of the nodes in $V(u)$ will be within transmission range of u, and thus, also in $T(u)$, while others will be farther away. The nodes in $V(u) \cap T(u)$ are said to be the *direct* Voronoi neighbors of u.

We assume that the sensor network is connected. I.e., for every pair of nodes u and v, there is a path of nodes $w_1, w_2, \ldots, w_k$, such that $w_1 = u$, $w_k = v$, and for each i, $1 \le i < k$, $w_{i+1} \in T(w_i)$.

Note that it is possible for $w \in T(u)$ but $w \notin V(u)$. This is because other nodes can be in between u and w, and thus, the Voronoi region of u does not overlap that of w. I.e., the fact that nodes can communicate directly does not imply that they are Voronoi neighbors, and vice versa.

In order to learn its set of Voronoi neighbors, each node must be able to communicate with each of them, often indirectly via direct neighbors. For efficiency, we expect each node u to keep as little information as possible, in particular, in the order of $|V(u)|$, which is much smaller than the number of nodes in the network. To do so, we restrict ourselves to *only communicate via direct Voronoi neighbors*, that is, only with nodes in $V(u) \cap T(u)$. Thus, between any pair of nodes in the network, there must exist a path using only direct Voronoi neighbors. Otherwise, the network becomes, in effect, disconnected. We show below that such a path always exists. Before doing so, we present some definitions.

Consider a pair of Voronoi neighbors (u, v). A *Voronoi path* is a sequence of edges in the DT starting at u and ending in v. A *direct Voronoi path* from u to v is a Voronoi path where all the edges are direct edges. That is, there is a sequence of nodes, $w_1, w_2, \ldots, w_k$, such that $w_1 = u$, $w_k = v$, and for each i, $1 \le i < k$, $w_{i+1} \in V(w_i) \cap T(w_i)$.

Theorem 1: (*Connectivity*) For every pair of nodes, u and v, there exists a direct Voronoi path from u to v.

Proof:
The proof is by contradiction. We assume that no such path exists. Therefore, as shown in Figure 2(i), there must exist a cut of the VD such that every pair of Voronoi neighbors have a distance greater than r between them.

From our network model, the sensor network is connected. Thus, there must exit a node a on one side of the cut and another node b on the other side of the cut such that $distance(a, b) \le r$. From the definition of the cut, a and b are not Voronoi neighbors. This pair of nodes is shown in Figure 2(ii). The vertical dashed line is the bisector between a and b.

Let t be the neighbor of a such that the face that R_a and R_t share crosses the line segment between a and b. In order for the face of R_t to prevent a and b from being Voronoi neighbors, it must be that $distance(a, t) < distance(a, b)$.

Consider then the cut of the VD. Recall that a and b are on opposite sides. We have two cases to consider: the cut crosses the line segment between a and t, or it crosses the line segment between t and b.

The former case is not possible. This is because a and t are Voronoi neighbors, and, being in opposite sides of the cut,

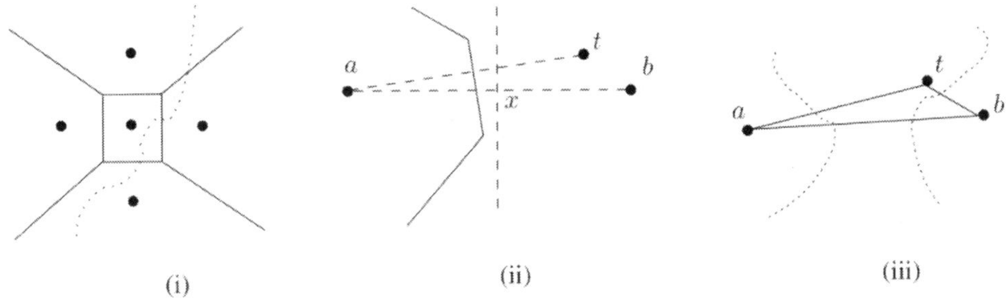

Figure 2. Voronoi path connectivity.

it must be that $distance(a, t) > r$. However, this contradicts what we have shown above, i.e., that

$$distance(a, t) < distance(a, b) \leq r.$$

In the latter case, we have a pair of nodes, t and b, on opposite sides of the cut, such that

$$distance(t, b) < distance(a, b) \leq r.$$

If t and b are Voronoi neighbors, then this is also a contradiction by the definition of the cut. If they are not, then we have found a pair of nodes, t and b, on opposite sides of the cut, such that their distance is smaller than the distance between a and b. Thus, the same argument can be applied again for t and b. I.e., either a contradiction is reached, or we obtain another pair of nodes with lesser distance. Since the different distances between nodes is finite, a contradiction must be reached. ∎

III. ROUTING ALONG TRIANGULATION EDGES

Recall that our objective is for each node to be aware of its Voronoi neighbors. However, some of those neighbors may not be direct neighbors. For example, consider Figure 1(ii). Assume that a has both x and w as direct neighbors. However, although x and w are Voronoi neighbors, they are not direct neighbors, due to their large distance between them. For x and w to learn about each other, it must be done through a.

In general, if Voronoi neighbors are not direct neighbors, they learn about each other via an intermediate node. As a node learns about its neighbors, it is then in a position to be an intermediate node and inform two of its neighbors about each other, and the process continues until all nodes are aware of all their Voronoi neighbors.

In this section, we show how to obtain a path between any pair of Voronoi neighbors, where the path consists only of direct edges in the DT. As shown earlier, such a path must exist. We begin by assigning a label to each edge in the DT, and use these labels to obtain the desired path.

A. Edge Labels and Neighbor Paths

Each edge in the DT can take part in at most two triangles. For example, in Figure 3, edge (b, h) takes part in triangle (i, b, h) and triangle (b, c, h). On the other hand, edge (i, g) belongs only to triangle (i, h, g).

We define a *Voronoi neighbor path* of an edge (a, z), denoted $VNP(a, z)$, as follows. If a and z are direct neighbors, then $VNP(a, z)$ is just the edge itself. Assume instead that they are not direct neighbors, and consider Figure 1(iv).

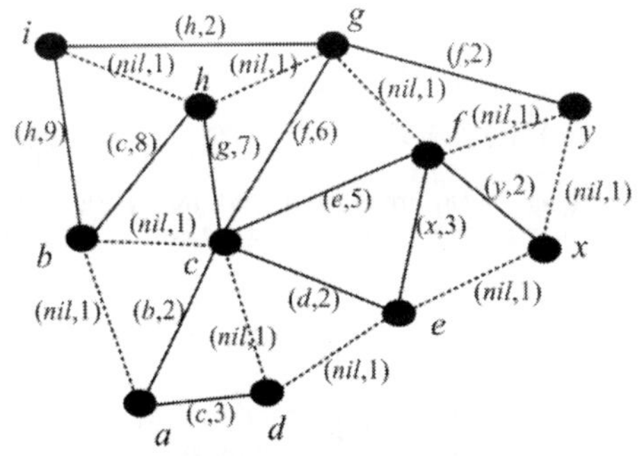

Figure 3. Edge label example.

Edge (a, z) takes part in two triangles: (a, y, z) and (a, w, z). Then, $VNP(a, z)$ is the concatenation of $VNP(a, y)$ with $VNP(y, z)$, or it is the concatenation of $VNP(a, w)$ with $VNP(w, z)$, whichever of these two yields the least number of direct edges.

Each edge is also considered to have a positive integer label that corresponds to the length, in direct Voronoi edges, of the Voronoi neighbor path. Labels can thus be defined recursively to be the smallest value that satisfies the following.

- If u and v are direct neighbors, then $label(u, v) = 1$.
- If u and v are not direct neighbors, and edge (u, v) takes part in triangles (u, x, v) and (u, y, v), then,

$$label(u, v) = min \begin{cases} label(u, x) + label(x, v) \\ label(u, y) + label(y, v) \end{cases}.$$

A simple induction proof can show that the label of each edge is well defined, and that edges with label $h+1$ can be computed once all edges with labels h or less have been computed.

Each non-direct edge is associated with a *hinge* node. The hinge node is the neighbor that defines the Voronoi neighbor path of the edge. In Figure 1(iv), the hinge node of (a, z) will be either y or w, in particular, it will be y if $VNP(a, y) : VNP(y, z)$ is shorter than $VNP(a, w) : VNP(w, z)$, where ':' denotes concatenation. In the event that both y and w provide the same length, we break ties alphabetically.

Figure 3 provides an example of the labels assigned to the DT of a group of nodes. Dashed edges indicate direct edges. All direct edges have no hinge and a label equal to one. Edge (c, a) has a label of two and its hinge is b, because b has a direct edge to each of c and a. Similarly, edges (c, e) and (i, g)

have labels equal to two. Edge (c, g) has a label of six with f as the hinge, because the labels of its edges (f, c) and (f, g) are five and one, respectively.

Finally, note that, in any triangle (u, v, w), there is one and only one node that can be the hinge of some edge in the triangle. For example, consider the triangle (f, c, g) in Figure 3. We have that $f = \mathit{hinge}(g, c)$, but $c \neq \mathit{hinge}(f, g)$ and $g \neq \mathit{hinge}(c, f)$. In general, we define the hinge of a triangle to be the node that is the hinge of the edge consisting of the other two nodes.

B. Finding Paths to Neighbors

We next address how to find a direct Voronoi path between any pair of Voronoi neighbors u and v. This path can be obtained recursively from the definition of edge labels as follows.

$$\mathit{path}(u, v) = \begin{cases} (u, v) & \text{if } \mathit{label}(u, v) = 1 \\ \mathit{path}(u, w) : \mathit{path}(w, v) & \text{if } w = \mathit{hinge}(u, v) \end{cases}$$

Consider again Figure 3, and finding a path from e to f. From the definition of $\mathit{path}(e, f)$, we have:

$$\begin{aligned} & \mathit{path}(e, f) \\ = \; & \mathit{path}(e, x) : \mathit{path}(x, f) \\ = \; & (e, x) : \mathit{path}(x, f) \\ = \; & (e, x) : \mathit{path}(x, y) : \mathit{path}(y, f) \\ = \; & (e, x) : (x, y) : \mathit{path}(y, f) \\ = \; & (e, x) : (x, y) : (y, f) \end{aligned}$$

A node does not need to know the entire topology in order to communicate with its neighbors. We show below that the only required information is the list of neighbors forming its Voronoi region, $R(u)$, and the label of each. Note that $R(u)$ is the same as the neighbors of u in the DT. E.g., in Figure 3, $R(h)$ consists of nodes i, b, c, and g. $R(f)$ consists of nodes c, g, y, x and e, while $R(a)$ consists of nodes b, c, and d.

Before discussing how neighboring nodes communicate, we begin by dividing a node's region into disjoint *segments*.

C. Segments of a Region

The set of direct neighbors of u will be denoted by $\mathit{core}(u)$. Node u can obtain this set from the convex-hull of nodes within transmission range of u.

$$\mathit{core}(u) = \mathit{convex\text{-}hull}(T(u))$$

That is, it is the subset of $T(u)$ obtained from the convex-hull of the bisectors from u to each element in $T(u)$. These nodes form the foundation for $R(u)$, as follows.

Lemma 1: (Core in region) For all u, $\mathit{core}(u) \subseteq R(u)$.

Proof:
If $v \in \mathit{convex\text{-}hull}(T(u))$, it implies that no node within transmission range can block the face of v in the convex-hull of $T(u)$. In order for v not to be in $R(u)$, the face that it provides to $R(u)$ must be blocked by other neighbors whose distance to u is closer than v's. Hence, these nodes must also be in $T(u)$. However, since v is also in the convex hull of $T(u)$, no node in $T(u)$ can block v. Hence, no node can block v from being in $R(u)$. ∎

For terseness, we use the terms *right* and *left* instead of clockwise and counter-clockwise, respectively. Additionally, we use *dir* to represent either *right* or *left*, and $\neg$*dir* to represent the opposite direction of *dir*.

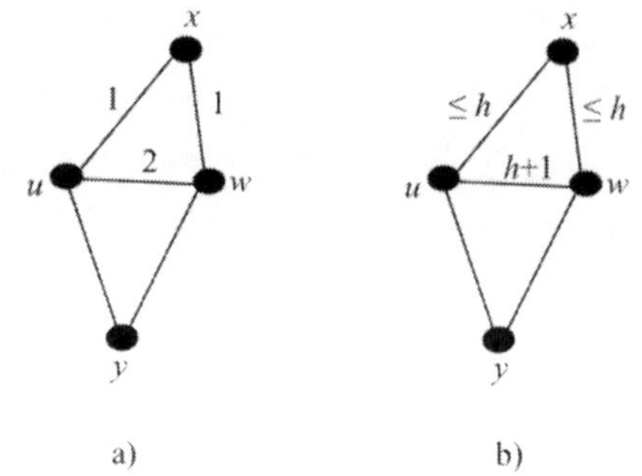

Figure 4. Segment structure induction.

Let v be any Voronoi neighbor of u. Let $\mathit{next}(u, v, \mathit{dir})$ be the next node along direction *dir* on region $R(u)$. For example, in Figure 3, $\mathit{next}(h, i, \mathit{right}) = g$, and $\mathit{next}(h, g, \mathit{left}) = i$. Also, for any pair of neighbors v and w of u, let $\mathit{bet}(u, v, w, \mathit{dir})$ denote the sequence of nodes found in $R(u)$ along direction *dir* starting from v and ending in w.

Let $\mathit{segment}(u, v, \mathit{dir})$ be the longest sequence of nodes, $w_0, w_1, \ldots, w_j$, along the periphery of $R(u)$, starting from core node v, $v \in \mathit{core}(u)$, such that:

- $w_0 = v$,
- for each i, $0 \leq i < j$, $w_{i+1} = \mathit{next}(u, w_i, \mathit{dir})$, and
- for each i, $0 \leq i < j$, $\mathit{hinge}(u, w_{i+1}) = w_i$.

As an example, consider node f in Figure 3. We have:

$$\begin{aligned} \mathit{segment}(e, x, \mathit{left}) &= \langle x, f \rangle \\ \mathit{segment}(e, d, \mathit{right}) &= \langle d, c \rangle \\ \mathit{segment}(f, y, \mathit{left}) &= \langle y \rangle \\ \mathit{segment}(f, y, \mathit{right}) &= \langle y, x, e, c \rangle \end{aligned}$$

Note that all nodes in $R(f)$ are contained in some segment of f. Also, the segments that make up $R(f)$ do not overlap with each other, other than at their starting core node or their last node. We argue below that this is true for all nodes.

From the definition of a segment, a few intuitive definitions follow. Given a neighbor w of u, we define the root, $\mathit{root}(u, w)$, to be the core neighbor v of u such that w is contained in $\mathit{segment}(u, v, \mathit{dir})$, for some $\mathit{dir} \in \{\mathit{left}, \mathit{right}\}$. We argue below that all neighbors must have a root. In the figure, $\mathit{root}(e, f) = x$, $\mathit{root}(e, c) = d$, and $\mathit{root}(e, d) = d$. Finally, let $\mathit{last}(u, v, \mathit{dir})$ be the final element in $\mathit{segment}(u, v, \mathit{dir})$. Thus, $\mathit{last}(e, x, \mathit{left}) = f$, and $\mathit{last}(e, d, \mathit{right}) = c$.

Theorem 2: (Segment structure): For every non-core node w in $R(u)$, there exists a core node v of u and a direction *dir*, such that:

- $w \in \mathit{segment}(u, v, \mathit{dir})$.
- all nodes in $\mathit{segment}(u, v, \mathit{dir})$, other than v, are not core nodes.
- Let p be the node previous to w in $\mathit{segment}(u, v, \mathit{dir})$, i.e., $p = \mathit{next}(u, w, \neg \mathit{dir})$. Then,
  - $\mathit{hinge}(u, w) = p$.
  - $\mathit{label}(u, w) = \mathit{label}(u, p) + \mathit{label}(p, w)$.

Proof:
The proof is by induction over the labels associated with the edges between u and neighbors in $R(u)$, that is, between u and w in the statement of the theorem.

Consider an arbitrary Voronoi edge, (u, w), with $label(u, w) = 2$, shown in Figure 4(a). There are only two possible nodes (one on each side) that can be the hinge, namely, x and y. Let x be the hinge node. Then, by the definition of a label, $label(u, x) = label(w, x) = 1$. Thus, x is a core node, and w belongs to the segment of x.

Assume now that the label of (u, w) is $h+1$, and all edges (u, v) in $R(u)$ with label at most h satisfy the theorem. Again, there are only two possible nodes that can be the hinge of this edge, as depicted in Figure 4(b). Without loss of generality, let x be the hinge node. From the definition of edge labels, the labels of (x, u) and (x, w) are both at most h.

From the induction hypothesis, there is a segment of u that contains x. This segment cannot begin from the direction of w and y, because all edges from any node in the segment to node u must have a label no greater than h, and edge (w, u) has label $h + 1$. Hence, the segment for x begins along the direction of x, and extending this segment by edge (w, u) with label $h + 1$ satisfies the theorem. ∎

IV. Segment Construction

The objective of the protocol is for each node u to become aware of its region $R(u)$. A consequence of Theorem 2 is that $R(u)$ is divided into disjoint segments. Consider Figure 5(a). It shows $R(u)$ and the different segments it comprises. Bold dashed edges belong to core nodes of $R(u)$, and thin dashed edges separate one segment from another. For example, $segment(u, i, right) = \langle i, j, k\rangle$, while $segment(u, m, left) = \langle m, l\rangle$. These two segments do not end at the same node; there is an edge, (k, l), along the rim of $R(u)$, that does not belong to either segment. From the theorem, neither k nor l can be the hinges of trianlge (k, u, l). Otherwise, the segments would both end at either k or at l. Thus, it must be that $hinge(u, k, l) = u$. Similarly, $hinge(u, i, p) = u$ and $hinge(u, m, n) = u$.

Consider $segment(u, i, right)$. From the theorem, $hinge(u, i, j) = i$ and $hinge(u, j, k) = k$. Because u is not the hinge of any of these triangles, information about the existence of these triangles is expected to be received from the root of the segment, i.e., from core node i. Similarly, information about the existence of triangle (u, l, m) is expected to be received from core node m. Once u learns of these segments, it makes the assumption that the hinge of (k, u, l) is itself. It is thus *its responsibility* to inform both k and l of the triangle (k, u, l). In this case, we say that *u is joining* nodes k and l.

To do this join, u will communicate with k and l via their root core nodes i and m, respectively. Node u must inform k that it has a neighbor l, and in addition, what u believes is the label of (k, l). This is represented by the following tuple:

$$\langle k, l, label(k, l)\rangle.$$

Node u must ensure this tuple reaches k. Similary, u sends the tuple

$$\langle l, k, label(k, l)\rangle$$

to node l. In general, joining tuples are of the form

$$\langle destination, neighbor, edge\text{-}label\rangle.$$

Tuple $\langle k, l, label(k, l)\rangle$ has to be routed towards k. To do so, u forwards it to the root node, i. Recursively, node i forwards it in the direction of k, in particular, first in the direction of j. Each of edges (i, j) and (j, k) may correspond to simply a direct edge (label one), or to a longer transmission path requiring crossing multiple direct Voronoi edges.

Note, however, that l may also desire to join a pair of nodes in its region $R(l)$, such as σ and ρ in Figure 5(b), and this join needs to be sent to σ. If u is in the segment of $R(l)$ that contains σ, then this join tuple created by l will eventually reach u. The task of u is to forward this join towards k, which is the next node along the segment of $R(l)$ containing σ. Thus, u has to forward *two* tuples to k (via core node i): a tuple created by u, and a tuple created by l (that was received via core node m). This argument can be extended further, because ρ may also be joining two nodes, r and s in the figure, and the join tuple may need to reach σ. Thus, the tuple is sent to l, who in turn has to send it to u, who in turn has to send it to k (via core node i).

In summary, u does not send an individual tuple to its neighbor k (via core neighbor i), it sends a *stack of tuples*. In this stack, the tuple generated by u is at the top. The remainder of the stack consists of tuples that l wants to forward to k. This in turn contains the tuple from l joining σ and ρ, plus the stack of tuples that ρ wants to send to σ, etc..

Finally, by symmetry, u has to forward to l (via core neighbor m) a stack of tuples that it received from k (via core neighbor i).

V. Hull Construction Protocol

Before presenting our method in more detail, we first give a brief overview of the notation.

A. Protocol Notation

The notation used originates from [10] [11], and is typical for specifying stabilizing systems. The behavior of each node is specified by a set of inputs, a set of variables, a set of parameters, and a set of actions.

The inputs declared in a node can be read, but not written, by the actions of that node. The variables declared in a node can be read and written by the actions of that node. For simplicity, a shared memory model is used, i.e., each node u is able to read the variables of nodes in $T(u)$. To maintain a low atomicity, and thus an easier transition to a message-passing model (see Section VII), each action is able to read the variables of a *single* neighbor.

Every action in a node u is of the form:

<guard> → <statement>.

The <guard> is a boolean expression over the inputs, variables, and parameters declared in the node, and also over the variables declared in a single node in $T(u)$. The <statement> is a sequence of assignment, conditional, and iteration statements that change some of the variables of the node.

The parameters declared in a node are used to write a set of actions as one action, with one action for each possible value of the parameters. For example, if the following parameter definition is given,

par g : 1 .. 2

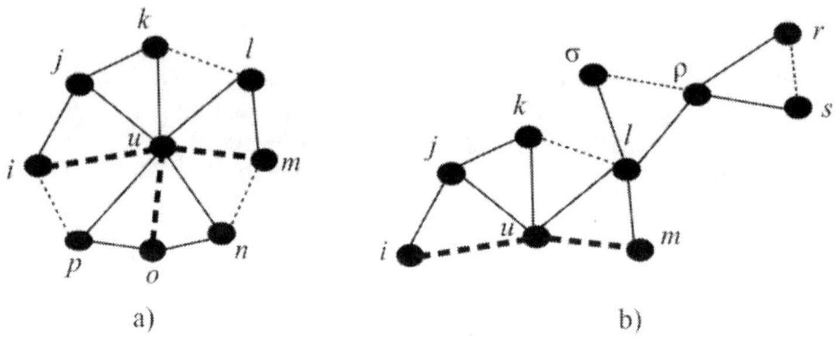

Figure 5. Segment construction.

then the following action

$$x = g \quad \rightarrow \quad x := x + g$$

is a shorthand notation for the following two actions.

$$x = 1 \quad \rightarrow \quad x := x + 1$$
$$\square \quad x = 2 \quad \rightarrow \quad x := x + 2$$

An execution step consists in evaluating the guards of all the actions of all nodes, choosing an action whose guard evaluates to true, and executing the statement of this action. An execution consists of a sequence of execution steps, which either never ends, or ends in a state where the guards of all the actions evaluate to false. All executions are assumed to be weakly fair, that is, an action whose guard is continuously true must be eventually executed.

To distinguish between variables of different nodes, the variable name is prefixed with the node name. For example, variable $x.v$ corresponds to variable v in node x. If no prefix is given, then the variable corresponds to the node whose code is being presented.

B. Method

We next present our protocol in more detail. In particular, we present the specification of an arbitrary node u.

Node u is aware of nodes in $T(u)$, and thus also of *core*(u), because they are within transmission range. We thus assume the core nodes are simply an input to node u.

We represent region $R(u)$ by the two-dimensional array E.

E : **array**[*core*][*left* . . *right*] **of sequence of ID**

The first index corresponds to the core nodes. Each core node can be the root of at most two segments: one in each direction. Thus, the second index is the direction. The element stored in $E[i][dir]$ corresponds to the sequence of nodes in *segment*(u, i, dir). For example, in Figure 5, *segment*$(u, i, right) = \langle i, j, k \rangle$, while *segment*$(u, i, left)$ = **nil** because there is no segment counter-clockwise starting at i. Note, however, that some core neighbors may be the root of both a *left* and a *right* segment, such as core neighbor o.

The labels of each neighbor of u are stored in array L. This is a one-dimensional array, with one element per neighbor.

As mentioned in Section IV, each node may have to send a stack of tuples to each of its core neighbors. These stacks are stored in array *send*.

send : **array**[*core*][*left* . . *right*] **of stack of** (**ID**, **ID**, **integer**)

The second dimension of the array is necessary because, as mentioned above, a core node can be the root of a segment in each direction. The complete algorithm is shown below.

```
node u
inp
    core  :  set of ID                              {core neighbors}
var
    E     :  array[core][left . . right]
               of sequence of ID                    {region edges}
    L     :  array[ID] of integer                   {edge labels}
    send  :  array[core][left . . right]            {forwarded edges}
               of stack of (ID, ID, integer)
    rcvd  :  stack of (ID, ID, integer)
    k, l  :  ID
par
    dir   :  left . . right
    i     :  ID
begin
  i ∈ core  →
        rcvd := i.send[u][dir];
        build-segment(rcvd, i, dir);
        m := next-core(i, dir);
        if last(i, dir) ≠ last(m, ¬dir) then {join segments}
            k := last(E[i][dir]);
            l := last(E[m][¬dir]);
            send[m][dir] := (l, k, L[l] + L[k]) : rcvd;
        else
            send[m][dir] := nil
        end if
end
```

Node u consists of a parameterized action. Since the action has two parameters, i and dir, it is a shorthand for many actions: one action for every combination of a core neighbor of u and a value from $\{left, right\}$. Node u reads the tuples that a neighbor i is sending to u along direction dir. These tuples are stored in a temporary array $rcvd$. Then, several steps are taken to build the segment whose root is i. These steps are captured in *build-segment*$(rcvd, i, dir)$ as shown in Figure 6.

Consider Figure 5 as an example. The stack of tuples expected to be received are, first, a tuple from i joining u and j, followed by a tuple from j joining u and k. These tuples are removed from $rcvd$ one at a time and the appropriate edges and labels are added to E and L (we denote concatenation via ':'). The remaining tuples do not have u as the destination,

build-segment$(rcvd, i, dir)$
    $E[i][dir]$:= **nil**; $L[i] := 1$;
    $(dst, neigh, label)$:= **top**$(rcvd)$;
    while $(dst = u)$ **do**
        $E[i][dir] := E[i][dir] : neigh$;
        $L[neigh] := label$;
        pop$(rcvd)$;
        $(dst, neigh, label)$:= **top**$(rcvd)$;
    end while

$$\textit{next-core}(v, dir) = w \Leftrightarrow$$
$$\langle \forall x : (x \in \textit{bet}(u, v, w, dir) \wedge x \notin \{v, w\}) \Rightarrow x \notin \textit{core}(u) \rangle$$

Figure 6. Auxiliary definitions.

and these are not processed by *build-segment*$(rcvd, i, dir)$.

The action continues by finding the next core neighbor along direction dir. Let m be this node (potentially i itself). The action checks if the segments of i and m need to be joined. If so, it sets $send[m][dir]$ to the single tuple $(l, k, L[l]+L[k])$. This tuple will be propagated by m along the segment until it reaches its destination l. In addition, the tuples remaining in $rcvd$ correspond to the tuples that k needs to forward to l via u. These tuples (if any left) are forwarded via core neighbor m. Thus, they are concatenated to the end of $send[m][dir]$.

VI. STABILIZATION

We next describe the changes that are necessary to strengthen our protocol and achieve stabilization. We begin with a formal definition of stabilization.

A *predicate* P of a network is a boolean expression over the variables in all nodes of the network. A network is called *P-stabilizing* iff every computation has a suffix where P is true at every state of the suffix [9] [11].

Stabilization is a strong form of fault-tolerance. Normal behavior of the system is defined by predicate P. If a fault causes the system to a reach an abnormal state, i.e., a state where P is false, then the system will converge to a normal state where P is true, and remain in the set of normal states as long as the execution remains fault-free.

We will add stabilization in two steps. First, local sanity checks ensure that the data currently available to a node meets the criteria of predicate P. Data that does not meet the sanity checks is simply discarded. Second, a method is introduced to ensure that information being propagated from node to node has a limit on the distance it can propagate from its source. In this way, incorrect information has a limit on its propagation. This, in combination with the sanity checks, ensures that the system returns to its normal operating state defined by P.

The variables of the updated protocol remain as before. The updated actions are given below. The specific predicate P and a proof of stabilization is given in Section VI.

begin
  {core sanity }
  $\textit{core} \neq \textit{convex-hull}(T) \quad \rightarrow$
      $\textit{core} := \textit{convex-hull}(T)$
▯
  {region sanity}
  $\neg\textit{region-sanity}(E, L) \quad \rightarrow$
      for $k \in core, d \in \textit{left} .. \textit{right}$, **do**
          $E[k][d]$:= **nil**
▯
  {receive edges from neighbor}
  $i \in core \quad \rightarrow$
      $rcvd := i.send[u][dir]$;
      build-segment$(rcvd, i, dir)$;
      $m := \textit{next-core}(i, dir)$;
      if $\textit{last}(i, dir) \neq \textit{last}(m, \neg dir)$ **then**
          $k := \textit{last}(E[i][dir])$;
          $l := \textit{last}(E[m][\neg dir])$;
          $send[m][dir] :=$
              $(l, k, L[l] + L[k], L[k]) : \textit{hops-1}(rcvd)$;
          $send[m][dir] := \textit{filter}(send[m][dir])$;
      else
          $send[m][dir]$:= **nil**
      end if
end

A. New Actions

The first action is for sanity of the set of core nodes. Because nodes may fail and new nodes may join the network, the set of core neighbors of a node u becomes a variable, rather than an input. In addition, node u is aware of $T(u)$ because it is in direct communication with these nodes. Thus, $T(u)$ becomes an input to u. The core sanity action simply ensures the correct membership of the core set.

The second action is for sanity on the region formed by the segments stored in $u.E$. Node u can perform local tests on $u.E$ to ensure its values are consistent. Once this action is executed, and $u.E$ is consistent, the remaining actions are written so that if $u.E$ is in a consistent state before the action, it will remain in a consistent state after the action. Therefore, $u.E$ will be in an inconsistent state only immediately after a fault.

Above, predicate *region-sanity*(E, L) is the conjunction of the following four conditions.

1) Let E^* be the union of all nodes contained in any segment of u. Then,
$$\textit{convex-hull}(T \cup E^*) = E^*.$$
That is, the segments themselves form a convex hull containing all the core nodes.
2) Segments have no nodes in common, except that adjacent segments may have the same last node.
$$\langle \forall x, (c, d) \neq (c', d') : x \in (E[c][d] \cap E[c'][d']) \Rightarrow (x = \textit{last}(E[c][d]) \wedge (x = \textit{last}(E[c'][d']) \wedge \textit{next-core}(c, d) = c' \wedge d \neq d') \rangle$$
3) Nodes within the same segment should be unique.
$$\langle \forall c, d, m, n : (m < n \wedge E[c][d](m) = E[c][d](n)) \Rightarrow E[c][d](n) = \textbf{nil} \rangle$$
Above, the mth element in the sequence $E[c][d]$ is denoted by $E[c][d](m)$.
4) Labels should be increasing from one node to the next.
$$\langle \forall c, d, n > 0 : E[c][d](n) \neq \textbf{nil} \rightarrow L(E[c][d](n)) > L(E[c][d](n-1)) \rangle$$

build-segment$(rcvd, i, dir)$
  $E[i][dir] :=$ **nil**; $L[i] := 1$;
  $(dst, neigh, label, hops) :=$ **top**$(rcvd)$;
  while $(dst = u)$ **do**
    $E[i][dir] := E[i][dir] : neigh$;
    $L[neigh] := label$;
    for each $x, x \in E \wedge x \notin$ *convex-hull*(E) **do**
      $E := E - x$;
    end for
    if $\neg$*region-sanity*(E, L) **then**
      $E[i][dir] := E[i][dir] - neigh$;
    end if
    pop$(rcvd)$;
    $(dst, neigh, label, hops) :=$ **top**$(rcvd)$;
  end while

Figure 7. Modified *build-segment* routine.

filter$(stack)$
  $temp := stack$;
  $stack :=$ **nil**;
  $hops := 1$;
  $label := 2$;
  while $temp \neq$ **nil**
    $(d, n, l, h) :=$ **top**$(temp)$;
    if $h \geq hops \wedge l \geq label$ **then**
      $stack := stack : (d, n, l, h)$;
      $hops := max(hops, h)$;
      $label := max(label, l) + 1$;
    end if;
    pop$(temp)$;
  end while

Figure 8. Ensuring sanity in *send* array.

B. Strengthening Existing Actions

Although some of the information that a node u maintains can be checked locally for consistency, u cannot determine if the tuples that it forwards from one node to another are consistent. To ensure that faulty information is not propagated indefinitely, each tuple is assigned a *hop count*, that is decremented each time the tuple is forwarded from one node to the next, and it is discarded if it reaches zero. Because the label of an edge (u, v) corresponds to the number of direct Voronoi edges for u to reach v, this label can be used as an initial hop count for tuples generated by u and destined for v.

Consider for example Figure 5. Node u creates a tuple that is to be sent to neighbor k via core neighbor i. This tuple is given a hop count of $L[k]$. Similarly, the tuple u creates for l and sent via core neighbor m is given a hop count of $L[l]$. In addition, when u forwards tuples from l to i, it decrements the hop count in each of them by one. The same is true for tuples from k to m.

There are two main changes in the action that receives edges from neighbors. The first consists of strengthening routine *build-segment*, as shown in Figure 7. The segment is constructed one node at a time, as before. However, there might be some nodes in E that do not belong to the convex-hull, i.e., they are covered by the new nodes being added. These nodes are removed from E. Another change to *build-segment* is that a node is not added to E if in doing so the region-sanity predicate is violated. This ensures that once region-sanity holds (by the earlier action), it will continue to hold.

The second change to the action is to check the stack in $send[m][dir]$ for sanity, before making it available to neighbor m. This is done by the *filter* routine in Figure 8. This routine ensures that the hops remaining in the tuples of the stack are in non-increasing order towards the top of the stack. In addition, the labels have to be in strictly decreasing order towards the top of the stack. Finally, no label can be less than two.

C. Convergence

We show that regardless of the initial state of the system, the following predicate will hold permanently for every u,

$$R(u) = E^*$$

where E^* is the union of all nodes in any segment of u.

We define an *execution round* to be a subsequence of an execution in which every action of every node has either been executed or its guard is not enabled. A round captures the notion of taking enough execution steps guaranteeing that every node makes progress.

We begin with some observations. The core neighbors of node u cannot change unless there is a fault. Thus, after one round, the core sanity action ensures that $core$ is correct. Note that no other action affects this set, and hence, it continues to have the correct values (unless a fault occurs).

After one execution round, the region sanity action ensures that predicate *region-sanity* holds. However, routine *build-segment* affects array E, and thus it affects *region-sanity*. The removal of a node from E does not affect the truth value of *region-sanity*. Furthermore, when a node is added to E, *region-sanity* is checked. Thus, *region-sanity* continues to hold.

Note that the action to receive edges is parameterized. Thus, every segment in E is rebuilt at least once in each round. Because of this, every stack in array $send$ is also rebuilt. As it is rebuilt, routine *filter* ensures that $send$ has sanity values.

Finally, after an execution round, $L[i] = 1$ for every core neighbor i, and due to sanity on the send array, $L[v] \geq 2$ for every node in E.

1) Eliminating Non-Existing Nodes: If a node u is aware of all nodes in the network, simply taking the convex-hull of these nodes will suffice to compute its Voronoi region. Our objective is to have each node learn the least possible number of other nodes and thus minimize communication. However, due to faults, this communication may contain nodes that no longer exist due to failures, or simply values that have been corrupted due to communication errors. We next argue that such non-existing nodes will disappear from arrays E and $send$. We do so by induction on the label.

Basis: Within one round, any node v in a segment of E with $L[v] = 1$ is a real node, and all tuples in the $send$ array with a label value of one also correspond to real nodes.

As argued above, $L[v] \geq 2$ for any non-core node in E, and furthermore, $L[c] = 1$ for all core nodes c, and from the core-sanity, the core nodes are real-nodes (due to having direct communication with them) and immutable. From sanity of array $send$, no tuple has a label less than two.

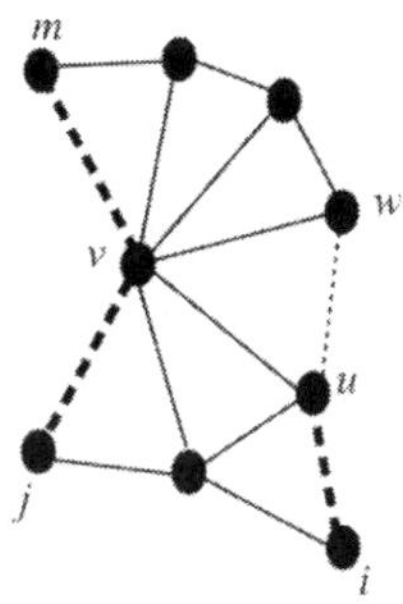

Figure 9. Stabilization induction step.

Induction Step: Assume now all nodes v in E with $L[v] \leq k$ are real nodes, and all tuples in array *send* with *label* $\leq k$ are real nodes. We argue the same holds for $k+1$.

Consider first array *send*, and consider tuples with label $k+1$. In each round, *build-segment* completely rebuilds array *send*. Any tuples created with label $k+1$ must be real because the nodes being joined have labels at most k. Tuples added to array *send* that are being forwarded from a neighbor have a hop count decreased by one. Thus, the maximum hop count of all tuples in the network that are not real nodes and have $k+1$ will decrease by one after each round. As this reaches zero, the tuples are eliminated by the *filter* routine. Thus, eventually all tuples with label $k+1$ correspond to real nodes.

For array E, once all tuples with label $k+1$ are real, the next time a segment is rebuilt, the nodes and labels come from the tuples of the send arrays. Hence, in one more round all nodes v in E with $L[v] = k+1$ are real nodes.

2) Constructing the Region: We next argue that within a bounded number of rounds $R(u) = E^*$. We assume that we have reached a state where all known nodes are real. We argue by induction on the label of edges in $R(u)$ that these edges are added to and preserved in E. Since the convex-hull of a set of nodes S does not change if we add to S nodes that are not in the convex-hull, then by the *region-sanity* predicate we will have that $R(u) = E^*$.

Recall that when a node processes the tuples from a neighbor, some are used to build the corresponding segment, and some are forwarded to the adjacent core node. The former are said to be *consumed* by the node. Note also that when forwarding tuples to a core neighbor, the first tuple is created by the node, and the remaining tuples are simply forwarded.

We use Figure 9 as reference for the induction, consisting of an arbitrary node u and neighboring core nodes i and m. Dashed lines correspond to core edges. The induction is based on the label of edges in $R(u)$, as follows.

a) For any node u and any core neighbor i, the sequence of nodes in $E[i][dir]$ with label at most l corresponds to the nodes in *segment*(u, i, dir) of $R(u)$ with label at most l.
b) If u has an edge of label l with a neighbor w, and u sends a tuple to core neighbor i of its segment containing w, and the tuple has a label of at least $l+1$, a hop count of at least l, and w as the destination, then the tuple reaches w and w consumes this tuple.
c) If u has an edge of label l with a neighbor v, and u sends a tuple to core neighbor i of its segment containing v, and the tuple has a label of at least $l+1$, a hop count of at least $l+1$, and a destination not equal to v, then v forwards the tuple to the core node of the adjacent segment to the one received.

We begin the induction with $l = 2$. Consider Figure 4, where x is the hinge of (u, w), and (u, w) has a label of two. Part a) requires that this edge will be added to the segment $u.E[x]$. Because u and w are core edges of x, from region-sanity, x is aware of them, and there can be no other nodes in x's segments $x.E[u]$ and $x.E[w]$. When x reads the tuples from w, it creates the tuple $(x, u, w, 2, 2)$ and sends it to u. Since this is the top tuple, it passes the send-sanity test at u, and u adds edge (u, w) to $u.E[x]$. Because (u, w) is in $R(u)$, no other node can block this edge, and the region sanity test is satisfied, making the edge permanent in $u.E[x]$.

For part b), assume u were to send a tuple to x with label $l > 2$ and hop count $h = 2$ and destined to w. Due to the label and hop count, the tuple passes the send sanity test at x. Node x receives it, and not being the destination forwards it to w. This tuple is below the tuple that x created to inform w of u. Node w processes the first tuple (adding u to its segment), and then processes the tuple from u.

Part c) is similar, except that the hop count is greater than two, and the destination is not w. In this case, w forwards it to the core neighbor opposite to x (not shown in the figure).

For the induction step, assume the statement holds for all values of l, $l \leq k$, and we show that it will also hold and continue to hold for label $l = k+1$.

Consider Figure 9, where *label*$(u, w) = k+1$, and *hinge*$(u, w) = v$. Let j and m be the roots of the segments of v containing u and w, respectively. From Theorem 2, all labels in these two segments of v are at most k. In addition, let i be root of the segment of u containing edge (u, v). Again, from Theorem 2, the labels in this segment are at most k. From the induction hypothesis and the labels being at most k, arrays E and L of nodes v and u permanently have the correct values for these three segments.

For part a), when v reads the tuples from m, it creates a tuple $(u, w, k+1, L[u])$ and sends it to k. From the induction hypothesis, this tuple is received and consumed at u adding the edge (u, w). Because this edge is in $R(u)$, it passes the region sanity test and no other node can displace this edge.

For part b), consider the case of u sending to i a tuple destined to w with label greater than $k+1$ and hop count of $k+1$. From part (b) of the induction hypothesis, and *label*$(u, v) \leq k$, this tuple is received at v (via j) and forwarded to core node m.

Note that, if the destination of this tuple were v rather than w, then, by the induction hypothesis, this tuple would have been consumed at v. This implies the tuple destined to w is at the top of the stack that v forwards to m. In particular, it is next to the top of the stack, which consists of the tuple created by v and sent to m to join edge (u, w). By the induction hypothesis, the tuple joining (u, w) is consumed at w. Recall that our tuple of interest is immediately below this tuple on the stack. Hence, since its destination is also w, this tuple will also be consumed at w, as desired.

For part c), the argument is similar, except that the label and hop count in the tuple that u sends to i are both greater than

$k+1$, and w is not the destination. Thus, when w processes the tuple, it forwards it to the core node adjacent to the core node from where the tuple is received, as desired.

VII. Conclusion and Future Work

We have developed a distributed algorithm that allows sensor nodes to learn their Voronoi region in a two-dimensional field. The algorithm is shown to be stabilizing, and thus, it is resilient to a wide variety of faults. It has the advantage of not assuming that there is an underlying routing protocol, and thus, there is no hidden communication cost. The low level of atomicity consists of only reading the variables of a single neighbor at a time. This is similar to receiving a message from the neighbor containing a copy of the neighbor's variables. We will extend the algorithm to the message passing model in future work.

Regarding communication overhead, each node receives a stack of tuples from each core neighbor. Each stack is of size at most $O(N)$ due to the requirement that labels decrease towards the top of the stack. Assuming that on average each node has g neighbors, then the overhead is $O(g \cdot N)$. It is known that if nodes are distributed in the plane according to a Poisson process with constant intensity, then each node in the DT has on average six surrounding triangles [16]. Thus, on average, the overhead is $O(N)$.

In general, a node u receives tuples from a source s to destination d if s and d are Voronoi neighbors and their VNP crosses u. If the area where the sensors are deployed is regular, as opposed to a long linear shape, then we expect the number of such pairs to be small, even of constant size. Thus, the overhead in most networks will be small, even smaller than $O(N)$. We will investigate this in future work, along with several variations of the problem such as obstacles that interfere with communication and having nodes with different transmission radius.

References

[1] J. Yick, B. Mukherjee, and D. Ghosal, "Wireless sensor network survey," Computer Networks, vol. 52, no. 12, 2008, pp. 2292 – 2330.

[2] P. Bose, P. Morin, I. Stojmenović, and J. Urrutia, "Routing with guaranteed delivery in ad hoc wireless networks," Wireless Networks, vol. 7, no. 6, Nov 2001, pp. 609–616.

[3] B. Karp and H. T. Kung, "Gpsr: Greedy perimeter stateless routing for wireless networks," in Proc. of the 6th Annual International Conference on Mobile Computing and Networking, ser. MobiCom '00. New York, NY, USA: ACM, 2000, pp. 243–254.

[4] S. S. Lam and C. Qian, "Geographic routing in d-dimensional spaces with guaranteed delivery and low stretch," SIGMETRICS Perform. Eval. Rev., vol. 39, no. 1, Jun. 2011, pp. 217–228.

[5] B. Leong, B. Liskov, and R. Morris, "Geographic routing without planarization," in Proc. of the 3rd Conf. on Networked Systems Design & Implementation, ser. NSDI'06. Berkeley, CA, USA: USENIX Association, 2006, pp. 25–25.

[6] S. Fortune, Voronoi Diagrams and Delaunay Triangulations, second edition, J. E. Goodman and J. O'Rourke, Eds. CRC Press, 2004.

[7] P. Bose and P. Morin, "Online routing in triangulations," in Proc. of the 10th International Symposium on Algorithms and Computation, ser. ISAAC '99. London, UK: Springer-Verlag, 1999, pp. 113–122.

[8] M. Schneider, "Self-stabilization," ACM Computing Surveys, vol. 25, no. 1, Mar. 1993, pp. 45–67.

[9] E. W. Dijkstra, "Self-stabilizing systems in spite of distributed control," Commun. ACM, vol. 17, no. 11, 1974, pp. 643–644.

[10] S. Dolev., Self-Stabilization. Cambridge, MA: MIT Press, 2000.

[11] M. G. Gouda, "The triumph and tribulation of system stabilization," in Proc. of the 9th International Workshop on Distributed Algorithms (WDAG). London, UK: Springer-Verlag, 1995, pp. 1–18.

[12] Y. Núnez-Rodrıguez, H. Xiao, K. Islam, and W. Alsalih, "A distributed algorithm for computing voronoi diagram in the unit disk graph model," in Proc. of the 20th Canadian Conference in Computational Geometry, Quebec, Canada, 2008, pp. 199–202.

[13] D. Y. Lee and S. S. Lam, "Protocol design for dynamic delaunay triangulation," in 27th International Conference on Distributed Computing Systems (ICDCS '07), June 2007, pp. 26–26.

[14] ——, "Efficient and accurate protocols for distributed delaunay triangulation under churn," in 2008 IEEE International Conference on Network Protocols, Oct 2008, pp. 124–136.

[15] R. Jacob, S. Ritscher, C. Scheideler, and S. Schmid, "A self-stabilizing and local delaunay graph construction," in Algorithms and Computation, Y. Dong, D.-Z. Du, and O. Ibarra, Eds. Berlin, Heidelberg: Springer Berlin Heidelberg, 2009, pp. 771–780.

[16] R. A. Dwyer, "Higher-dimensional voronoi diagrams in linear expected time," Discrete & Computational Geometry, vol. 6, no. 3, Sep 1991, pp. 343–367.

Delay Optimization for URLLC in Software Defined Networks: A Case Study on Platooning

Müge Erel-Özçevik*, Berk Canberk*†, V. Çağri Güngör‡, Yeşim Bayramlı§

*Computer Engineering Department of Istanbul Technical University, Istanbul, TURKEY
† Electrical and Computer Engineering Department of Northeastern University, Boston, USA
‡Computer Engineering Department of Abdullah Gül University, Kayseri, TURKEY
§Havelsan, Ankara, TURKEY
Emails: erelmu@itu.edu.tr, canberk@itu.edu.tr, cagri.gungor@agu.edu.tr, yesimb@havelsan.com.tr

Abstract—**The autonomous driving in a platoon network requires reliable data transfer and strict latency on downlink traffic. These two requirements have been addressed in 5G under the Ultra-Reliable Low Latency Communication (URLLC) specification. In this study, we focus on this 5G service, and we design a novel Software-Defined Platoon Network (SDPN) to optimize the end-to-end Delay (e2eDelay). Our SDPN defines the e2eDelay in a closed-form expression that covers Data and Control planes. To optimize e2eDelay, we propose a Mixed Integer Linear Problem (MILP) that jointly considers the constraints in the vehicle to vehicle (V2V) and the vehicle to infrastructure (V2I) links. Due to the NP-hard characteristic of our MILP optimization and to reduce the computational complexity of the optimization at the same time, we propose a novel Centralized Set Cover algorithm that finds the optimum set cover of vehicles by building platoons. According to the results, our SDPN serves e2eDelay under 3.5 msecs with a 45% improvement over the conventional approach.**

Keywords–SDN; URLLC; e2eDelay; Platooning; MILP.

I. Introduction

According to the European Commission, the carbon emission has been aimed to decrease the fuel-consumption in transportation by 60% level by 2050 [1]. To reduce it, "eco-driving" is newly defined as avoiding aggressive acceleration, keeping optimal space, driving in steady-state speed according to road dynamics [2]. Therefore, this has led us to investigate a new Intelligent Transport Systems (ITS) with higher fuel efficiency in highways with an approach: *Platooning*.

In a platoon, there is one leader and there are also followers just behind it. Thanks tothe vehicle to infrastructure (V2I) link, a leader takes the dynamic rules for traffic flow control and accident data from the remote control center in virtual Evolved Packet Core (vEPC). By vehicle to vehicle (V2V) link, the leader forwards these rules to the following vehicles [2]-[4].Therefore,it decreases fuel consumption in different road dynamics enhances traffic efficiency and ensures safety by controlling the space between vehicles [2]. Such a fully automated driving in a platoon requires reliable data transfer and strict latency in downlink traffic flow during mobility. Here,this flow is called Ultra-Reliable Low Latency Communication (URLLC) in 5G services [3].

According to International Mobile Communications (IMT-2020), URLLC services require a radio-latency of 1 msec and an end-to-end Delay (e2eDelay) of a few msecs [4] [5]. E2eDelay is measured by the concatenation of V2V and V2I communications in the downlink URLLC service from a remote source to a vehicle. Therefore,by considering both edge

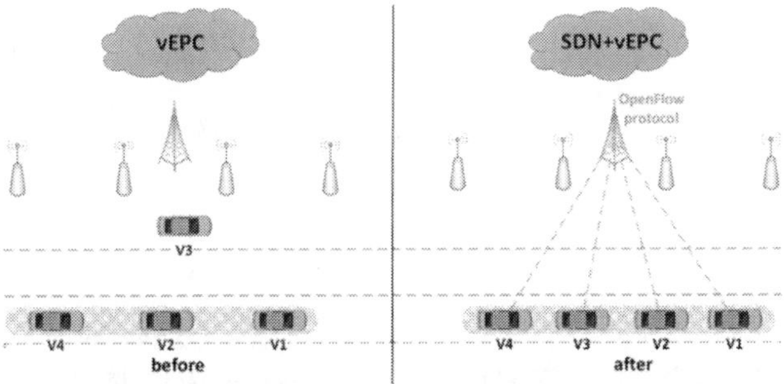

	before	after
Approach	AdHoc	Centralized
Comm. Tech.	DSRC, IEEE 802.11p	4G+5G, OpenFlow with SDN
Traffic Type	Reliable Data Transfer	URLLC

Figure 1. The Comparison of Vehicle Platooning Approaches.

and core in the platoon networks, we study e2eDelay into two parts as V2V and V2I.

A. Problem Definition

For V2V case, Figure 1 showstwo proposed approaches for platooning. Before,there has been an AdHoc approach that vehicles communicate with each other by Dedicated Short-Range Communication (DSRC) over IEEE 802.11p. A vehicle platoon has been built locally according to the vehicle-centric decision. There are many studies that try to build a platoon via an AdHoc approach [6] [7]. However,there have been such challenges as frequency reuse and interference between vehicles during the V2V communication and platoon building. Under extremely increased 5G background traffic [8], these challenges cause many packet retransmissions and this negatively affects the e2eDelay of URLLC service [9]. Therefore,the platoon should be built as long as possible by decreasing the number of independent vehicles exemplified as V3 in the figure. However,the size of the platoon cannot increase after a certain level because of depending AdHoc approach. To overcome these problems, the centralized orchestration of platooning and control of the vehicles are required.

Thanks to the global view of the centralized controller, an optimal platoon can be built that offers such advantages: The fuel efficiency is increased for the whole vehicular network. The frequencies per vehicle can be assigned to them previously from a centralized pool, and therefore,the data transfer would become reliable without any packet retransmission in a platoon [10]. Therefore,a centralized approach for the vehicle platooning is taken into consideration.

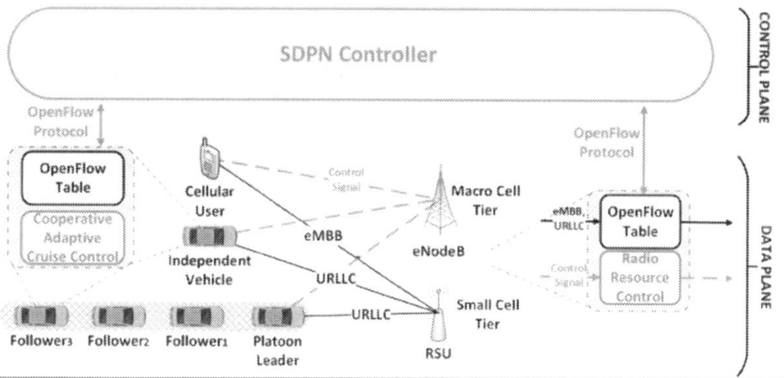

User Type	Application	5G Traffic	Velocity	Mobility Characteristic
Platoon Vehicle	Fully Automated Driving	URLLC	50-130 km/h	Fluid-Flow Direction
Independent Vehicle	Fully Automated Driving	URLLC	50-130 km/h	Fluid-Flow Direction
Cellular User	Video Content Apps	eMBB	0-2 km/h	Random Way Point

Figure 2. System Architecture and User Types in Proposed SDPN.

However,the centralized approach is only seen in 3% of the recent studies that try to solve such platooning challenges in the literature. The main reason for it is the lack of V2I technology investments in 5G [11]. Therefore,to keep the advantages of the centralized approach, we investigate also the V2I part of URLLC services in the platoon networks. In V2I part,the load in vEPC has increased because there is huge traffic intensity on core network [8] and the whole signaling of the platoon is now routed over V2I as mentioned in Figure 1. Therefore,the closed-form expression of e2eDelay is also proposed with a traffic load effect due to increasing the queuing and processing delay in the core devices.

B. *Contributions*

We propose a Software-Defined Platoon Networks (SDPN) that considers both Data and Control parts of URLLC services. It optimizes e2eDelay (D) with a Mixed Integer Linear Problem (MILP) for platoon networks by jointly considering V2V and V2I constraints. Thanks to the global view of SDPN, it builds an optimal platoon as long as possible. The decisions are embedded in each dummy devices without touching the physical plane with open source OpenFlow(OF) protocol. The whole contributions can be found below:

- A novel closed-form expression of e2eDelay (D) by covering Data and Control Planes,
- A MILP that jointly considers the constraints in both V2V and V2I links,
- A novel Centralized Set Cover for Platooning algorithm to optimize e2eDelay.

The rest of the paper is organized as follows: Section II gives the proposed system architecture of SDPN by considering the mathematical model of e2eDelay in terms of Data and Control Planes. Section III shows the comparison of proposed and conventional model in terms of e2eDelay (D). Finally, Section IV concludes the paper by giving summary.

II. Proposed System Architecture of SDPN

The system architecture of SDPN is shown in Figure 2. The Data and Control planes are separated from each other. Data plane includes two tiers. In small cells and macrocells, end-users are served over RSUs (5G) and eNodeBs (4G), respectively. There is a Dense-Urban (eMBB-UMx) [12] topology in Data Plane. It is based on four outdoor small cells per macrocells. The end-users have Control and Data signals to keep communications alive. Control signals, shown in dashed line,are routed over macrocells; whereas, Data signal shown in solid line, can be served over small cells.

A. *Data Plane*

In this paper, there are three user types named as platoon vehicle, independent vehicle and cellular user. A vehicle can be a platoon vehicle as either a platoon leader or follower in a platoon.The cooperative automation system in a platoon requires highly reliable service and ultra-low latency during this communication. Then,we assume predecessor-leader controller strategy in V2V communication. The leader communicates via V2I to take fully automated driving data over URLLC traffic type and also forwards it to the followers via V2V links in a platoon. Follower vehicle only communicates with the preceding one to know its relative position and to take road characteristics. For those vehicles, we only consider vehicle communication by ignoring end-user in a car who can generate multimedia traffic; i.e., eMBB.

In highways, the velocities are assumed as uniformly distributed between 50-130 km/h. In this study,we consider the speed limits in the German Autobahn road network (130 km/h). Then,the mobility characteristic is determined as Fluid-Flow direction. The reason for it is that the fuel-efficiency of platooning only makes sense in highways. According to Larsson et al. [1],the long and low-traffic roads are mostly suitable for platooning. Therefore, it is not preferred to use in the dynamic road characteristics with multi-lane scenarios. Moreover,the independent vehicle is a vehicle that communicates via V2I to take fully automated driving data over URLLC traffic. Here, it has no V2V communication around. Its velocity and mobilitycharacteristics are the same as platoon vehicles on highways. On the other hand,there are cellular users as background traffic in Core. They run video content applications over mobile-devices, which generates eMBB traffic. Due to being pedestrian, the velocity is assumed as uniformly distributed between 0-2 km/h. The mobility characteristic is determined as Randow WayPoint. The total number of the users is defined as N.

Each vehicle, macrocells, and small cells have also OpenFlow (OF) switch capability to communicate with Control plane via OF protocol. In the Data plane, each OF device has two main layers, such as Radio Resource Control (RRC) and OF table. Control signaling is performed via the RRC

TABLE I. AN EXAMPLE OPENFLOW SWITCH TABLE IN SDPN.

Match Fields				ACTION	STATISTICS
IN_PORT	IP_PROTO	IP_SRC	IP_DST	Output	TX Packets
port1	6 (URLLC)	10.0.0.1	10.0.0.3	port3	5260759
port2	17 (eMBB)	10.0.0.2	10.0.0.4	port4	34506

layer for assigning to radio resources. The resources for RSUs, eNodeBs, and vehicles are previously allocated from a resource pool. Especially in a platoon, it enables short inter-vehicle distance and low transmission power to enable spatial reuse of V2V links [13]. Moreover,the handover is only performed during inter-macrocell transitions.

URLLC and eMBB traffics are routed according to embedded rules in OF table as exemplified in Table I. The match fields of OF table include 44 components in OF basic class that can be matchable with the incoming packet header. This part is in OpenFlow Extensible Match (OXM) format, which is also defined as type-length-value (TLV) format and it has 5 to 259 bytes long [14]. In each OF table as exemplified in Table I, we consider statistics parts to take data periodically; such as user type, traffic load (ρ), current position and velocity. Firstly,the user type is defined according to the protocol type of the matched field which is directly mapped with URLLC and eMBB services. We differentiate the traffic flows according to the protocol number of IP packet (IP Proto=6 for TCP based URLLC, IP Proto=17 for UDP based eMBB). These flows should also match with such fields: Ethernet type (0x800 IP packet), different Ethernet source, destination, and different IPv4 source, the destination address in OF table. Secondly, the counter of TX packets is directly used to calculate traffic load (ρ) per OF switch. Thirdly, the current position of a mobile user is determined if the related flow is matched with specific OF switch (The static position of RSUs is already known). Finally, the velocity of end-user can be easily calculated by using periodically taken statistics, which will be used while building a platoon.

B. Control Plane

Control plane has centralized SDPN controller. It calculates proposed e2eDelay (D) per URLLC services and runs the proposed e2eDelay optimization algorithm by considering the whole topology thanks to the global view. It takes statistics via OpenFlow protocol 1.5.1 for each period of time. As a result; according to the output of SDPN decisions, OF rules are embedded to specific OF switches. The details of SDPN controller can be found into following subsections:

*1) **E2eDelay (D) Calculation:*** A novel e2eDelay(D) for SDPN is defined by considering two planes in the following equation:

$$\mathrm{D} = \overbrace{\sum P_{mm'} \cdot W_s}^{\text{Control Plane Delay}} + \overbrace{\sum P_j \cdot W_j}^{\text{Data Plane Delay}} \qquad \forall\, j \in (m, s) \qquad (1)$$

where P_j is serving probability over OF_j, W_j is queuing and processing delay per macro or smallcells which are also OF switch. j is an index of macro (m) or smallcell (s). W_s is delay caused by SDPN Controller processing and is executed for each macrocell to macrocell transition ($P_{mm'}$=1) called handover procedure. Here,the propagation delay is ignored. It is calculated by using d/s equation where d is the distance in meters and s is the speed of light (3x10^9 m/sec) [15]. By considering 10 m distances between vehicles in a platoon, the delay becomes at most 3x10^{-8}secs. This can be disregarded even if the length of the platoon may be increased too much ($\leq 10^5$ vehicles). Moreover,such an increase on platoon length is not realistic. It enables V2V communication in platoon simultaneously [11]. On the other hand, the propagation delay between eNB and a centralized SDN controller is taken as 1 msec. This propagation delay is calculated by the coverage of the SDN controller that is responsible for a highway. In this study,we assumed that 600 km long highway is orchestrated by a centralized controller. By using the speed of light and d/s equation, the propagation delay is measured as 1 msec [16]. Moreover, because of only controlling URLLC traffic which has a packet size equal to approximately one-tenth of the eMBB packets, the processing time can be kept under 5G requirements (1 sec response time).

*a) **Control Plane Delay:*** The control part of e2eDelay (D) is triggered when the macrocell to macrocell transition ($P_{mm'}$) occurs, which calls a handover procedure when the probability is 1. For the whole topology, the distribution function for the topology is calculated for all type of user such as Pedestrian, Platoon or Independent Vehicle as in the following equation:

$$P_{mm'} = \frac{\sum P_{mm'}(t < T)}{N} \qquad (2)$$

where$N$ is the total number of usersand $P_{mm'}(t)$ is discrete probability of the handover execution between macrocells at simulation time t and T is the total period of time as follows:

$$P_{mm'}(t) = \begin{cases} 1, & \text{macrocell transition} \\ 0, & \text{otherwise} \end{cases} \qquad (3)$$

On the other hand,there is an extra delay (W_s) caused by the handover execution in centralized SDPN controller. The handover procedure is taken as 15 msecs for each requirement of inter macrocell transitions [15] [16]. Therefore,the $P_{mm'}$ per vehicle should be minimized by platooning them as long as possible. We mapped this part with Control part of e2eDelay.

*b) **Data Plane Delay:*** In Level 2 of the proposed equation, e2eDelay (D) is performed per URLLC flow by considering each packet process. To understand where the flow is performed at a specific time t, the match of OF_j table should be checked. If a flow is matched with OF_j table, that means it is served over this cell which can be either macrocell or small cell. This is mathematically formalized as in following discrete probability function:

$$P_j = \begin{cases} 1, & flow \text{ matches in } OF_j \text{ table} \\ 0, & \text{otherwise} \end{cases} \qquad (4)$$

On the other hand,in each OF switch, Data packets of end-user are directly affected by the load in Core due to queuing and processing delay (W (sec)). Wemodel each cell by queuing theory. In M/M/c/K Markov model, the probability density function (P_n) has a Poisson distribution for $0 \leq n < c$ and a Geometric distribution for $c \leq n \leq K$. As in general aspect, the summation of each probability (P_n) should be equal to 1. Here, the computation is nearly the same as the M/M/c (infinite queue) Markov model. However, both Poisson and Geometric series of M/M/c/K are finite; Therefore,in the computation, there is no constraint such that ρ defining as $\frac{\lambda}{c \cdot \mu}$ must be less than 1 [17]. Thanks to that, the waiting time in a queue while $1 \leq \rho$ can be also analytically calculated. While working on

$$
D = \begin{cases} \sum_0^M P_{mm'} \cdot W_s + \\ \sum P_j \cdot \dfrac{r_j(1 - \frac{(r_j)^K}{(c_j)^{(K-c_j)} c_j!} P_0) + \frac{P_0 (r_j)^{(c_j)} \rho_j}{c_j!(1-\rho_j)^2} \cdot [1 - (\rho_j)^{(K-c_j+1)} - (1-\rho_j) \cdot (K - c_j + 1)(\rho_j)^{(K-c_j)})]}{\lambda_j (1 - \frac{(r_j)^K}{c_j^{(K-c_j)} c_j!} P_0)} & , (\forall j \in (m,s)), (\rho_j \neq 1) \\ \sum_0^M P_{mm'} \cdot W_s + \\ \sum P_j \cdot \dfrac{r_j(1 - \frac{(r_j)^K}{(c_j)^{(K-c_j)} c_j!} P_0) + \frac{P_0 (r_j)^{(c_j)}}{c_j!} \cdot \frac{(K-c_j)(K-c_j+1)}{2}}{\lambda_j (1 - \frac{(r_j)^K}{(c_j)^{(K-c_j)} c_j!} P_0)} & , (\forall j \in (m,s)), (\rho_j = 1) \end{cases} \tag{7}
$$

Dense Urban topology, this case should be also considered. Therefore,each macrocell and small cells are modeled with M/M/c/K Markov model. The probability density function of this model is given in (5) [17].

$$
P_n = \begin{cases} \frac{r^n}{n!} \cdot P_0 & , 0 \leq n < c \\ \frac{r^n}{c^{n-c} \cdot c!} \cdot P_0 & , c \leq n \leq K \end{cases} \tag{5}
$$

where r is calculated as $\frac{\lambda}{\mu}$, c is channel number of small cell or macro cell and K-c is the length of the queue. With the help of $\sum P_n = 1$ general aspect, P_0 is calculated as in [17]. By implementing L'Hospital rule on $\sum n \cdot P_n$, the number of packets that are waiting in a queue (L_q) is calculated. Then,the number of packets in the whole system (L) is performed by using $L = Lq + r \cdot (1 - P_K)$ formula. $P_K$is the probability of being a drop from the queue. The total waiting time (W) in the whole M/M/c/K system is calculated as [17]:

$$
W = \frac{L}{\lambda \cdot (1 - P_K)} \tag{6}
$$

where λ is dynamically changed in the Data Plane, which also alters traffic load ($\sum \rho$) per cell. Therefore,e2eDelay (D) optimization should consider the traffic load in Core. We mapped the Data part of e2eDelay (D) analytical formula with Level 2. The whole formula of proposed D is shown in (7).

*2) **E2eDelay (D) Optimization**:* The e2eDelay optimization problem in SDPN is defined as follows:

$$
\begin{aligned}
&\text{min e2eDelay (D):} && \text{(8a)} \\
&\text{s.t.} \quad |V_j| > 1, \quad V_j \in Platoon && \text{(8b)} \\
&\forall \ |V_j V_j'| < 20 \ \ m, \quad V_j \in Platoon && \text{(8c)} \\
&\sum W_j < 4 \ \ msecs, \forall j \in (m,s) && \text{(8d)}
\end{aligned}
$$

The objective function is minimizing average D as in (7). It is calculated by considering all end-users in a platoon. Due to having both discrete and continues variables in the constraints, this problem is called a Mixed Integer Linear optimization problem (MILP). In the first constraint in (8b), the number of vehicles in a platoon should be higher than 1. Otherwise,a vehicle is called an independent vehicle because it cannot build a platoon alone. In the second constraint in (8c), the inter-vehicle spacing in a platoon should be under 20 m while considering optimal SINR values and path-loss models to keep V2V communication alive [13] [18] . In the third constraint in (8d), the data part of D should be under 4 msecs.

The optimal solution of this problem can be found by using the Branch and Bound algorithm, however, it is NP-hard. The spent time can reach up to 20 mins for German Autobahn as mentioned in [1]. In our scenario, the proposed optimization algorithm should be met by 5G requirements:

Require: Graph G
Ensure: Set of Platoons P and the size of it M

1: Initialize empty set for the platoons $P = \{\{\}\}$
2: **while** Platoon P is feasible **do** ▷ Check (8d)
3:     **while** Graph G is not empty **do**
4:         **for** Each Vehicle v in G **do**
5:             Find v' where |vv'| <20+penalty
6:             Add v' into the platoon of v in P
7:             Remove v from G
8:     $M \leftarrow$Calculate the size of P
9: **return** P, M

Figure 3. Centralized Set Cover for Platooning.

e2eDelay should be kept under a few msecs for URLLC traffic and SDPN controller should give dynamic decisions under 1 sec period [4] [19]. Therefore,we propose a greedy algorithm called Centralized Set Cover for Platooning that builds a platoon as long as possible. The pseudocode is given in Figure 3.

This algorithm finds minimum set cover in a graph G where all vehicles are platooned in a set P. However, the response time of the set cover is not acceptable because it exceeds 1 sec.. Therefore,we use the indirect constraint handling in e2eDelay(D) optimization. The static penalty function violates the constraint in (8c)enabling local search on infeasible solutions. In the proposed SDPN, these infeasible solutions would be feasible by dynamic alteration on velocities and positions of the vehicles in a platoon for the next period of the controller. It takes graph G including all vehicles in a highway as an input and returns the number of sets M and the minimum set covers as platoons P. After initializing empty set P, it checks the feasibility of the decision of the algorithm in terms of third constraint in (8d)in line 2. Between lines 3-7, there is a loop executing until there is no vehicle in a Graph G. Between lines 4-7, there is another loop for each vehicle v in dynamically reduced graph G. In line 5, the algorithm tries to find another vehicle v' of which euclidian distance to v is lower than 20+penalty. In this study, the penalty function is selected as 80 m and the performance evaluation is executed by using this value.If there is such v', it is added to the platoon of v in set P as in line 6 and the vehicle v is removed from graph G due to already being in a platoon as in line 7. Finally, the size of P is calculated as M in line 8 and the algorithm returns a greedy platoon P in line 9.

III. Performance Evaluation

The performance of the proposed SDPN is evaluated by a simulation environment shown in Figure 4. It is separated into two parts: Level 1 and Level 2. Firstly,in MATLAB©2018a, the Data Plane of SDPN is built by using uniformly random generation for mobility data according to Level 1 parameters in

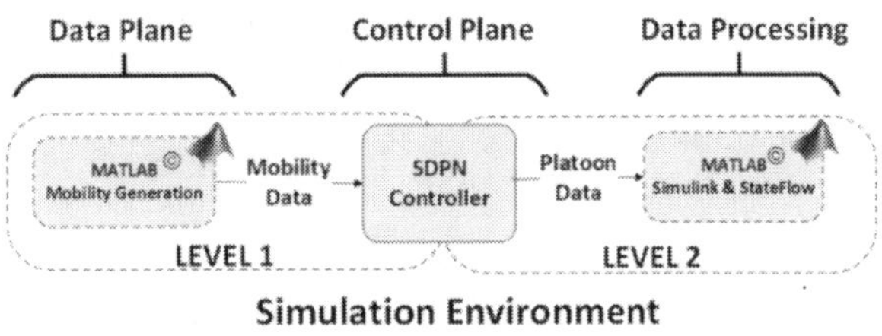

(A). MOBILITY PARAMETERS.

LEVEL 1 Parameters	Values
Random Way Point	Pedestrains
Speed Interval	[0 2 km/h]
Pause Interval	[0 1 sec]
Walk Interval	[2.00 6.00 sec]
Direction Interval	[-180 180 degree]
Fluid Flow Direction	Vehicles
Highway Length	[0 24200 m]
Highway Exit Interval	2000 m
Speed of Vehicles	110 km/h
Cell Ranges	
Macrocell (R_m):	200 m
Smallcell (R_s)	100 m
Per macrocell	4 smallcells
Simulation Time	200 secs

(B). MARKOV PARAMETERS, AND THE DETAILS OF URLLC AND EMBB.

LEVEL 2 Parameters	Values
Spectrum, Bandwidth	
Macrocell:	4GHz, 200MHz
Smallcell:	30GHz, 1000MHz
V2V:	5.9GHz, 100 Mhz
Channels in Macro/Smallcell:	20, 7
Serving Rates	
of Macrocell $1/\mu_m$:	6,00E-005 secs/packet
of Smallcell $1/\mu_s$:	1,20E-005 secs/packet
Flow Parameters	
Packet generation	Poisson Traffic
λ per URLLC flow:	60 packets/sec
λ per eMBB flow:	1000 packets/sec
Total λ per macrocell:	33333 - 8333333 packets/sec
Queue size	10000

(C). TOTAL NUMBER OF URLLC AND EMBB WHEN TOPOLOGY UTILIZATION γ IS INCREASED.

γ	N	10 % URLLC	90 % eMBB	50%URLLC	50 % eMBB	90%URLLC	10 % eMBB
0.005	121	12	108	60	60	108	12
0.5	12100	1210	10890	6050	6050	10890	1210
1	24200	2420	21780	12100	12100	21780	2420
1.5	36300	3630	32670	18150	18150	32670	3630

Figure 4. Simulation Environment and Dense Urban (eMBB-UMx) [12] Topology Parameters in Platoon Network.

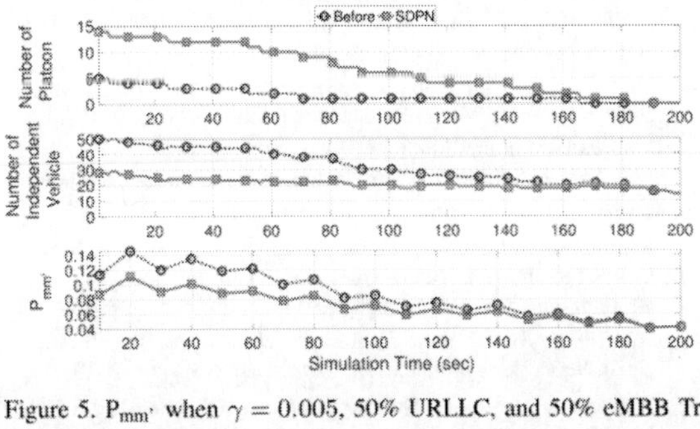

Figure 5. $P_{mm'}$ when $\gamma = 0.005$, 50% URLLC, and 50% eMBB Traffic.

sub-table 4a. Then,the mobility data is given to Control Plane which runs algorithm in Figure 3. These results are interpreted in the following Level 1 sub-section. Secondly,the data analysis is executed in Level 2 part by using Simulink and StateFlow libraries of MATLAB. The Level 2 parameters are given in sub-table 4b. The results are shown in the following Level 2 sub-section. Moreover,the traffic types during simulation are differentiated as given in sub-table 4c. Here, γ is the topology utilization changing by the total number of the users (N).

A. Level 1

In Level 1 of performance evaluation, two methods are compared: Before (conventional AdHoc platooning) and SDPN (proposed centralized platooning). In AdHoc platooning, each vehicle locally decides to enter or exit a platoon in terms of (8c). In Centralized platooning, SDPN executes Centralized Set Cover for Platooning algorithm in Figure 3 that globally tries to find minimum set cover of vehicles. In the Figure 5, the number of platoons and the effect on $P_{mm'}$ are shown by comparing Before and SDPN approaches. When the topology utilization is $\gamma = 0.005$, there is 50% URLLC and 50% eMBB, i.e., 60 URLLC (vehicles) and 60 eMBB (pedestrian). Initially, all vehicles are active in the highway, and after a randomly determined duration per vehicle, they leave the topology. In the first sub-graph, in Y-axis the number of platoons and in X-axis the simulation time are shown. Initially, SDPN builds 50% more platoons than Before. During the simulation, the number of leaving from the highways increase. Therefore,the number of platoons decreases. In the middle graph, there are further 20 independent vehicles in Before that create a handover request to SDPN controller per macrocell transition. It directly increase $P_{mm'}$. Thanks to SDPN, $P_{mm'}$ can be decreased by approximately 0.04 (33%) as given in third sub-graph. This directly decreases Control part of D, as in (1).

B. Level 2

In Level 2 of performance evaluation, the effect of Level 1 is studied on e2eDelay (D). As seen in Figure 6, e2eDelay (msec) is given according to different topology utilization (γ) during a first 15 seconds of the simulation. In each sub-graph,left one shows the results of the Before (conventional) and SDPN (proposed) approaches when $\gamma = 0.005$ and $\gamma = 0.5$, whereas,the right one shows the outputs when $\gamma = 1$ and $\gamma = 1.5$. Before performs AdHoc platooning, the SDPN executes proposed Centralized Set-Cover algorithm in Figure 3. In each case when $\gamma <= 0.5$, the SDPN can decrease

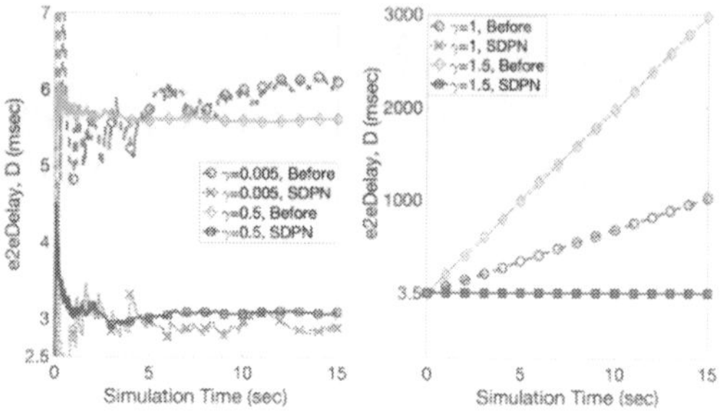

(a) 10% URLLC, 90% eMBB.

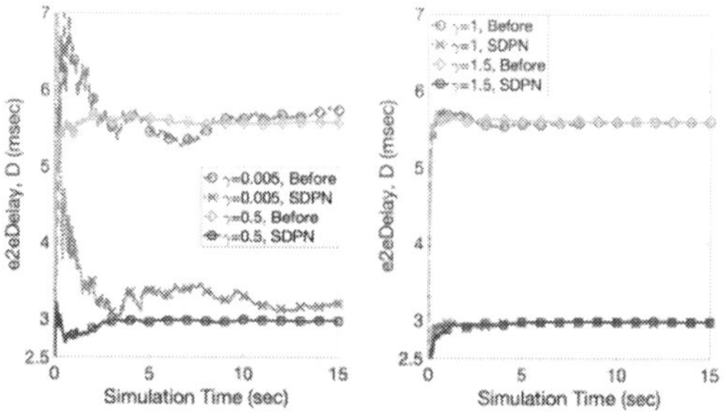

(b) 50% URLLC, 50% eMBB.

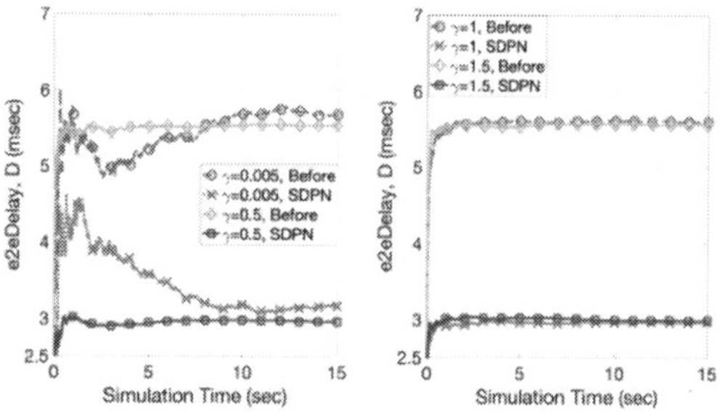

(c) 90% URLLC, 10% eMBB.

Figure 6. e2eDelay, D (sec) for different Topology Utilization γ.

e2eDelay nearly 2.5 msecs from 5.5 to 3. The fluctuationsare caused by the handover request during macrocell transition ($P_{mm'}$=0.3) to SDPN controller where W_s takes approximately 15 msecs as in (1). As the rate of eMBB services is increased from 10% to 90% in Figures 6a-6c, the URLLC service is further squeezed by the background traffic. In the right subgraph of Figure 6a, Before cannot serve URLLC services and e2eDelay increases up to 3 secs,whereas the proposed one can keep it under 3.5 msecs. As a result,thanks to centralized view SDPN improves e2eDelay 45% by keeping it under 3.5 msecs even if the topology utilization is too high ($\gamma >> 1$).

IV. Conclusion and Future Work

In this paper, we proposed a Software-Defined Platoon Network (SDPN) dynamically optimizing e2eDelay of URLLC services. A closed-form expression of e2eDelay (D) was newly defined by considering Data and Control planes. This objective function was optimized via Mixed Integer Linear Programming (MILP) by jointly considering the constraints in V2V and V2I links of a platoon. Due to being NP-hard and to reduce the computational complexity of the optimization, we proposed a novel Centralized Set Cover for Platooning algorithm that built a platoon as long as possible. According to the performance evaluation, e2eDelay was improved by 45% by keeping it under 3.5 msecs even if the topology utilization was too high. As future work, the load effect of the core on platoon networks will be investigated due to the lack of V2I investments in 5G.

Acknowledgment

This work is supported by TUBITAK TEYDEB 1501 program with project no 3180114.

References

[1] E. Larsson, G. Sennton, and J. Larson, "The vehicle platooning problem: Computational complexity and heuristics," *Transportation Research Part C: Emerging Technologies*, vol. 60, pp. 258 – 277, 2015.

[2] K. Y. et al., "Model Predictive Control for Hybrid Electric Vehicle Platooning Using Slope Information," *IEEE Trans. on Intelligent Transportation Systems*, vol. 17, no. 7, pp. 1894–1909, July 2016.

[3] C. Campolo, A. Molinaro, G. Araniti, and A. O. Berthet, "Better Platooning Control Toward Autonomous Driving : An LTE Device-to-Device Communications Strategy That Meets Ultralow Latency Requirements," *IEEE Vehicular Tech. Magazine*, vol. 12, no. 1, pp. 30–38, March 2017.

[4] E. Hossain and M. Hasan, "5G cellular: key enabling technologies and research challenges," *IEEE Instrumentation Measurement Magazine*, vol. 18, no. 3, pp. 11–21, June 2015.

[5] S. Y. Lien, S. C. Hung, D. J. Deng, and Y. J. Wang, "Efficient Ultra-Reliable and Low Latency Communications and Massive Machine-Type Communications in 5G New Radio," in *IEEE Global Communications Conference*, Dec 2017, pp. 1–7.

[6] S. Santini, A. Salvi, A. S. Valente, A. Pescap, M. Segata, and R. L. Cigno, "Platooning Maneuvers in Vehicular networks: A Distributed and Consensus-Based Approach," *IEEE Transactions on Intelligent Vehicles*, vol. 4, no. 1, pp. 59–72, March 2019.

[7] A. Bibeka, P. Songchitruksa, and Y. Zhang, "Assessing environmental impacts of ad-hoc truck platooning on multilane freeways," *Journal of Intelligent Transportation Systems*, vol. 0, no. 0, pp. 1–12, 2019.

[8] "Visual Networking Index Report: Global Mobile Data Traffic Forecast Update, 2016-2021," Cisco, Tech. Rep. C11-738429-00, Feb. 7, 2017.

[9] R. Hall and C. Chin, "Vehicle sorting for platoon formation: Impacts on highway entry and throughput," *Transportation Research Part C: Emerging Technologies*, vol. 13, no. 5, pp. 405 – 420, 2005.

[10] J. B. et al., "Road Side Unit Deployment: A Density-Based Approach," *IEEE Intelligent Transportation Systems Magazine*, vol. 5, no. 3, pp. 30–39, Fall 2013.

[11] K. T. E., "A Comparison of Approaches for Platooning Management," Master's thesis, Vorgelegt am Lehrstuhl fr Wirtschaftsinformatik II, Universitt Mannheim, 24 February 2017.

[12] "Recommendations for NGMN KPIs and Requirements for 5G," NGMN Alliance, Tech. Rep. P1 WS#3 BBTS, June 2016.

[13] J. Karedal, N. Czink, A. Paier, F. Tufvesson, and A. F. Molisch, "Path Loss Modeling for Vehicle-to-Vehicle Communications," *IEEE Trans. on Vehicular Technology*, vol. 60, no. 1, pp. 323–328, Jan 2011.

[14] "OpenFlow Switch Specification, Version 1.4.0 (Wire Protocol 0x05)," Open Networking Foundation, Tech. Rep., October 2013.

[15] J. Prados-Garzon, O. Adamuz-Hinojosa, P. Ameigeiras, J. J. Ramos-Munoz, P. Andres-Maldonado, and J. M. Lopez-Soler, "Handover implementation in a 5G SDN-based mobile network architecture," in *2016 IEEE 27th Annual International Symposium on Personal, Indoor, and Mobile Radio Communications (PIMRC)*, Sept 2016, pp. 1–6.

[16] J. P.-G. et al., "Modeling and Dimensioning of a Virtualized MME for 5G Mobile Networks," *IEEE Tran. on Vehicular Technology*, vol. 66, no. 5, pp. 4383–4395, May 2017.

[17] D. Gross, J. F. Shortle, J. M. Thompson, and C. M. Harris, *Fundamentals of Queueing Theory*, 4th ed. New York, NY, USA: Wiley-Interscience, 2008.

[18] T. Zeng, O. Semiari, W. Saad, and M. Bennis, "Joint Communication and Control for Wireless Autonomous Vehicular Platoon Systems," *CoRR*, vol. abs/1804.05290, 2018.

[19] C. Chen, Y. T. Lin, L. H. Yen, M. C. Chan, and C. C. Tseng, "Mobility management for low-latency handover in SDN-based enterprise networks," in *2016 IEEE Wireless Communications and Networking Conference*, April 2016, pp. 1–6.

Genetic Algorithm for Time-Effective IoT Service Function Placement

Arvind Kalyan
Westview High School
San Diego CA 92129
email: arvindkrishnakalyan@gmail.com

***Abstract*—This paper focuses on the concept of IoT Service Function Chains (IoTSFC): a set of Internet of Things (IoT) Network Functions that must be allocated and implemented on IoT nodes in a specific order. Our problem is of Integer Linear Programming (ILP) type and therefore NP-Hard, so an optimal solution cannot be found in polynomial time. Therefore, we attempt to devise a heuristic method to solve the problem at a lower time complexity. The paper develops a solution using a genetic algorithm that attempts to minimize the total processing time and incurred transmission delay time required to execute a group of network functions across IoT nodes. The genetic algorithm is run on a string denoting placement of the network functions and runs a set of genetic operators in order to work toward an optimal solution. Our experimental results are encouraging, however, remain in progress.**

Keywords – Internet of Things; IoT Service Function Chaining; Minimax Problem; Genetic Algorithm; Natural Selection; Fitness.

I. Introduction

With the rise of network technologies in the last decade, the progress of the Internet of Things (IoT) has ramped up. Using various devices, such as sensors, remote monitors, etc., IoT networks can collect and process data on a massive scale. Services offered by an IoT device consist of various IoTSFC, and each IoTSFC itself contains a set of Network Functions (NFs). As opposed to less stringent network structures, IoTSFC functions must be implemented and executed in a specific order in order to carry out the appropriate service. With a rising amount of data, the efficiency of deployment becomes paramount. Traditional solutions involve function implementation on both hardware in the IoT gateway and in the cloud. However, this has proved unsuitable due to exorbitant costs and inflexibility. The introduction of Network Function Virtualization (NFV) has helped alleviate these concerns. Instead of implementation in the gateway, NFV allows for various NFs to be rendered through software on IoT nodes. This allows for programmability, as well as the required flexibility of network function assignment. Performance time can be improved by altering the site of implementation of a certain IoTSFC. However, high complexity and volume of these network functions can bring about challenges. The assignment of functions in IoTSFCs to viable IoT nodes is crucial to keep up with the increasing demands of today's age.

Section II delves into our contributions with this paper as compared to existing solutions. Section III establishes the mathematical model of the IoT problem. We specify the constraints and objective function that we look to minimize. Section IV introduces the proposed genetic algorithm we have devised, and it is further illustrated with a pseudo-code model. Section V depicts experimental setup and testing of our proposed algorithm, featuring a Gantt chart to illustrate these results. Finally, Section VI contains the conclusion and final remarks.

II. Our Contributions

Our problem presents an approach to minimizing the combination of processing time and incurred transmission delays through the placement of IoT network functions across a set of IoT nodes. We utilize a genetic algorithm to discover a minimum solution, returning a full placement scheme for a set of network functions.

Ren et al. [1] delved into a new scheme for the placement of IoT service functions, attempting to deploy these functions on nodes that are as close to their data source as possible. Doing so allows them to minimize total resource costs and maximize system performance. Qu et al. [2] introduced the concept of delays in their paper regarding NFV. The authors explored two different types of delay, one of them being a transmission delay incurred by a switch in virtual machines. They looked to find a scheme to minimize the maximum time as well, treating the service function chain problem as a "flexible job-shop scheduling problem". The authors also utilized a genetic algorithm to discover a minimum solution. Gao et al. [3] developed a genetic algorithm to solve the job-shop problem, using various genetic operators to add diversity. Moghadam et al. [4] brought up the concept and execution of a POX crossover to be used in the offspring generation in a genetic algorithm.Kouah et al. [5] have developed an energy-aware optimization model to solve the placement of IoTSFC problem and proposed a genetic algorithm heuristic solution and an energy-agnostic algorithm, with the goal to avoid exhausting nodes with limited energy capacities and providing an optimal solution for energy consumption for a small network topology. Wang [6] has considered an IoTSFC placement problem from the perspective of minimizing the number of VNF instances implemented and proposed a genetic algorithm based solution.

Our paper is unique in its inclusion of transmission delays in an IoTSFC placement scheme problem, utilizing a modified genetic algorithm in order to work toward a solution that minimizes the maximum time of implementation. While Ren et al. [1] attempt to minimize the distance from functions to a data source, we instead attempt to minimize the overall processing time and incurred transmission delay between network nodes. Wang [6] has considered an overall processing delay not to exceed a certain acceptable delay threshold, however has not accounted for transmission delay. Our problem formulation models closer to a real life IoT network as we take into account the varied transmission delays between network nodes. To our best knowledge, we are not aware of other research that has taken this into account, and this is a novel approach for solving IoTSFC placement problem. Our solution appears promising, but has not been fully tested. This remains the next step in the authors' research.

III. Mathematical Formulation of the Problem

This section presents a mathematical representation of the problem, including constraints and the objective function that will be solved using a genetic algorithm.

A. Model

We represent a graph of IoT nodes $G = (V, E)$, where V is the set of nodes on the graph and E is the set of traversable edges connecting these nodes. We create a set of service requests $\{s_1, s_2, s_3, ..., s_N\}$, where each of these service requests consist of network functions $\{f_{i1}, f_{i2}, ..., f_{ik_i}\}$. Each node that implements these requests is denoted by $k \in V$. These network functions must be implemented in the exact order as specified in the IoTSFC.

We define $i \in \{1, 2, ..., N\}$ as an index of service requests. $j \in \{1, 2, ..., k_i\}$ is an index for each service request that denotes the network function in the necessary order. For a service request i, the processing time required to implement network function j on node k is defined as $t_{i,j,k}$. The time that this implementation begins is represented by $s_{i,j}$, and the time it ends is denoted by $e_{i,j}$. In addition, we include a transmission delay when a request implements network function j on node k and implements function $j+1$ on another node k', denoted by $d_{i,j,k,k'}$.

We denote $x_{i,j,k}$ to be a binary variable representing whether or not a network function j contained in service request i is implemented on node k. We denote $y_{i,j,k,k'}$ as another binary variable for service i, network function j is implemented on a node k while function $j+1$ is implemented on separate node k' (i.e., the node is switched from k to k').

B. Objective

We treat this problem as a "minimax" problem, attempting to minimize the combination of processing time and incurred transmission delays through the placement of IoT network functions across a set of IoT nodes. We must take into account both the time of implementation of each network function, as well as transmission delays incurred by switching nodes.

$$\min C$$

where C = max $\sum_i \sum_j (t_{i,j,k} \cdot x_{i,j,k} + d_{i,j,k,k'} \cdot y_{i,j,k,k'})$

C. Constraints

First, we must define binary variable $x_{i,j,k}$ to represent whether a network function j contained in service request i is implemented on node k.

$$x_{i,j,k} = \begin{cases} 1 \text{ if implemented} \\ 0 \text{ else} \end{cases} \tag{1}$$

Similarly, $y_{i,j,k,k'}$ as another binary variable that represents whether a service i, network function j is implemented on a node k while function $j+1$ is implemented on separate node k' (i.e., the node is switched from k to k').

$$y_{i,j,k,k'} = \begin{cases} 1 \text{ if (k, k') is traversed} \\ 0 \text{ else} \end{cases} \tag{2}$$

To prevent a network function j of service request i from being implemented on an underresourced node, we create a constraint governing the start time $s_{i,j}$ across all nodes $k \in V$. In addition, the function must be implemented after the previous function has ended, ensuring that the necessary order of functions is preserved.

$$s_{i,j} + \sum_k t_{i,j,k} \cdot x_{i,j,k} \leq e_{i,j}, \forall i, j \tag{3}$$

Furthermore, when switching nodes within a request, we must ensure that the next function is implemented following the incurred transmission delay, preserving the order of implementation.

$$e_{i,j} + \sum_k d_{i,j,k,k'} \cdot y_{i,j,k,k'} \leq s_{i,j+1}, \forall i, j \tag{4}$$

When switching a service i from function j to $j+1$ through node k to k', we assure the $j+1$ is implemented on k'.

$$\sum_k y_{i,j-1,k,k'} = x_{i,j,k'}, \forall i, j \tag{5}$$

Additionally, we create a constraint that makes sure we can only switch to one other node at each function in a request.

$$\sum_k^{'} y_{i,j,k,k'} \leq 1, \forall i, j, k \tag{6}$$

The final constraint governs the implementation of each service function i for a request j, allowing each to be implemented only once on a node.

$$\sum_k x_{i,j,k} = 1, \forall i, j \tag{7}$$

Our problem is ILP and therefore NP-Hard, so an optimal solution cannot be found in polynomial time [6]. Therefore, we attempt to devise a heuristic method to solve the problem at a lower time complexity.

IV. Genetic Algorithm for IoT Function Placement

This section proposes a genetic algorithm that will allow the scheduling of a set of network functions onto IoT nodes, using pseudo-code to visualize this solution.

A. Proposed Solution Setup

We attempt to minimize the combined processing time and incurred delay times of IoT service function chains assigned across IoT nodes. In order to do so, we designate two strings [3] representing the function placement to be utilized by the algorithm. The first is the Operation Selection (OS) string, listing a set of functions given in the order they are meant to be implemented in. A service request i with j network functions, for example, is listed j times in the total string in various positions. The first network function will be listed as the first appearance, the second network function the second, and so on. The nth listing of a service request is the nth network function it contains, for example. This string cannot be edited, and is given as an input into the algorithm.

The second string, known as the Machine Selection (MS) string, outlines the nodes that each of the functions will be placed on. It has the same length as the OS string, however, it is split up into its i components, one for each service request. The jth element of the ith component represents the node on which jth function of service function i is to be implemented, as defined by the OS string. Each smaller component, denoting a service request, represents a chromosome. Each element, containing the node of implementation, is a gene. A solution is represented by placements dictated by an MS string.

To decode the MS string and return a set of $x_{i,j,k}$ and $y_{i,j,k,k'}$ values, we iterate through the string. If the value of the jth network function in the ith service request chromosome is equal to some value k, we set $x_{i,j,k} = 1$. For all network functions in a gene, if the value is a different value k' from the previous, indicating a different node used to implement, we set $y_{i,j,k,k'} = 1$.

For example, we consider a set of 3 jobs containing 2 functions each. These $f \in f_{1,1}, f1, 2, ..., f_{3,1}, f_{3,2}$ may be implemented on one of 3 virtual nodes.

We randomly designate an OS String, in this case, to 131223, denoting the order of function placement. The initial value is the first repetition of 1, so we implement $f_{1,1}$ first. The second function to implement is $f_{3,1}$, third is $f_{1,2}$, and so on. Similarly, we create a MS String of 213122. $f_{1,1}$ is implemented on Node 2, $f_{1,2}$ on Node 1, $f_{2,1}$ on Node 3, and so forth.

B. Proposed Genetic Algorithm

We begin by setting an arbitrary population size to store the MS strings. We define a simple fitness function as the maximum time taken to implement all the functions on the nodes denoted by the string. We generate two MS strings randomly, and unpartitioned to begin. To generate a population, it must satisfy each of the constraints listed previously. We select a node at random for each network function of each service request. Going in the order dictated by the OS string, we create a suitable starting time for each function after the previous function has been implemented, using the idle times available on each node. If there is enough time in an idle slot, we may add the next function in it. If not, it will be implemented at the end. These strings are stored in a sorted queue of length equal to the previously selected population size.

Inside the loop, we begin by evaluating the fitness of our population. This fitness test is done by calculating the time required for implementation, and a lower time entails a higher fitness score. We also define termination criteria; in this paper, the algorithm terminates when we reach the maximum generation or the maximum step with no significant improvement. If the termination criteria are satisfied, we exit and return the MS string that provides the optimal time at the beginning of the queue. If not satisfied, we select the two MS strings that provide the lowest maximum time to implement all functions in the OS string. These strings are crossed over to create two new offspring. We utilize a POX crossover [4] that will allow us to remain within the given constraints. First, the service requests contained in the string are partitioned at random into two groups. An element in the first parent string that is sectioned into the first group is placed in the same position in the first offspring, then removed from the first parent string. Meanwhile, elements in the second parent string that are in the second group occupy the same position in the second offspring and are removed from the parent. Elements that remain in the first parent string are placed in that order in the remaining spots of the second offspring, and vice versa.

We also introduce simple swapping mutations to the offspring after crossover. Two elements chosen at random in the offspring strings may be swapped, adding another layer of randomness to the selection process. After the offspring are completed, we evaluate their fitness as well. If any offspring are deemed to be more fit than any elements in the population, we add these offspring to the population and remove the least fit members of the population in order to maintain the constant population size. After the loop is completed, the algorithm will return the updated values of $x_{i,j,k}$ and $y_{i,j,k,k'}$ for all i, j, k.

V. Experimental Results

We have begun to test our algorithm using the network graph depicted in Fig. 1. The topology features six IoT nodes, with links connecting each node to its adjacent neighbors. We also removed the link from Node 1 to 3, so a service request may not switch between the two. Along each connected node pair, we labeled the transmission delay that would be incurred by switching across the two nodes. As suggested earlier, this closely models a real IoT network as we take into account the varied transmission delays between network nodes.

For this topology, as shown in Fig. 2, we created a set of four requests with a random amount of network functions contained in each. For example, Service Request 1 contains both f_{11} and f_{12}, while Service Request 3 contains three functions f_{31}, f_{32}, and f_{33}. We then defined a random implementation

Algorithm 1 Genetic Algorithm for IoTSFC Placement

Input: $G(V, E)$; $t_{i,j,k}$; $d_{i,j+1,k,k'}$; OS string
Output: $x_{i,j,k}$, $y_{i,j,k,k'}$
population = empty sorted queue of length $popsize$
MS1, MS2 = randomly generated MS strings
population = population $\cup$ MS1, MS2
while TRUE **do**
  evaluate fitness of all elements in population
  if termination criteria are met **then**
    optimalString = MS string with highest fitness score in population
    for all element in optimalString **do**
      update $x_{i,j,k}$, $y_{i,j,k,k'}$ using element
    end for
  end if
  P1, P2 = two MS strings from population with the highest fitness, implementing network functions in lowest times
  O1, O2 = POX crossover on P1, P2
  randomly mutate O1, O2
  if fitness of O1 $\geq$ lowest fitness in population **then**
    add O1 to population
    remove least fit element of population
  end if
  if fitness of O2 $\geq$ lowest fitness in population **then**
    add O2 to population
    remove least fit element of population
  end if
end while
return $x_{i,j,k}, y_{i,j,k,k'} \forall i, j, k$

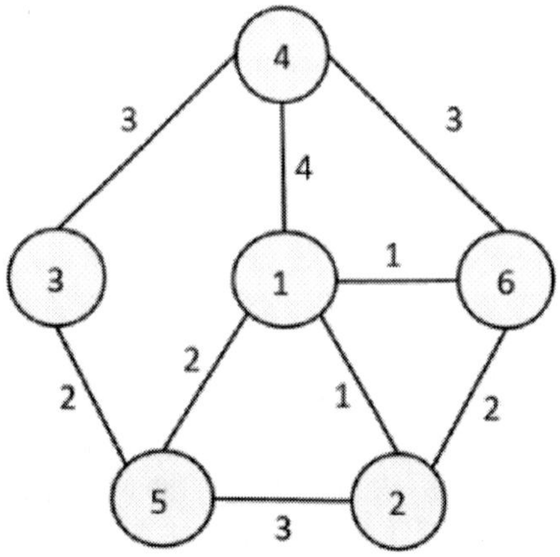

Fig. 1. 6 IoT-node topology

time for each network function on the six nodes given by the topology. Some of the functions cannot be implemented on all nodes; for example, f_{31} can only be implemented on Nodes 3 and 6. During simulations, we set the processing time for any unimplementable function on a certain node to be a very large integer, preventing the cost-reducing algorithm from implementing there.

		Node 1	Node 2	Node 3	Node 4	Node 5	Node 6
Service Request 1	f_{11}	5	-	4	-	-	-
	f_{12}	-	1	5	-	3	-
Service Request 2	f_{21}	-	6	-	6	-	-
	f_{22}	1	6	-	-	-	5
Service Request 3	f_{31}	-	-	4	-	-	2
	f_{32}	2	6	-	-	-	5
	f_{33}	-	3	4	-	-	6
Service Request 4	f_{41}	2	6	-	-	-	5
	f_{42}	-	1	5	-	3	-

Fig. 2. Set of 4 service requests with NF implementation times in each node

A. Simulation Results and Discussion

As shown in Fig. 3, our test was able to execute each network function contained in each service request in a total time of 7 units. The final and optimal string requires five node switches, incurring delays each time. Node 1 implements the most service functions, with three, while Nodes 3, 4, 5, and 6 are only tasked with implementing 1 function each. The algorithm took 15.55 seconds to run, creating additional generations until this solution was reached.

While these initial results are promising, our testing remains a work in progress. The authors look to test the algorithm on a variety of different topologies, as well as different functions which take a random time to implement on each of the nodes.

VI. CONCLUSIONS

We attempted to minimize the combination of processing time and incurred transmission delay of the placement of IoT network functions across a set of nodes. Since this problem falls under the classification of ILP problems, it is NP-Hard and therefore cannot be solved in a polynomial time. We utilized a genetic algorithm to discover a solution to the problem at a lower complexity. The algorithm takes into account both execution time and transmission delays incurred by a request switching nodes. Our testing is a work in progress, however, the initial results have been promising. We hope to reach an acceptable optimal solution in a time-efficient manner.

REFERENCES

[1] W. Ren, Y. Sun, H. Luo, and M. Obaidat, A New Scheme for IoT Service Function Chains Orchestration in SDN-IoT Network Systems, *IEEE Systems Journal*, pp. 1-12, July 2019.
[2] L. Qu, C. Assi, and K. Shaban, Delay Aware Scheduling and Resource Optimization with Network Function Virtualization, *IEEE Transactions on Communications*, pp. 3746-3758, Sept. 2018.
[3] L. Gao and X. Li, An Effective Hybrid Genetic Algorithm and Tabu Search for Flexible Job Shop Scheduling Problem, *International Journal Production Economics*, pp. 93-110, Dec. 2015.
[4] A.M. Moghadam, K. Wong, and H. Piroozfard, An Efficient Genetic Algorithm For Flexible Job-shop Scheduling Problem, *2014 IEEE International Conference on Industrial Engineering and Engineering Management*, pp. 1409-1413, Dec. 2014.
[5] Xin-Gang Wang, An Effective Solution Based on Genetic Algorithm for Virtual Network Functions Placement, *ICEIT*, pp. 21-31, 2017.
[6] R. Kouah, A. Alleg, A. Laraba, and T. Ahmed, Energy-aware placement for IoT-Service Function Chain, *IEEE 23rd International Workshop on Computer Aided Modeling and Design of Communication Links and Networks*, pp. 1-7, 2018.
[7] S. Skiena, The Algorithm Design Manual, *Springer-Verlag*, 1998.

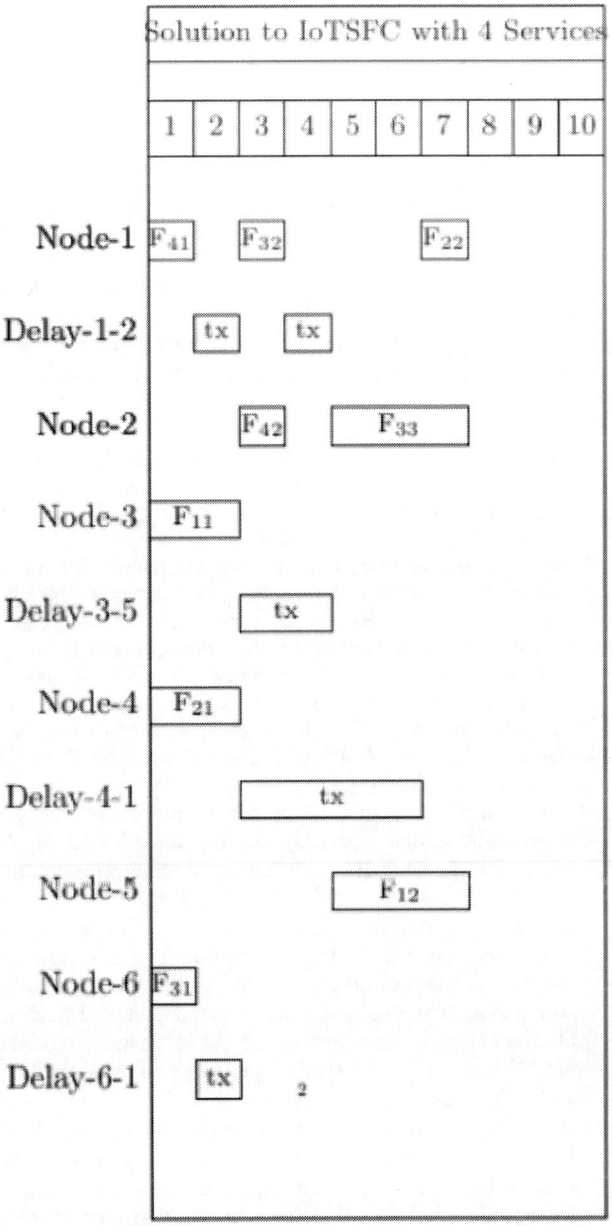

Fig. 3. GA Algorithm solution for IoTSFC Placement for 4 service requests on 6 IoT-node topology

Multiple Conditions-aware Dynamic Switch Migration in SDN Large Area Networks

Eugen Borcoci, Silviu – Gabriel Topoloi, Serban Georgica Obreja
University POLITEHNICA of Bucharest - UPB
Bucharest, Romania
Emails: eugen.borcoci@elcom.pub.ro, silviu.topoloi@elcom.pub.ro, serban@radio.pub.ro

Abstract —**Distributed control plane solutions are adopted in large SDN-controlled networks, to improve control plane scalability. Many studies exist, on Controller Placement or Selection Problem (CPP/CSP) using different optimization criteria. Most of them consider static solutions to optimize controller placement. However, in a dynamic context, (i.e., traffic flows variation, possible failures of links, nodes, or controllers, etc.) the initial controller placement and controller-to-forwarders mapping could be no more optimum. Additionally, in practice, the controllers have limited processing capacity so, their overload is possible. A solution for the above problems could be a partial dynamic switch migration, e.g., when detecting some controllers' overload. The contribution of this work-in-progress paper is an enhancement proposal of a dynamic migration solution (recently proposed in the literature), by introducing a multiple condition-aware migration complex decision. The proposed approach could solve the trade-offs between different optimization objectives of the network operator.**

Keywords — Software Defined Networking; Controller placement; Multi-condition-aware switch migration; Multi-criteria optimization; Forwarder nodes assignment; Reliability.

I. INTRODUCTION

The usual solution to assure the scalability of the *Software Defined Networking* SDN control plane is a distributed multi-controller implementation (flat or hierarchical organization), e.g., in [1][2].

Basically, a *SDN controller* (SDN-C) is placed in a geographically distinct location, i.e., physical network node. However, the recent *Network Function Virtualization* technologies [3] allow that SDN-Cs virtualization (notation for such a controller will be vSDN-C); several vSDN-Cs can be collocated in the same physical node. In the following text we suppose the basic approach, but the models developed in this paper can be as well applied to a virtualized environment.

A major issue in SDN large networks is the *Controller Placement Problem* (CPP). A lot of studies already exist dedicated to this problem [4-12]. Recent works are still elaborated, given that many associated issues exist together with CPP itself. Some examples are: network topology - flat or clustered; what are the criteria used to solve the CPP; number of controllers; failure-free or failure-aware metrics (controllers and/or node/link failures); controller-forwarder/switch mapping (in a static or dynamic way, i.e., depending on actual network conditions and network provider policies), etc. The optimality of the different solutions can be studied on some simplified topologies – in order to compare the approaches or, on real specific network topologies. The CPP is a non-polynomial NP-hard problem [4]; therefore, many pragmatic static/dynamic solutions have been proposed, using specific optimization criteria, targeting good performance in failure-free or failure-aware approaches.

Given the complexity of a real network environment, there is no unique best placement rule for CPP. Many of the current existing CPP solutions consider static mapping switches-controllers, thus having no capability of adaptation to dynamic load. However, during the network run-time, dynamic nodes addition and deletion can happen, or traffic variation (consequently, controller loads fluctuation appear), link/node/controller failures can appear, etc. In such cases, one can apply *dynamic switch migration* from the current controller to a new more appropriate controller, if enough pertinent and updated information exist at run-time [13-17]. This migration can be included in a more general *Controller Selection Problem* (CSP) and can be considered as an extension of the CPP [5].

The main parameter to be taken into account when deciding on switch migration is the current *load of the controllers*, dynamically evaluated by a monitoring system [13-17]. The switching objective is to achieve better load balancing and avoid controllers' overload. However, other individual parameters might be important, like controller-switch communication latency, inter-controller communication throughput, reliability-related properties, etc. Other specific optimization goals could be added to the above list, depending on specific network context (wire-line, wireless/cellular, cloud computing and data center networks) and on some specific business targets of the SDN-controlled network owner. A major problem is that different optimization criteria could naturally lead to non-convergent solutions; therefore, *a multi-criteria global optimization* could be a useful approach.

The contribution of this paper is a proposal to enhance a single criterion dynamic switch migration algorithm, recently proposed in the literature, [13][14], by *introducing a multiple condition-aware migration complex decision*. The procedure used is an extension of the method developed in [18] based on *multi-criteria decision algorithms* (MCDA)

[20]. Therefore, the goal here is not to develop some new optimization algorithm based on a single criterion, but to prove the value of multi-criteria CPP/CSP optimization approach, both statically, or performed during run-time. The input of MCDA is the set of candidates (e.g., an instance of controller placement and implicit a switch-controller mapping is called a candidate solution). Examples have been illustrated in the paper, on some simple network topologies, proving the usefulness of the approach. This work is still in progress; a simulation model is currently in development and its results will be reported in a future paper.

The paper structure is described here. Section II is a short overview of related work. Section III presents a flow-aware dynamic switching algorithm recently proposed [13][14]. Section IV shortly recalls the framework for MCDA-RL (the "*reference level*"). Section V contains the main paper contribution i.e., an enhancement proposal of the dynamic migration solution (described in Section III), by introducing a multiple condition-aware switch migration complex decision which could solve the trade-offs between different objectives of such optimization. Simple examples are given to prove the value of multi-criteria optimization. Section VI presents conclusions and future work.

II. Related Work

This short section is included mainly for references. In works [4-8][19], specific optimizations based generally on a single criterion are proposed, while comprehensive surveys on CPP/CSP are overviewed in [9-12]. The general goal is to find those controller placements that provide high performance (e.g., low delay for controller-switch communications) and also create robustness to controllers and/or network failures. The studies [13-17] are oriented on CSP issues i.e., switch migration and load balancing algorithms. The work [18] applies MCDA [20] in order to consider several criteria in a static CPP approach.

An early work of Heller et al. [4], has found optimal CPP solutions for realistic network instances, in failure-free scenarios, by analyzing the entire solution space, with off-line computations (the metric is switch-to-controller latency). The works [6-8][19] additionally considered the resilience as being important with respect to events like: *controller* failures, *network links/paths/nodes* failures, *controller overload, load imbalance*. The *inter-controller latency* is also important; generally, it cannot be minimized while simultaneously minimizing controller-switch latency- therefore - a tradeoff solution could be the answer.

K.Sood and Y.Siang [5] propose to transform the CPP problem into *Controller Selection Problem* (CSP), i.e., consider the dynamics of the network and make controller selection for group of forwarders. They explore the relationship between traffic intensity, resources requirement, and QoS requirements. They search solutions which are topology-independent and adaptive to the needs of the underlying network behaviour. The optimal number of controllers is calculated, to reduce the individual workload, of a controller; the paper investigates the placement/location of the controllers. However, the first declared objective in [5] has been to motivate the CSP and not to determine the optimal placement of controllers in the network.

The work [6] they developed several algorithms for real topologies, considering the reliability of SDN control, but still looking for keeping acceptable latencies. The controller instances are chosen as to minimize connectivity losses; connections are defined according to the shortest path between controllers and forwarding devices.

Hock et.al. [7] adopted a multi-criteria approach for some combinations of the metrics (e.g., max. latency and controller load imbalance for failure-free and respectively failure use cases). Muller et.al. [8] eliminate some restrictions of previous studies, like: single paths, *on-demand* only processing (in controllers) of the forwarders requests, and some constraints imposed on failover mechanisms.

Yang Xu, Marco Cello et al., [13]14] recently developed a comprehensive solution for dynamic switch migration, based on run-time information delivered by a monitoring system. This approach will be further described in Section III as the starting point for work presented in this paper.

The paper [15] proposes a switch migration method, where switch migration is seen as a signature matching problem and is formulated as a 3-D earth mover's distance model to protect strategically important controllers in the network. A heuristic method is proposed, time-efficient and suitable to large-scale networks. Simulation results show that one can disguise strategically important controllers by diminishing the difference of traffic load between controllers. The proposed methods can relieve the traffic pressure of controllers and prevent saturation attacks.

In [18] a multi-criteria based algorithm is used (applicable for an arbitrary number of decision criteria) to solve the CPP.

This paper extends the solution of [13][14] and is based on [18] work. A multiple condition-aware switch migration complex decision is introduced which could solve the trade-offs between different objectives (thus solving a dynamic selection problem - CSP).

III. A Flow-aware SDN Dynamic Switch Migration Algorithm

This section will shortly present (as a starting point) a recent solution developed by Yang Xu, Marco Cello et al. in [13][14], for dynamic SDN switch migration, to avoid controller overload. Then, in the next section we will propose an enrichment of the decision for SDN switch migration, considering that in practice multiple conditions could actually exist, to influence the switch-to-controller assignment, i.e., not only the controller overload. Other criteria to take a decision can also be important, like switch-controller communication delay, reliability capabilities, etc. A multiple criteria optimization algorithm could offer a better trade-off solution.

A. The SDN switches migration problem

In [13][14], the switch migration scenario is analyzed, starting from a given switch-to-controller assignment and partition (based on some criteria) of the network, in domains; each one is controlled by a single controller. Also, a realistic assumption is considered, i.e., limited processing capacity of the controllers. During run-time, if some controllers are overloaded (such events are dynamically observed by a monitoring system), then a heuristic algorithm is applied, to optimally move (re-assign) a number of the switches coordinated by the overloaded controller to another controller less loaded. In order to reduce the control plane signaling (needed to govern the migration) between controllers, the migration is *cluster-based*. In other words, not a single switch is migrated, but a cluster of switches are moved from an overloaded controller, e.g., CT_i, to another less loaded controller CT_j. Thus, the algorithm realizes a controller load balancing (the name *BalCon* is coined for this algorithm [13]). The [13][14] works do not assume a predictable traffic or well-known traffic patterns among the SDN switches. Instead, the network load level is learned from monitored values of the input or transited flows through the network of SDN switches.

The scenario supposes a set *S* of SDN switches, managed by a set *CT* of controllers. Let Si be a SDN switch controlled by the SDN controller CT_m. The following flow arrival rates are considered:

$f_{o,Si}$ at *Si* from outside (e.g., from some hosts) the SDN network,

$f_{Si,o}$ flows leaving the network from *Si*,

$f_{Si,Sj}$ - current arrival rate of new flows going on the link between the two connected switches, from *Si* to *Sj*.

All the above flows generate processing tasks in the controller CT_m. Here, it is assumed the case which produces the highest controller's load: reactive SDN control behavior is applied. This means that for each new flow coming to a switch, a *packet_in* message is uploaded to the controller. The message is asking the controller to process the flow information and then to install in the switch Si new rules for that flow.

The SDN network of switches was previously partitioned (using some algorithms) in disjoint "control-domains", each one controlled by a single controller. The total load $L(CT_m)$ at controller CT_m is composed of three main components:

- the path computation load of new flows arriving from outside the SDN network, to the switches "belonging" to CT_m
  another SDN domains of the same SDN network
- the rule installation load at each switch controlled by CT_m, for all flows crossing the domain controlled by CT_m.

To evaluate in a generic way the computational effort of a controller due to the instantiation of the new flows, the work [14] considered that path computation for a single flow requires α units of load, whereas the rules installation of a single flow in a single switch requires β units of load. So, the overall computation load for each controller can be evaluated, given the flow arrival rates at the switches coordinated by it.

If the CT_m has in its partition/domain a set $Sw(CT_m)$ of SDN switches, then its overall load $L(CT_m)$ (see detailed formulas in [14]), is:

$$L(CT_m)=L_{cmp}(CT_m) + L_{inst}(CT_m) \quad (1)$$

where the index *cmp* denotes the computation load and *inst* denotes the installation load. The two components are:

$$L_{cmp}(CT_m) = L_{cmp}(CT_m)_{in}+L_{cmp}(CT_m)_{transit}$$

$$L_{inst}(CT_m) = L_{inst}(CT_m)_{out}+L_{inst}(CT_m)_{transit} \quad (2)$$

The notations are explained below.

$L_{cmp}(CT_m)_{in}$ and $L_{cmp}(CT_m)_{transit}$ are the sums of all computation loads associated to input flows for all switches in $Sw(CT_m)$, related to $f_{o,Si}$ and respectively to $f_{Sj,Si}$, where $Si \in Sw(CT_m)$.

$L_{inst}(CT_m)_{out}$ and $L_{inst}(CT_m)_{transit}$ are the sums of the installation loads for all switches in $Sw(CT_m)$, in order to instruct each switch about flows going out of it, outside of the SDN network, or flows going out to another switch of the SDN network.

An SDN controller is overloaded or even congested when its overall computational load is $L(CT_m) > L$, where L is the maximum load to be admitted for CT_m. Note that in [14], the same value L is supposed for all controllers (this can be seen as a limitation of the method).

The *Optimal Controller Load Balancing (OCLB)* problem is defined in [14] as *to find the partition which minimizes the worst case of load of a controller CTm, among the set CT of all controllers*. It is stated in [13] that the OCLB problem is NP-complete. Therefore, a heuristic algorithm is proposed.

The OCLB problem is actually to partition a network graph. The computation of $L(CT_m)$ for each CT_m can be induced directly from the graph. The SDN network is modeled as a directed edge-weighted and vertex-weighted graph G(S, E) in which SDN switches are the vertices with weights $l(Si)$, where $Si \in S$ and edges $E = \{(Si, Sj) : Si, Sj \in S, l(Si, Sj) > 0\}$, are the inter-connections among SDN switches. The value $l(Si, Sj)$ is the edge weight of (Si, Sj). Equivalently, the overall load at CT_m is the sum of the weights of the vertices belonging to its partition plus the sum of weights of the edges directed to the partition of CT_m. Specifically, the switch Si placed in the partition of CT_m, produces the following load for its controller CT_m:

$$l(Si) = L_{cmp}(CT_m)_{in,Si} + {}_{inst}(CT_m)_{out,Si}+L_{inst}(CT_m)_{transit,Si,Sj} \quad (3)$$

The l(Si) is the sum of computing load in CT_m, for flows coming into Si from external networks added to the installation load of the CT_m, in order to install rules in Si for flows going out of Si (to external networks/hosts, or to other switches).

$$l(Sj, Si) = L_{cmp}(CT_m)_{transit,Sj,Si} \quad (4)$$

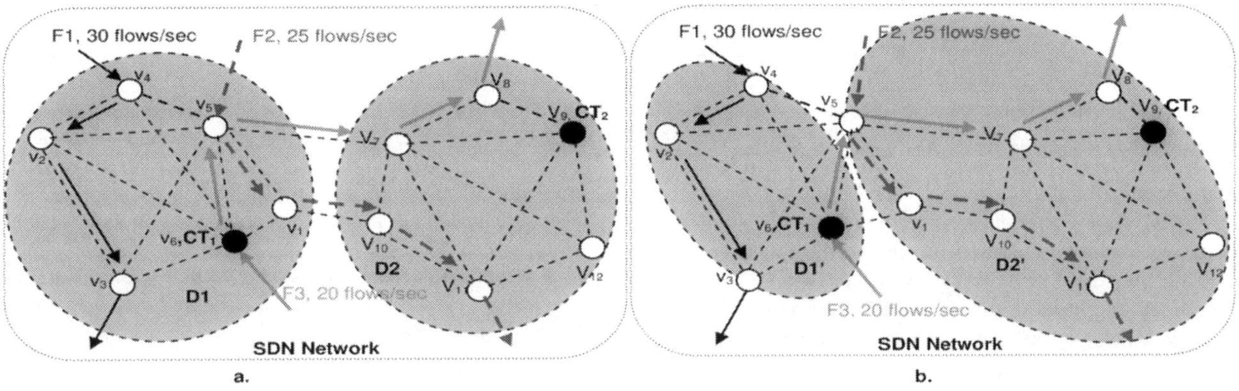

Figure 1. Switch migration from D1 to D2 – example; a. before migration; b. after migration

The weight l(Sj, Si) = $L_{cmp}(CT_m)_{transit,Sj,Si}$ is the computation load in CT_m, induced by the Si when it receives a new flow from Sj.

BalCon is a heuristic algorithm, operating during the network runtime. It detects and solves congestion at the SDN controllers through optimized SDN switch migrations. BalCon can be implemented as a northbound application of the SDN controller. BalCon consists of three phases:

1) *Monitoring and congestion detection*: BalCon monitors the congestion level at each controller. If the load of a controller CT_m reaches a given threshold, then BalCon computes a list of switches that may be migrated. The list is ordered by a priority based on a pre-determined metric.

2) *Clustering and migration evaluation*: starting from the SDN switches in the priority list, BalCon analyzes the traffic pattern among switches to find clusters of heavily connected switches.

3) *Cluster migration*: the best cluster is found and the migration is evaluated; the switches belonging to the cluster are migrated to the new SDN controller.

Figure 1 a. shows a SDN network partitioned in two domanins D1 and D2, controlled by the controllers CT_1 and respectively CT_2. Each vertice V_i of the graph is a network node accommodating a switch or a switch and a controller. The example shows three set of flows going into the network, routed as in the figure and producing F1: 40 flows/sec; F2:25 flows/sec and F3:20 flows/sec. We assume that α=1 and β = 0.1 [14]. Then, computing the loads for CT_1 and CT_2 (formulas (1) and (2) are applied), we get :

$L(CT_1) = (30+25+20)\alpha + (3*30 +2*25 + 2*20)\beta = 75 + 18 =93$ units of load

$L(CT_2) = (25 + 20)\alpha + (2*25 + 2*20)\beta = 45+9 = 54$ units of load.

Supposing that L=80 (maximum load for a controller) one can see that the CT_1 is overloaded. If for instance, V_5 and V_1 migrate to CT_2 then the loads will be modified (see Figure 1 b.). This simple example qualitatively proves that an appropriate migration can realize better load balancing.

$L(CT_1) = (30+20)\alpha + (3*30 +2*25 + 2*20)\beta = 50 + 18 =68$ units of load.

$L(CT_2) = (25 + 20)\alpha + (3*25 + 4*20)\beta = 45+15.5 = 60.5$ units of load.

This second partition provides better load balance.

B. The BalCon Algorithm

This sub-section summarizes the BalCon algorithm proposed in [14]. It is activated when an overload is detected for a controller, by a monitoring system. The input data in the algorithm are: the network graph G(S, E); the identity of a congested controller CTm and its load; the set of switches Sw(CTm) controlled by CTm. A cluster of switches to be migrated is started to be defined and then expanded via iterations (*IncreaseCluster* function). The migrations to different target SDN controllers of the selected cluster are evaluated by a function *ComputeMigrationAlternatives*. For each controller, it computes the controller load and the migration size (the number of switches to be migrated). Finally, the function *Evaluate-BestMigrationAlternative* evaluates the best alternative (based on some optimum criteria). The computation steps are [see details in 14]:

```
A=Ø; A is the set of cluster switches
A = ComputeStartingSwitchesList(Sw(CTm))
foreach Si ∈ A do
    T = {Si}; T is the cluster
    alternatives =
        alternatives U ComputeMigrationAlternatives(T );
   while 1 do
       newT = IncreaseCluster(T );
       if size(T ) >mcs_ newT = T then break;
       T = newT ;
       alternatives = alternatives U
                 ComputeMigrationAlternatives(T );
     od
  od
[T^0, Target_SDN_controller^0] ←
   EvaluateMigrationAlternatives (alternatives);
```

Starting from the cluster *T*, the function *IncreaseCluster* constructs the set *neighborsT* composed of all SDN switches that are neighbors to *T*. An SDN switch *Si* is a neighbor of *T* if $\exists Sj \in T : l(Si, Sj) \neq 0, l(Sj, Si) \neq 0$. The function selects the neighbour that maximizes the relative density *Density* [11] of the newly created cluster. The rationale is that only SDN switches with strong inter-connections should be grouped into the same cluster. Then the cluster will be migrated between controllers as a whole, to reduce the overall computation complexity (related to migration) of controllers.

The algorithm halts if the cluster reaches a predefined size *mcs* (max cluster size), or the increased cluster is equal to the old one ($newT = T$). The next switch in *A* is then selected and inserted in an empty cluster *T*. When the max starting switch list size is reached, all the migration alternatives are evaluated (*AlternativeEvaluation*). The best alternative composed by the cluster and the target SDN controller are chosen and the migration can be executed.

Given the alternatives vector, the function *EvaluateMigrationAlternatives* chooses the best alternative ($[T^0$,Target_SDN_controller$^0]$) among them, that optimizes one of the following *Evaluation-Method* like:

minMax - minimize the maximum controllers' load:

$$\underset{alternatives}{argmin}\ (\ max\ [L(CT_1), \ldots, L(CT|_{CT|})\ ]) \quad (5)$$

minSum - minimize the sum of controllers' load:

$$\underset{alternatives}{argmin} \sum_{CTm \in CT} L(CTm) \quad (6)$$

Note that the optimization criteria presented above is the unique *load balancing objective*, based on the current load of the controllers. This can be considered as a limitation of this method.

IV. MULTI-CRITERIA OPTIMIZATION ALGORITHMS

The placement of the SDN controllers and/or selection, or switch migration may involve several particular metrics. The migration of switches can use the metric defined by formulas (5) or (6). So, to achieve particular objectives, appropriate static and/or dynamic optimization algorithms can be applied. However, the CPP, CSP and switch migration problems have naturally multiple conditions characteristics; therefore, the MCDA is a good approach to achieve a convenient trade-off solution.

This paper uses the same variant of MCDA implementation i.e., the *reference level (RL) decision algorithm* (MCDA-RL) [20]. Here, the MCDA will be applied as to enhance the solution for dynamic switch migration, by adding the possibility to obtain a trade-off between load balancing objective and some other possible criteria. The MCDA-RL selects the optimal solution based on normalized values of different metrics. For the sake of completeness we summarize the MCDA-RL model.

The MCDA assumes *m* objectives functions (whose positive values, should be minimized). A solution is represented as a point in a space R^m of objectives; the decision parameters/variables are: v_i, i = 1, ..m, with $\forall i$, $v_i \geq 0$; the image of a candidate solution is $Sl_s=(v_{s1},v_{s2}, ..,v_{sm})$, represented as a point in R^m. The number of candidate solutions is S. The value ranges of decision variables may be bounded by given constrains. The optimization selects a solution satisfying a given objective function and conforming to a particular metric.

The MCDA-RL [20], defines two reference parameters: r_i =*reservation level*=the upper limit, not allowed to be crossed by the actual decision variable v_i of a solution; a_i=*aspiration level*=the lower bound, below which the decision variables (i.e., the associate solutions) are seen as similar (i.e., any solution can be seen as "good"- from the point of view of this variable). For each decision variable v_i, one can define two values named r_i and a_i, i= 1, ..m, by computing among all solutions s = 1, 2, ..S:

$$r_i = \max\ [v_{is}],\ s = 1, 2, ..S \qquad a_i = \min\ [v_{is}],\ s = 1, 2, ..S \quad (7)$$

Normalization can make the algorithm agnostic versus different nature of criteria; the normalized non-dimensional values can be numerically compared despite their different nature. The absolute value v_i of any decision variable is *replaced* with *distance from it to the reservation level*: r_i-v_i; (so, increasing v_i will decrease the distance). For each variable v_{si}, a ratio is computed:

$$v_{si}' = (r_i - v_{si})/(r_i - a_i), \quad \forall s,i \quad (8)$$

The factor $1/(r_i-a_i)$ - plays also the role of a weight. A variable having high dispersion of values (i.e., *max* – *min* has a high value in formula (7)) will have lower weight and so, greater chances to be considered in determination of the minimum in the next relation (9). On the other side, if the values *min, max* are rather close to each other, then any solution could be enough "good", w.r.t. that respective decision variable.

The basic MCDA-RL algorithm steps are (see also [18]):

Step 0. Compute the matrix $M\{v_{si}'\}$, s=1…S, i=1…m

Step 1. Compute for each candidate solution *s*, the minimum among all its normalized variables v_{si}':

$$\min_s = \min\{v_{si}'\};\ i=1...m \quad (9)$$

Step 2. Select the best solution:

$$v_{opt} = \max\ \{\ \min_s\ \},\ s=1, ..S \quad (10)$$

Formula (9) selects for each candidate solution *s*, the worst case, i.e., the closest solution to the reservation level (after searching among all decision variables). Then the formula (10) selects among the solutions, the best one, i.e., that one having the highest value of the normalized parameter. One can also finally select more than one solution (quasi-optimum solutions in a given range).

Different policies can be applied for selection; some decision variables could be more important than others. A simple modification of the algorithm can support a variety of provider policies. The new normalized decision variables will be:

$$v_{si}' = w_i(r_i - v_{si})/(r_i - a_i) \quad (11)$$

where $w_i \in (0,1]$ is a weight (priority), depending on policy considerations. Its value can significantly influence the final selection. A lower value of w_i represents actually a higher priority of that parameter in the selection process.

V. MULTIPLE CONDITIONS-AWARE DYNAMIC SWITCH MIGRATION

This section will develop the main contribution of this paper, i.e., to consider several conditions to decide upon SDN switch migration and therefore, to transform the BalCon algorithm (shortly described in Section III, [13][14]) in a multi-criteria one, by making a trade-off optimization based on several weighted criteria. The idea is that the switch migration will change the controller-switch mapping and therefore, it can be seen as a new optimization problem derived from CPP/CSP.

Examples of several metrics of interest have been presented in [18]. A selection of them (at network provider choice and policies) can be included in the function *EvaluateMigrationAlternatives* of the BalCon algorithm, thus offering the possibility to decide upon a solution determined by multiple conditions and not only by the controller overload. The MCDA methodology will be applied. Some examples of such metrics are given below.

A. Other metrics examples

The SDN-controlled network can be abstracted by an undirected graph G(V, E), with V - set of nodes, E – set of edges and n=|V| the total number of nodes. Note that this graph is different from the flow-based graph considered in the Section III. The edges weights may represent an additive metric (e.g., *average propagation latency*).

A basic metric is *d(v, c): shortest path* distance from a forwarder node $v \in V$ to a controller $c \in V$. We denote by C_i a particular placement of controllers; $C_i \subseteq V$ and $|C_i| < |V|$. The number of controllers can be limited to $|C_i| = k$ for any particular placement C_i. The set of all possible placements is denoted by $C = \{C_1, C_2 \ldots\}$. Some metrics are basic, i.e., failure-free; others could take into account failure events of links or nodes. It is assumed that the controllers are installed in particular positions of the set of network nodes V. A few examples are given below:

Example 1:

Worst_case_latency

$$L_{wc} = \max_{v \in V} \min_{c \in C_i} d(v,c) \quad (12)$$

Average_latency:

$$L_{avg}(C_i) = \frac{1}{n} \sum_{v \in V} \min_{c \in Ci} d(v,c) \quad (13)$$

The CPP algorithm should find a placement C_{opt}, where *either average latency* or *the worst case latency is minimized.* The limitations of the optimization process based on the above metrics (12) and (13) consist in: static values assumed for latencies, despite that delay is a dynamic value in IP networks; only free-failure case are considered; no upper limit exists on the number of forwarders/switches assigned to a controller; not taking into account the inter-controller connectivity. Another possible metric in failure-free case is *maximum cover,* [4]. The algorithm should find a controller placement, as to *maximize the number of nodes within a latency bound,* i.e., to find a placement of *k* controllers such that they cover a maximum number of forwarder nodes, while each forwarder must have a limited latency bound to its controller.

Example 2:

Nodes/links failures (Nlf)

This example will consider a failure-aware metric. Links or nodes failures can cause some switches to loose access to controllers. Therefore, a particular optimization objective could be to find a switch-to-controller mapping that minimizes the number of switches possible to get into controller-less situations, in various scenarios of link/node failures. A realistic assumption is to limit the number of possible simultaneous failures at only a few (e.g., two [7]).

For *any given placement* C_i of the controllers, an additive integer value metric $Nlf(C_i)$ could be defined: consider a failure scenario denoted by f_k, with $f_k \in F$, where F is the set of all network failure scenarios. Suppose that in an instance scenario, at most two link/nodes are down; initialize $Nlf_k(C_i) = 0$; then for each node $v \in V$, add one to $Nlf_k(C_i)$ if the node v has no path to any controller $c \in C_i$ and add zero otherwise; in other words, count the number of isolated nodes; compute the maximum value (i.e., consider the worst failure scenario). One obtains the formula (14) where *k* covers all scenarios of F.

$$Nlf(C_i) = \max Nlf_k(C_i) \quad (14)$$

The *optimization algorithm* should find a *placement which minimizes (14).* It is expected that increasing the number of controllers, will decrease the *Nlf* value. Note that the optimum solution based on the metric (14) could be very different from those provided by the algorithms using the metrics (12) or (13).

B. Multi-condition algorithm

Transformation of the BalCon algorithm in a MCDA type is realized by modifying the final BalCon phase and is summarized below. Note that positions of the controllers in the network is fixed; only the mapping switch-to-controller can vary.

The function *ComputeMigrationAlternatives* provides several solutions of switch assignment to controllers, to avoid controller overload.

The function *EvaluateMigrationAlternatives* will be replaced by a new function *Multi-condition_Eval_Migration_Alternative* in which the inputs are:

- migration alternatives provided by the original *ComputeMigrationAlternatives*
- solutions of switch-to-controller mapping provided by other algorithms based on several criteria of interest, selected from, e.g.: to minimize the maximum controllers' load (5); minimize the sum of controllers' load (6); worst case latency (12);

average latency (13); node/link failure (14) and maybe others. Note that the detailed algorithms for the metrics (12-14) are not presented here.

We also stress the idea that this study will not aim to select a given set of "best" criteria and use them for optimization. The reason is that such a selection is actually dependent on the particular SDN network characteristics and, more important on the policies of the SDN network provider/owner in defining the goals of the optimization process. So, this study shows the applicability and usefulness of multi-criteria in solving dynamic CSP problems.

The working phases are the following:

(1)*Phase 1*:

1.1. Define the additional criteria, (other than the controller load) i.e., the decision variables of interest and their priorities.

1.2. Consider all solutions C1, C2, .. (a solution is a particular switch-to-controller mapping provided by the *ComputeMigrationAlternatives* function (these would result after migration of a cluster).

1.3. Compute the values of the *normalized metrics for each candidate solution* (i.e. future MCDA candidate solution), by using specialized algorithms and their associated metrics.

The Phase 1 phase has as outputs the set of candidate solutions and values to fill the entries of the matrix M defined in Section IV.

(2) *Phase 2*: MCDA-RL: define r_i and a_i, for each decision variable; eliminate those candidates having parameter values out of range defined by r_i; define – if wanted – convenient weights w_i for different decision variables; compute the normalized variables (formula (8)); run the MCDA Step 0, 1 and 2 (formulas (9-11)).

The Phase 2 provides the migration solution.

C. Simple numerical example

This subsection will present a simple numerical example to illustrate the multi- criteria switch migration solution. The network has three domains D1, D2, D3, each one controlled by a controller.

The network is described by a graph, in which three sets of flow rates F1, F2, F3 are represented. The links could be physical or overlay links. The numbers written on some links show the estimated average latency between those vertices (this is an additive metric).

The loads for CT_1, CT_2, CT_3 (applying the formulas (1) and (2)) with α=1, β=0.1:

$L(CT_1) = (30+25+20)\alpha + (3*30 +2*25 + 3*20)\beta = 75 + 20 = 95$ units of load.

$L(CT_2) = (25 + 20)\alpha + (2*25 + 2*20)\beta = 45+9 = 54$ units of load.

$L(CT_3) = (20)\alpha + (3*20)\beta = 20+6 = 26$ units of load.

Supposing that L=80 (maximum load for a controller) one can see that the CT_1 is overloaded. Therefore a cluster of switches migration from the domain of CT_1 would make a better load balance and solve the overload of CT_1.

Solution M1. Suppose that the cluster $\{V_1, V_5\}$ would migrate to CT_2. The new loads would be:

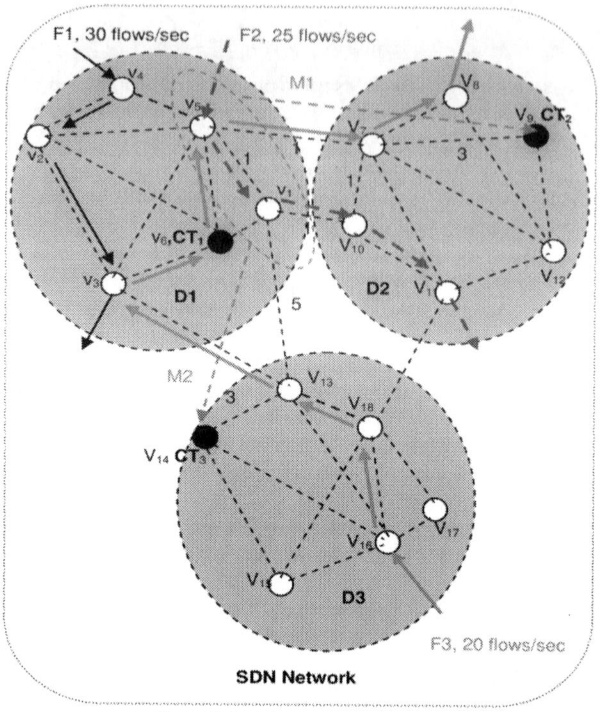

Figure 2. Switch migration example

$L(CT_1) = (30+20)\alpha + (3*30 + 2*20)\beta = 50 + 13 = 63$

$L(CT_2) = (25 + 20)\alpha + (3*25 + 3*20)\beta = 45+13.5 = 58.5$

$L(CT_3) = 26$ (not modified)

Solution M2. If the cluster $\{V_1, V_5\}$ would migrate to CT_3, then the new loads would be:

$L(CT_1) = (30+20)\alpha + (3*30 + 2*20)\beta = 50 + 13 = 63$

$L(CT_2) = 54$ (not modified).

$L(CT_3) = (25+20)\alpha + (2*25+3*20)\beta = 45+11 = 56$

If a single criterion (BalCon: e.g., considering the formula (5)), then the migration solutions M1 and M2 are equally acceptable (max load = $L(CT_1)$ = 63).

However if one consider additional multi-criteria then the best solution selected by a multi-criteria algorithm could be different. Examples are given below (see Figure 2).

Worst case latency (formula (12))

Let us suppose that shortest path from vertices V_1, V_5 to controllers are: $d(V_1, CT_2) = 5$; $d(V_5, CT_2) = 4$; $d(V_1, CT_3) = 8$; $d(V_5, CT_3) = 9$. So, the MCDA for the criterion *worst case latency* will prefer the M1 solution as better.

Nodes/links failures (Nlf)(formula (14))

It can be seen that M2 solution is better than M1, if link failures are considered. In D2 domain, a failure scenario with links V_7-V_9 and V_9-V_{12} out of order, will isolate the controller CT_2 and consequently, *Nlf = 5*. On the other side in D3 domain, the maximum value of this metric is *Nlf* = 1.

If multiple other criteria are included in a MCDA based decision, then the final solution will depend on weights assigned to different criteria.

Of course, other criteria (see [18]) could be added to MCDA with different weights for the decision variables. We limited our numerical example above to a simple case, just to illustrate the idea of the approach, i.e., to prove the usefulness of the multi-criteria in deciding upon SDN switch migration. Complete calculations could be performed using the full BalCon algorithm enriched with MCDA procedures.

We have to acknowledge the limitations of this study as a work in progress. This paper does not include the study of the control plane signalling between controllers, in order to achieve awareness of the controllers about the new situation of their domains; this is a separate problem. No quantitative performance evaluations of the migration procedures are presented here. The limit of controller acceptable load has been considered to be the same for all controllers; actually these values can be different. These topics could be subjects of additional studies.

VI. CONCLUSIONS AND FUTURE WORK

This paper extended the studies [13][14] on dynamic switch migration, by enriching the final decision on the migration solution based, i.e., based not only on controllers load values but on multiple conditions and using multi-criteria decision algorithms (MCDA), as in [18]. The advantage of MCDA is that it can produce a tradeoff (optimum) result, while considering several weighted criteria, part of them even being partially contradictory.

The goal here was not to select a given set of "best" criteria and use them for optimization. The reason is that such a selection is actually dependent on the particular SDN network characteristics and, more important on the policies of the SDN network provider/owner in defining the goals of the optimization process. So, this study is focused to show the applicability and usefulness of multi-criteria in solving CPP/CSP problems not only in static context but also during run-time of the SDN network.

This is still a work in progress; a simulation model is currently in development. An initial proof on concept has been performed in Section V by using some simple but relevant examples.

Future work will be done to complete and run the simulation model and considering more extended network topologies.

A more deep study should consider the amount of signaling between controllers while switch migration occurs. Another open issue is to get a trade-off between the frequency of switch migration events and stability of the network (i.e., to avoid excessive migration of switches) - versus the rate of traffic changes in the data plane of the network. The dynamic of the data plane after switches migration (e.g. in multicast context) is still an open research issue.

REFERENCES

[1] A. Tootoonchian, and Y. Ganjali, "Hyperflow: a distributed control plane for openflow" in Proc. INM/WREN, 2010, https://pdfs.semanticscholar.org/f7bd/dc08b9d9e2993b3639 72b89e08e67dd8518b.pdf, [retrieved: 5, 2019].

[2] T. Koponen, M. Casado, N. Gude, J. Stribling, L. Poutievski, et.al., "Onix: a distributed control platform for large-scale production networks," in Proc. OSDI, 2010, https://www.usenix.org/legacy/event/osdi10/tech/full_papers /Koponen.pdf, [retrieved: 5, 2019].

[3] B.Han, V. Gopalakrishnan, L. Ji, and S. Lee, "Network Function Virtualisation: Challenges and Opportunities for Innovations", IEEE Communications Magazine, pp. 90-97, February 2015.

[4] B. Heller, R. Sherwood and N. McKeown, "The controller placement problem," in Proc. HotSDN, pp. 7–12, 2012, https://dl.acm.org/citation.cfm?id=2342444, [retrieved: 5, 2019].

[5] K. Sood and Y. Xiang, "The controller placement problem or the controller selection problem?", Journal of Communications and Information Networks, Vol.2, No.3, pp.1-9, Sept.2017.

[6] Y. Hu, W. Wendong, X. Gong, X. Que, and C. Shiduan, "Reliability aware controller placement for software-defined networks," in Proc. IM. IEEE, pp. 672–675, 2013, https://ieeexplore.ieee.org/document/6573050/, [retrieved: 4, 2019].

[7] D. Hock, M. Hartmann, S. Gebert, M. Jarschel, T. Zinner, and P. Tran-Gia, "Pareto-Optimal Resilient Controller Placement in SDN-based Core Networks," Proceedings of the ITC, Shanghai, China, pp. 1-9, 2013, https://ieeexplore.ieee.org/document/6662939/, [retrieved: 4, 2019].

[8] L. Muller, R. Oliveira, M. Luizelli, L. Gaspary, and M. Barcellos, "Survivor: an Enhanced Controller Placement Strategy for Improving SDN Survivability", IEEE Global Comm. Conference (GLOBECOM), pp.1909 - 1915 12/2014, https://ieeexplore.ieee.org/document/7037087/, [retrieved: 4, 2019].

[9] G. Wang, Y. Zhao, J. Huang, and W. Wang, "The Controller Placement Problem in Software Defined Networking: A Survey", IEEE Network, pp. 21- 27, September/October 2017.

[10] S.Yoon, Z. Khalib, N. Yaakob, and A.Amir, "Controller Placement Algorithms in Software Defined Network - A Review of Trends and Challenges", MATEC Web of Conferences ICEESI 2017 140, 01014 DOI:10.1051/matecconf/201714001014, 2017.

[11] A.K. Singh and S. Srivastava, "A survey and classification of controller placement problem in SDN", Int'lJournal of Network Management, March 2018, DOI: 10.1002/nem.2018, pp.1-25, https://www.researchgate.net/publication/323974224 [retrieved: 4, 2019].

[12] A. Kumari and A.S. Sairam, "A Survey of Controller Placement Problem in Software Defined Networks", May 2019, https://arxiv.org/abs/1905.04649 [retrieved: 7, 2019]

[13] M. Cello, Y. Xu, A. Walid, G. Wilfong, H. J. Chao, and M. Marchese, "Balcon: A distributed elastic SDN control via efficient switch migration", in Proc. IEEE Int. Conf. Cloud Eng. (IC2E), pp. 40–50, April 2017.

[14] Yang Xu, et. al., "Dynamic Switch Migration in Distributed Software-Defined Networks to Achieve Controller Load Balance", IEEE Journal on Selected Areas in Communications , Vol. 37, No. 3, pp.515-528, March 2019.

[15] Y. Zhou, K. Zheng, W. Ni, and R. P. Liu, "Elastic Switch Migration for Control Plane Load Balancing in SDN", IEEE Access, Vol. 6, DOI 10.1109/ACCESS.2018.2795576, pp. 3609-3618, 2018.

[16] N. Mouawad, R. Naja and S. Tohmé, "Optimal and Dynamic SDN Controller Placement", July 2018, DOI: 10.1109/COMAPP.2018.8460361, https://www.researchgate.net/publication/326246703, [retrieved: 7, 2019].

[17] J. Cui, Q. Lu, H. Zhong,M.Tian, and L.Liu, 'A load-balancing mechanism for distributed SDN control plane using response time', IEEE Transactions on Network and Service Management, pp. 1-10, doi: 10.1109/ TNSM.2018.2876369, 2018.

[18] E. Borcoci, T. Ambarus, and M. Vochin, „Multi-criteria based Optimization of Placement for Software Defined Networking Controllers and Forwarding Nodes," The 15th International Conference on Networks, ICN 2016, Lisbon, http://www.iaria.org/conferences2016/ICN16.html, [retrieved: 5, 2019].

[19] Y. Zhang, N. Beheshti, and M. Tatipamula, "On Resilience of Split-Architecture Networks" in GLOBECOM 2011, http://citeseerx.ist.psu.edu/viewdoc/download?doi=10.1.1.691.795&rep=rep1&type=pdf, [retrieved: 6, 2019].

[20] A. P. Wierzbicki, "The use of reference objectives in multi-objective optimization". Lecture Notes in Economics and Mathematical Systems, vol. 177. Springer-Verlag, pp. 468–486, 1980.

DCM+: Robust Congestion Control Protocol for Mobile Networks

Rushdi A. Hamamreh
Al-Quds University
Jerusalem, Palestine
Email: rushdi@staff.alquds.edu

Derar Khader
Al-Quds University
Jerusalem, Palestine
Email: cedkhader@gmail.com

Abstract—**This paper aims at presenting a new robust congestion control protocol for mobile networks. It also can be used for mixed networks and mobile adhoc networks (MANETs). The proposed protocol is called *Dynamic Congestion Control Protocol for Mobile Networks* (DCM+). It makes use of the bandwidth estimation algorithm used in Westwood+ algorithm. We evaluate DCM+ on the basis of known metrics like *throughput, average delay, packet loss* and *Packet-Delivery-Ratio (PDR)*. New metrics like *Normalized Advancing Index (NAI)* and *Complete-Transmission-Time (CTT)* have been introduced for a comprehensive comparison with other congestion control variants like NewReno, Hybla, Ledbat and BIC. The simulations are done for a one-way single-hop-topology (*sender->router->receiver*). The findings in this paper clearly show excellent properties of our proposed technique like robustness and stability. It avoids congestions, increases performance, minimizes the end-to-end delay and reduces the transmission time. DCM+ combines the advantages of the protocols NewReno and Westwood+. The simulation results show high improvements, which make this approach extremely adequate for different types of networks.**

Keywords-Congestion control; DCM+; wireless; ns3 simulator.

I. INTRODUCTION

Congestion control is a vital process for data networks, especially those that rely mainly on TCP (Transmission Control Protocol) traffic. It has a central role for achieving high performance and throughput through managing congestions. This results in preventing the global networks like the Internet from collapse [2][3]. Since 1986, many protocols have been proposed and implemented for controlling data transmission between hosts. TCP NewReno is one of the most prominent variants of the old days [4][9][13][25], which though has some drawbacks and limitations, especially in wireless, mobile and mixed networks [3][5][7][20]. Another limitation of TCP NewReno is its little support for mobility [3][7][9], which makes it unusable in MANETS. TCP NewReno has been implemented in the TCP protocol stack of different applications and operating systems. Recently, newer TCP variants like TCP Westwood+, BIC, CUBIC, HighSpeed, Scalable, Hybla and Ledbat are available in modern applications and operating systems like Linux [6][8][10][11]. TCP Ledbat, for example, is implemented under MS Windows Server 2019, and also in MS Windows 10 [12].

TCP DCM+ is a new end-to-end approach that we have proposed in [1]. It stands for dynamic congestion control for mobile systems. It uses the Bandwidth Estimation (*BWE*) algorithm of TCP Westwood+, and hence comes the (+) sign. DCM+ is designed to avoid the congestion events in wireless and mobile networks. It also improves the performance in wired and mixed networks.

Despite the appropriate design for managing congestions in old (wired) networks, the main weakness of TCP NewReno is that it cannot distinguish the reasons for packet losses [3][5]. Two main reasons are known for packet losses. The first reason is a "full buffer" of the intermediate router, which is known as "network congestion". In this case, the data packet could be dropped intentionally from the router [13]-[18] like in Random-Early-Discard (RED). The aim of this strategy is to mitigate the large number "queue" of packets waiting for entrance into the router interface. The second reason is a signal error on the wireless channel, which is known as Link-Error (*LE*) [3][5][19][20][23]. In both cases, TCP NewReno drops its Congestion Window (*cwnd*) to the half, even if no real congestion exists and the packet was only dropped because of a bad wireless link [3][4][22]-[25]. This is the main reason for the bad performance of TCP NewReno in wireless and mobile networks.

This paper contains 5 sections. It is structured as follow: In section 2, works related to congestion control are mentioned. In section 3, we present our proposed technique. In section 4, the results and the simulations are shown. Section 5 is the conclusion and possible future work.

II. RELATED WORK

Many approaches dealing with modelling and identification of packet losses have been suggested [19][24], but this problem is still an active research topic. Fuzzy Logic (***FL***) and Machine Learning (***ML***) are some of the fields that have been used and tested to answer the question: "why is the packet lost?". Fuzzy inference systems [26][27], ANFIS [28], ML classification [29][30], neural networks [31][32] and random forests are just some of the modern approaches and algorithms to distinguish between *true* and *false* congestion events in mixed and mobile networks. The correctly identified congestion events are known as TP or "*True Positives*". In this case, Congestion-Avoidance (***CA)*** phase will be launched and new values for both Slow-Start Threshold (***ssth)*** and ***cwnd*** will be calculated. Otherwise, if the packet is dropped because of a link error, then the transmission continues without any change [27][29][30]. Hence, no or little false drops will occur, and thus, throughput will not suffer as in old TCP variants.

DCM+, on the other hand, is not causing any congestions during the transmission. It increases its *cwnd* size during the *CA* phase depending on the values of previous and current Round-Trip Times (***RTT***). Hence, DCM+ high performance is achieved because of using *RTT* as implicit feedback to predict the probability of a congestion, and thereafter to put the appropriate *cwnd* on the channel. This way, DCM+ reduces the probability of a congestion to an extremely low level. As a result, theoretically, the number of *cwnd* drops will be zero or very small. This results in high Packet-Delivery-Ratio (PDR), even when the packet-error-rates is too high. An example of the dynamics of TCP transmission using DCM+ is shown in Figure 1.

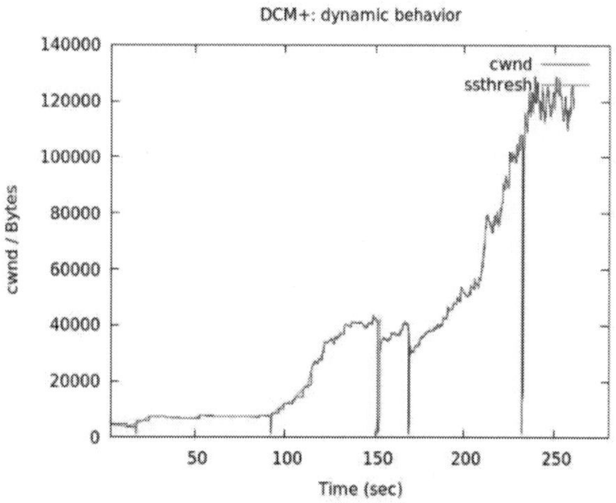

Figure 1. dynamic behavior of cwnd in DCM+

We see that ***cwnd*** is always tracking the actual state of slow-start-threshold (***ssthresh***). This causes a speedup in the transmission and hence, outperforms other TCP variants. Except at countable time points, which represent the lost packets, ***cwnd*** is tracking the state of ***ssthresh***. When a packet is lost because of a bad link conditions, the timeout counter signals this through a drop in the window size. This simulation is done using ns-3 with the following parameters:

- Bottleneck Bandwidth = 10 Mbps
- Access Bandwidth at the destination = 100 Mbps
- Packet-error-rate = 0.01
- Maximum Transmission Unit (MTU) = 1500 Bytes.

III. PROPOSED APPROACH

DCM+ is an End-To-End approach that uses the same algorithm explained in TCP Westwood+ [5][11][21][22] to find the accurate estimation of available bandwidth on the link. It describes a sender-side modification of ***CA*** phase of TCP Westwood+ protocol. Depending on the current discrete values of ***BWE***, DCM+ calculates the values for the next interval. The behavior of ***cwnd*** is observed to be dynamical. If a change (increase/decrease) of ***ssthresh*** has been observed within a specific time interval, then ***cwnd*** of DCM+ keeps using the same value of ***ssthresh*** until a newer state of ***ssthresh*** has been reached. After that, ***cwnd*** moves and remains at the new state for a new time interval. This way, ***cwnd*** will never (barely) exceed the available ***ssthresh***. Hence, congestion events will be extremely minimized. Figure 1 shows this behavior for packet-error-rate = 0.01, MTU =1500 bytes, bottleneck BW=10 Mbps and access-BW=100 Mbps.

Steady-state and stability for packet error rates lower than (0.05) can be observed from the simulations. Higher packet error rates, different MTU sizes and different sizes of TCP buffer can affect the dynamics of DCM+. Hence, the number of the packet drops is affected as shown in Figure 2 and Figure 3. The simulations are executed under ns-3.29 using the file 'tcp-variants-comparison.cc'. The used topology is a simple one-hop network. The topology is built of (TCP Source-> Router -> TCP Destination). The traffic is one-way TCP traffic only. No reverse traffic is used. The simplicity of this topology is vital to show the best performance that can be achieved by the different TCP variants. The used TCP variants are part of the simulator. NewReno, Hybla, Ledbat, BIC, Westwood/Westwood+ are implemented as C++ files. DCM+ has been implemented as a modified TCP Westwood+. The wireless channel is represented as a channel with high variable sporadic packet error rates.

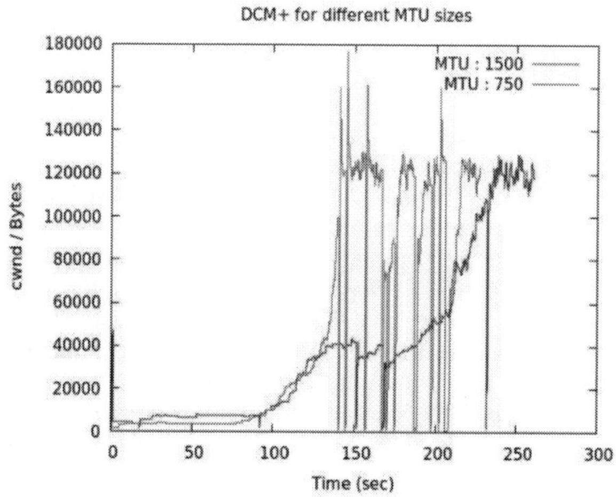

Figure 2. DCM+ behavior for different MTU

The design of DCM+ is similar to NewReno, which is detailed as an RFC [25]. DCM+ uses the same 4 phases like NewReno (***SS***, ***CA***, fast retransmission (***FR***) and fast recovery (***FV***)). In DCM+, the behavior in ***CA*** has been so modified to enforce the ***cwnd*** to track ***ssth*** in the next time interval. TCP timing parameters ***RTT*** and ***RTO*** have been used as feedback signals to control the values of ***ssth*** and ***cwnd*** in the next interval.

$$rateCA = RTT\_old / RTT\_new \qquad (1)$$

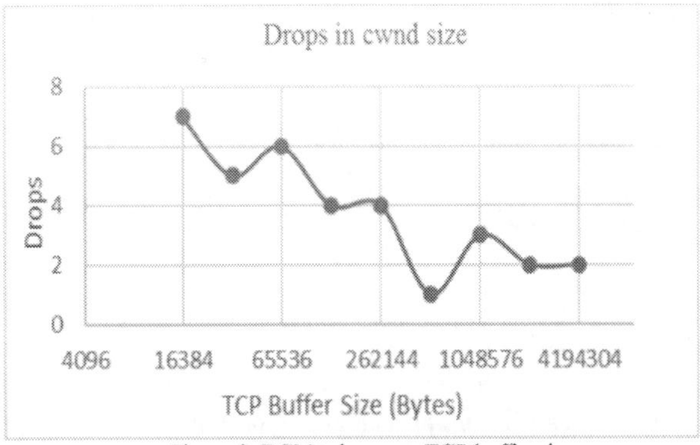

Figure 3. DCM+ drops vs. TCP buffer size

Figures 3 and 4 are shown for different TCP buffer sizes of the intermediate node. Figure 3 shows how many ***cwnd*** drops occur depending on the buffer size. According to [1], these drops occur only if a packet is lost because of a bad wireless link as no congestion events are allowed. We see that we get a minimum of drops when the buffer size is equal 512 KB. On the other hand, in Figure 4, we have the complete transmission time (***CTT***) as a function of TCP buffer size. Per definition, ***CTT*** is the difference between the arrival time of last ACK and first ACK segments:

$$\text{CTT} = \text{last\_ACK\_time} - \text{first\_ACK\_time} \qquad (2)$$

Figure 4 shows that for TCP buffer sizes equal or higher than 512KB, the TCP connection will have the shortest possible CTT.

DCM+ follows the following principle: it considers values of ***rateCA*** higher than **1** as ***advance*** or "Link Capacity Increasing", and values lower than **1** as ***danger*** or "Link Capacity Decreasing". Depending on the conditions stated in the algorithm of ***CA*** phase in [1], if ***cwnd*** is less than ***ssth***, then ***rateCA*** will be used to start the retransmission in wide steps, otherwise, retransmission goes slowly, which prevents any possible congestions. Please, refer to Figure 5 to see the changing of ***rateCA*** during the transmission.

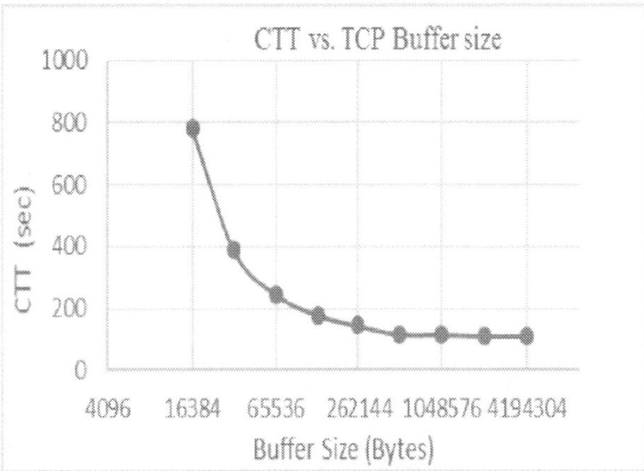

Figure 4. CTT vs. TCP buffer size

Figure 5 depicts the timing parameters for the simulation in Figure 1. We see that ***cwnd*** drops occur at the points: 21 sec, 90 sec, 151 sec, 168 sec and 240 sec. These points coincide with the spike points in Figure 5.

We discovered that if current ***RTT*** value is less than previous ***RTT***, then we have an increase in the ***cwnd*** size. Otherwise, if a spike occurs, then a packet is lost, and this is signaled through a spike on the RTT curve. When a spike occurs, RTO counter is exceeded, and a packet is lost. Hence, RTO timer is reset to 1, and this leads to the ***cwnd*** size to be reset to 1 packet. Look at Figure 5, and compare the time points of spikes and the ***cwnd*** drops.

At each time point during the transmission, the value of the next ***RTO*** is affected by the newly calculated ***rateCA***. If the current ***RTT*** is decreasing, then ***RTO*** shall be also reduced, as no congestion is expected. As described in the algorithm of ***CA*** phase in [1], next value of ***ssth*** depends on the available channel capacity, which is calculated regarding TCP Westwood+ algorithm [5],[21],[22]. The calculation of next ***cwnd*** depends on current ***rateCA*** and previous ***cwnd***.

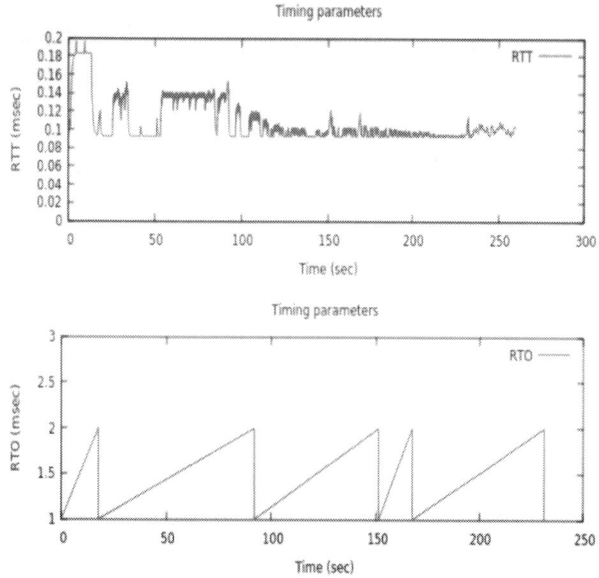

Figure 5. Timing parameters during the transmission

After we executed 1000's of simulations with different parameters, we found that our technique poses excellent stability and robustness properties.

Our simulations of the mentioned topology for many cases with different parameters show that next ***cwnd*** does not exceed the available ***ssth***. According to the theoretical results of the simulations, we make the assumption that DCM+ does not suffer or cause any congestion events, because it estimates the available channel capacity before sending data. More complex simulations are still to be executed to intensively study fairness and friendliness in the presence of other TCP sources and destinations.

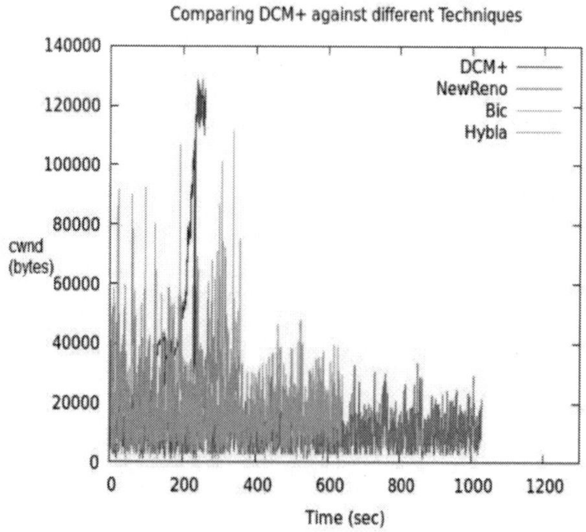

Figure 6. DCM+ performance compared with other techniques

We see that the quick tracking of the state of ***ssth*** and the smart way of selecting the transmission size are the main reasons for the improved performance and robustness of DCM+, as depicted in Figure 6, which is created with same parameters as Figure 1. Even better results are expected for higher bandwidth-delay-products due to the quick dynamic behavior of ***cwnd*** that is not available in other techniques.

IV. RESULTS

Table 1 depicts the used parameters to create Figures 7, 8 and 9. The simulations are executed for different packet error rates (1e-6 to 0.05). The used environment is ns-3.29 [33] under Ubuntu Linux VM inside Oracle VirtualBox 5.2.22.

TABLE I. PARAMETERS OF THE SIMULATION ENVIRONMENT

Data size	BW	Access BW	MTU Size	Duration (sec)
100 MB	1 Gb/sec	100 Mbps	1500 Bytes	2000

Figures 7, 8 and 9 below show the performance metrics for some TCP congestion control protocols (DCM+, NewReno, BIC, Ledbat and Hybla). Newer approaches like TCP CUBIC, TCP PCC and TCP ex Machina are to be compared against our approach in other works.

A. Throughput

In Figure 7, we see the throughput of different protocols, and we clearly see the advantage of DCM+ over other protocols. The high throughput extends nearly over the complete range of error rates, which is from 1e-6 to 0.05. For error rates less than 1e-3, only BIC protocol performs better, but that is at the expense of other metrics like PDR, average delay and packets losses, where BIC performs worst. Lost packets of BIC are highest in the range 1e-5 to 1e-3.

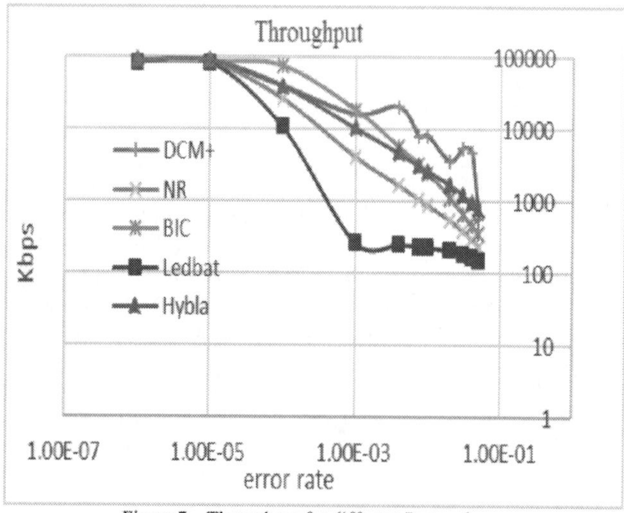

Figure 7. Throughput for different Protocols

B. Normalized Advancing Index (NAI)

For the reason of detailed comparison, we introduced a new metric, which we called *normalized advancing index* (***NAI***). It is defined as the ratio of throughput divided by the product of lost packets (given in bytes) and error rates. Its unit is (1/sec), and should indicate the speed of delivering the complete size of data from one end to the other despite the existence of lost packets at a specific error rate.

The robustness of DCM+ is visible in Figure 8. It shows that DCM+ performs better than all other protocols mentioned in this paper. This robustness is a result of less packet losses, lower average delay and a higher throughput than other approaches.

$$NAI = \frac{\text{Throughput}}{(\text{ErrorRate} \cdot \text{LostPackets} \cdot \text{MTUsize})} \quad (3)$$

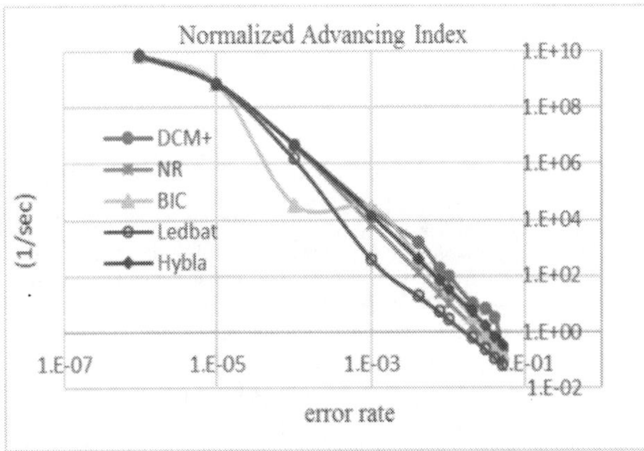

Figure 8. NAI as robustness indicator for different protocols

We clearly see that DCM+ has the best results over the whole range of simulated error rates. This reflects the best transmission speed and quality for the underlying TCP applications.

C. Complete Transmission Time (CTT)

It is a good advantage to finish transmission in short time without causing congestions, if possible. This is the case with DCM+ protocol as depicted in Figure 9. It has the lowest (***CTT***) among all tested protocols. ***CTT*** is defined as the time needed for the last ACK segment to arrive at the sender. We see from Figure 4 that the performance of ***CTT*** can be improved through changing the size of TCP buffer in the sender, receiver and intermediate router.

Based on the results presented above, TCP applications and devices that use DCM+ can extremely accelerate the data transmission and hence finish using the link earlier. This results in less power consumption.

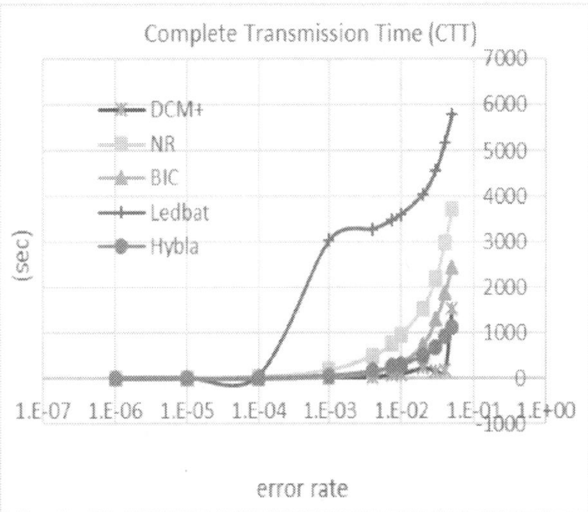

Figure 9. CTT for different protocols

V. CONCLUSION

We have demonstrated a new approach (DCM+) that has better performance than all other used approaches. We made the assumption that it does not cause any congestions as DCM+ is TCP fair and friendly. It is usable in the different types of networks, but more adequate for mobile/wireless and MANET networks. In this research work, we have shown that our approach is robust. It has the ability to minimize the average delay and packet losses, but also to improve the throughput and the speed of the transmission under high error rates. It is designed in similar fashion like TCP NewReno. It is an end-to-end technique, which will be used from the TCP sender to control the sent amount of data on the transmission link. It has a modified behavior in ***CA*** phase. It uses the ***BWE*** algorithm described in TCP Westwood+ protocol to estimate the available channel capacity. Thereafter, it calculates the appropriate values for both ***ssth*** and ***cwnd*** depending on the feedback signals ***RTT*** and ***RTO***, the parameter ***rateCA***, and whether the calculated ***cwnd*** is less than ***ssth*** or not. As feedback signals, we used previous states of both ***RTT*** and ***RTO.***

We found through intensive simulations that DCM+ has improved properties like high throughput, low delay, low drops and extremely fast speed in delivering data to the end device. We also introduced new performance metrics, *NAI* and *CTT* to show the advantages of the dynamic behavior of DCM+. In the future, these results are to be validated through more complex topologies in the presence of different traffic types. Also, a comprehensive mathematical model will be presented to show the theoretical limits of this approach. A comparison with newer techniques like CUBIC and ex Machina is planned as a future work.

REFERENCES

[1] R. Hamamreh and D. Khader, "DCM+: a multi-purpose protocol for congestion control", 2019 IEEE 7th Palestinian International Conference on Electrical and Computer Engineering (PICECE), Date of Conference: 26-27 March 2019, DOI: 10.1109/PICECE.2019.874723.

[2] V. Jacobson and M. J. Karels, "Congestion Avoidance and Control", Computer Communication Review, 18(4), pp. 314 – 329, Aug. 1988.

[3] Y. Tian, K. Xu and N. Ansari, "TCP in Wireless Environments: Problems and Solutions", IEEE Radio Comm., pp. S27 – S32, March 2005.

[4] S. Floyd and T. Henderson, "The NewReno Modification to TCP's Fast Recovery Algorithm", RFC 3782, 2004.

[5] L. Grieco and S. Mascolo, "Performance Evaluation and Comparison of Westwood+, New Reno, and Vegas", ACM SIGCOMM Computer Communication Review, Volume 34 Issue 2, pp. 25-38, April 2004.

[6] K. Miller and L. Hsiao, "TCPTuner: Congestion Control Your Way", Stanford University, 2016.

[7] P. Kaushika and R. Jagdish, "A survey on effectiveness of TCP Westwood in mixed wired and wireless networks", International Journal of Scientific & Engineering Research, Volume 4, Issue 6, pp. 197 – 205, June-2013.

[8] S. Arianfar, "TCP's Congestion Control Implementation in Linux Kernel", Aalto University, 2012.

[9] T. Henderson, S. Floyd, A. Gurtov and Y. Nishida. "The NewReno Modification to TCP's Fast Recovery Algorithm", RFC 6582. April 2012.

[10] P. Sarolahti and A. Kuznetsov, "Congestion Control in Linux TCP", *Institute of Nuclear Research at Moscow, 2002.*

[11] A. Dell'Aera, L. A. Grieco and S. Mascolo, "Linux 2.4 Implementation of Westwood+ TCP with rate-halving: A Performance Evaluation over the Internet", Tech. Rep. No. 08/03/S , 2004.

[12] Microsoft Networking Blog. Category- "Ledbat". https://blogs.technet.microsoft.com/networking/category/windows-transports/ledbat/, [retrieved: September-2019].

[13] A.E. Eckberg and D.T. Luan, "Meeting the challenge: congestion and flow control strategies for broadband information transport", 1989 IEEE Global Telecommunications Conference and Exhibition 'Comm. Technology for the 1990s and Beyond'. 1989.

[14] C. Yang and A.V.S. Reddy, "A taxonomy for congestion control algorithms in packet switching networks", IEEE Network, Volume: 9, Issue: 4, pp. 34 – 45, 1995.

[15] K Bala, I. Cidon and K. Sohraby. "Congestion control for high speed packet switched networks", IEEE INFOCOM, 1990.

[16] M. May, J. Bolot, C. Diot, and B. Lyles, "Reasons not to deploy RED", Inria, Sprint Labs.

[17] R. Torres, J. Border, J. Xu and J. Jong, "Congestion control using RED and TCP window adjustment", MILCOM 2012 - 2012 IEEE Military Comm. Conf., 2012.

[18] S. Floyd and V. Jacobson, "Random Early Detection Gateways for Congestion Avoidance", IEEE/ACM Transactions on Netw., Vol. I, No. I, pp. 397 – 413, 1993.

[19] J. Olsen, "On Packet Loss Rates used for TCP Network Modeling", Dep. of Math., Uppsala Univ., Sweden. 2004.

[20] K. Tan, F. Jiang and Q. Zhang, "Congestion Control in Multihop Wireless Networks", IEEE Transactions on Vehicular Technology, Vol. 56, No.2, March 2007.

[21] S. Mascolo, L.A. Grieco, R. Ferorelli, P. Camarda and G. Piscitelli, "Performance evaluation of Westwood+ TCP congestion control", ResearchGate, uploaded in May 2014.

[22] S. Mascolo, "Testing TCP Westwood+ over Transatlantic Links at 10 Gigabit/Second rate", (2005).

[23] C. Parsa and J.J. Garcia-Luna-Aceves, "Differentiating Congestion vs. Random Loss: A Method for Improving TCP Performance over Wireless Links", Computer Engineering Dep., Baskin School of Engineering, University of California.

[24] M. Allman, V. Paxson and E. Blanton, "TCP Congestion Control", RFC: 5681. 2009.

[25] M. H. Yaghmaee, F. Fatemipour. M. Bahekmat and A. Barasani, "A New Fuzzy Logic Approach for TCP Congestion Control", Researchgate, 2015.

[26] H. Elaarag and M. Wozniak, "Using Fuzzy Inference to improve TCP congestion control over wireless networks", BSc. Thesis, Stetson University, DeLand, Florida. 2010.

[27] S. M. Hosseini and B. N. Araabi, "A Neuro-Fuzzy Control for TCP Network Congestion", Advances in Intelligent and Soft Computing, Springer Verlag, Sep. 2009.

[28] I. Elkhayat, P. Geurts and G. Leduc, "Enhancement of TCP over wired/wireless networks with packet loss classifiers inferred by supervised learning", Tech. Report. Montefiore Inst., Belgium. 2004.

[29] P. Geurts, I. Elkhayat and G. Leduc, "A Machine Learning Approach to Improve Congestion Control over Wireless Computer Networks", University of Li`ege, Belgium, 2005.

[30] S. Alavandar, "ANN Based Intelligent Congestion Controller for High Speed Computer Networks", Journal of Electrical Engineering. 2015.

[31] L. Niu, "Applying the Linear Neural Network to TCP Congestion Control", Fuyang Teachers College, china, Published by Atlantis Press, 2015.

[32] P. Yang, J. Shao, W. Luo, L. Xu, J. S. Deogun and Y. Lu, "TCP Congestion Avoidance Algorithm Identification", CSE Journal Articles, IEEE/ACM Transactions on Networking, Vol. 22, No. 4, August 2014.

[33] Ns-3 network simulator. Website: https://www.nsnam.org/, [retrieved: September-2019].

Basic Concepts of Buried Wireless Sensor under Ballasted Layer

Nagateru Iwasawa, Satoko Ryuo, Koki Iwamoto,
Nariya Iwaki, and Akio Hada
Signalling and Transport Information Technology Division
Railway Technical Research Institute
Tokyo, Japan
e-mail: iwasawa.nagateru.81@rtri.or.jp

Akiko Kono
Railway Dynamics Division
Railway Technical Research Institute
Tokyo, Japan
e-mail: kono.akiko.43@rtri.or.jp

Abstract— **The impact of train loading deteriorates ballasted track that has differential settlement of ballasted layer primarily around rail joints. However the formation process of settlement has not yet clarified. With the development of Information and Communication Technology (ICT), the research on applying the remote monitoring system using Wireless Sensor Network (WSN) has become prevalent in railway equipment. This study focuses on the track monitoring, especially ballast condition, and conducted experiments of WSN to apply that monitoring. From a result of the experiments, the large attenuation by ballast was not confirmed, therefore, WSN can be used to monitor the condition of ballast.**

Keywords-railway tracks; ballast; monitoring system; raido wave propagation.

I. Introduction

Ballasted track is a general track structure on railways; it consists of a ballast, such as gravel and crushed stone, sleepers, and rails. Ballast settlement is normally caused by the repeated loading of train traffic and its progression occurs sparsely and locally, which has been a long-standing problem, as a challenge in the track maintenance. It is known that ballast settlement progresses rapidly particularly where impact load occurs, such as rail joint, see Figure 1. Uneven ballast settlement leads to "Hanging Sleeper," which induce sleeper vibration. To provide safety running of trains and comfortable riding, regular track maintenance is required, such as ballast maintenance by ballast tamper, which takes a lot of cost and effort. Therefore, the research of reducing maintenance work has been studied, for example, the method of elastic bottom sleepers to disperse the load transmitted from sleepers to ballast [2] and prevention of ballast settlement to fix the ballast by grout [3]. Also, the vibration acceleration of the ballasted layer is measured by embedding a "ballast sensing stone" with piezoresistive triaxle acceleration sensors in a track ballast [4] to observe the relationship of dynamic response of ballasted layer and ballast settlement. The ballast sensing stone has to be embedded in a track ballast for each measurement, but this will loosen the track.

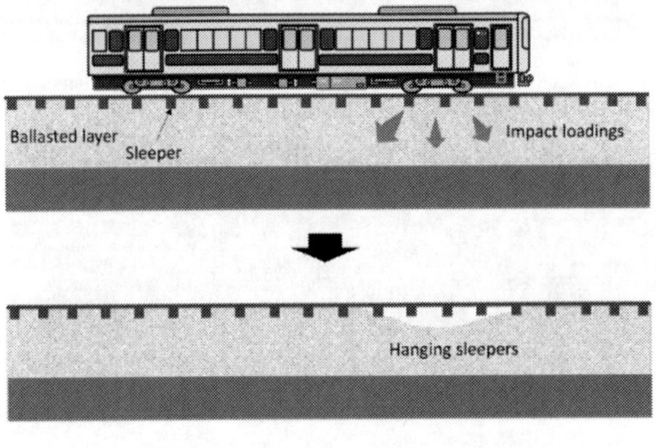

Figure 1. An image of the ballast settlement

With the development of ICT, the research on a condition monitoring system for remotely monitoring the condition of equipment using WSN has proceeded in a railway field. In WSN, the measurement data from sensors can be acquired over a long period of time by the installed wireless sensor node on a monitoring target. Thus, applying WSN can be expected to reduce maintenance and measurement work. By developing a device that integrates vibration acceleration and wireless sensor with respect to the ballast sensing stones installed inside the ballast which mentioned in the above, it is possible to reduce loosening of the track. In this paper, the sensor node, which is buried in the ballast in the long term for condition monitoring and is applied to the wireless sensor network, is examined.

The rest of the present paper is organized as follows: Section II introduces related work about monitoring track. In Section III, we propose the measuring system for the ballast layer. In Section IV, we introduce our verification test for communication between sensor nodes buried under ballasted layer and receiver placed outside of the ballast, and we indicate its result. Finally, Section VI concludes the present paper.

II. Monitoring Track

This section introduces conventional researches and problems for adapting them for monitoring tracks.

A. *Related Work*

As the research on the condition monitoring of track, the framework for monitoring tracks, with a network where sensor nodes transmit to base stations via wireless transmission, was proposed [5], see Figure 2. In Figure 2, the data collected by WSN is transmitted to the server via the Internet, and this data is stored in the database at the server and also can be checked on the monitor.

It is required to monitor various points and items for recognizing the condition of tracks in [6], shown in Figure 3. According to [6], it can be seen that the monitoring point exists below the ballasted layer. Correspondingly, track condition monitoring systems have been already proposed with wired or wireless transmission.

As an example of using a wired transmission, a remote monitoring system shown in [7] collects the data under ballast into a laptop pc installed along a track wayside using wired cable called probe and transmits the collected data to a remote place via Internet, shown in Figure 4. As an instance of using wireless transmission, a system for transmitting the sensing data of rail using wireless sensor was proposed in [8]. However, the research on a remote monitoring for points below the ballasted layer using wireless sensor nodes has not been presented. Therefore, it is necessary to verify that the sensor node buried below the ballasted layer can transmit the data to the base station using wireless communication.

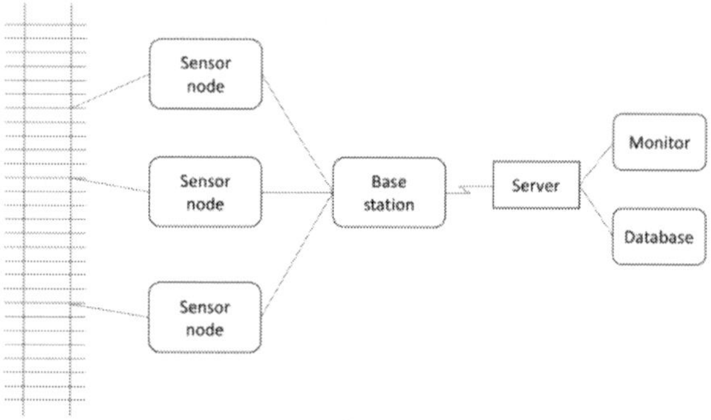

Figure 2. System framework for monitoring tracks [5]

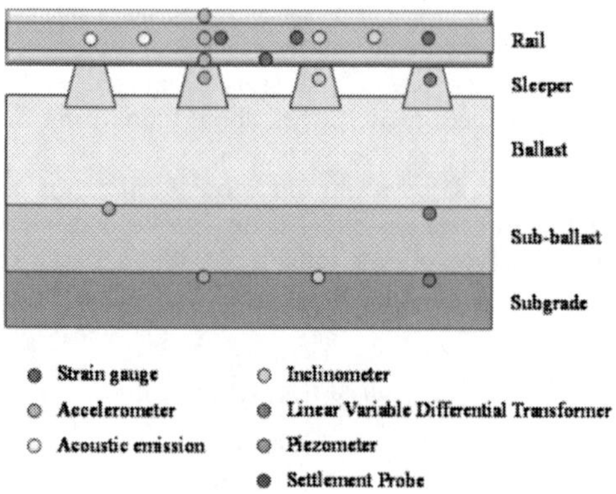

Figure 3. Schematic location of the sensors used for condition monitoring [6]

B. *Problems*

In the railway system in Japan, the periodic patrol that the maintenance worker carries out inspections by walking on the patrol path provided along tracks is generally conducted. Therefore, in addition to the problems, such as cable break, passages for workers may not be cleared due to the wires for the monitoring system. The wired system can also be expensive to maintain, as they have external damage as described in [6].

When considering a sensor that transmits data by wireless, it is necessary to verify the communication between below ballasted layer and outside ballast. Therefore, this paper proposes the monitoring system collecting data under ballast and its sensor node and discusses the possibility of their application.

III. PROPOSED MEASURING SYSTEM

This section introduces the concept of sensors in ballast layer for monitoring tracks.

A. *Overview of the system*

The overview of the proposed monitoring system is shown in Figure 5 [9]. As before, we define network from sensor nodes to the base station as WSN.

In the proposed WSN for monitoring under the ballasted layer, sensor nodes installed in the ballast transmit the data to the base station. In cases where a sensor node cannot directly transmit the data to the base station and consume the large power due to frequent communication failure, a relay node is installed in the ballast shoulder, receives the data from the

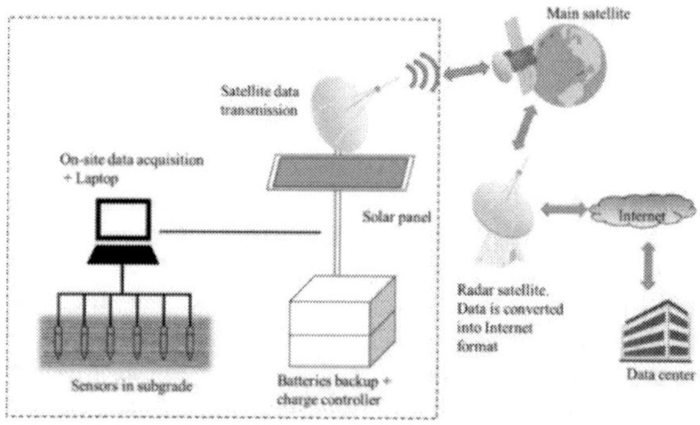

Figure 4. Remote monitoring system package [7]

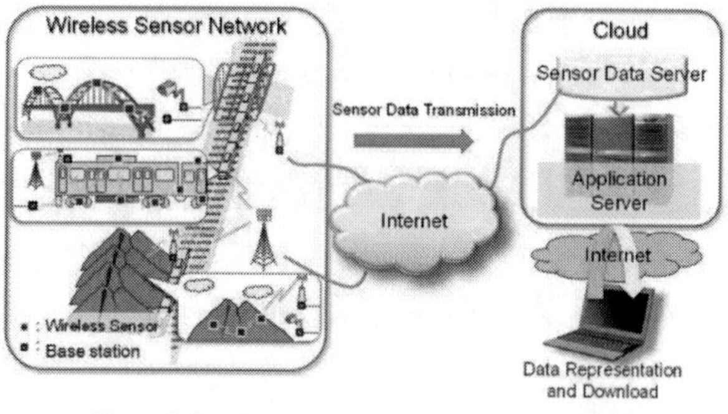

Figure 5. Condition monitoring system for Railway [9]

sensor nodes, and appropriately sends their data to the base station.

B. Buried wireless sensor node under ballasted layer

The following shows the sensor node buried under ballasted layer. Figure 6 shows the position of the sensor under the ballast and its composition. The sensor node consists of a sensor for measurement, memory for temporarily storing sensing data, a wireless module for transmitting sensing data, a CPU for controlling them, and a battery. It has the memory to store the sensing data, so it can transmit when there is no train passing, for example, the time zone of train operation. We suppose that the sensor node is installed under ballasted layer and left to monitor, so its maintenance, such as battery changing is not needed. However, there is some possibility of the sensor node trouble, so it is necessary to consider how to grasp its condition and reliability of sensing data, and so on.

IV. FUNCTIONAL VERIFICATION

429 MHz, 920 MHz, and 2.4 GHz band, which does not need a license, are mainly used for WSN in Japan. We made experiments to verify the reachability of 429 MHz band radio wave and 920 MHz band radio wave from inside of the ballast to outside of the ballast. Both of the frequencies of 429 MHz and 920 MHz band have good diffraction properties, compared with 2.4 GHz band. Although those bandwidths are narrow so those transmission speeds are lower than 2.4 GHz's, those speeds are enough to transmit data several times a day. Moreover, those frequency bands have wireless modules of the radio communication standards classified as Low Power Wide Area (LPWA). We use MU-2-429 (Figure 7 left side) [10] as a 429 MHz band wireless module and BP35A1 (Figure 7 right side) [11] as a 920 MHz band wireless module for the experiment.

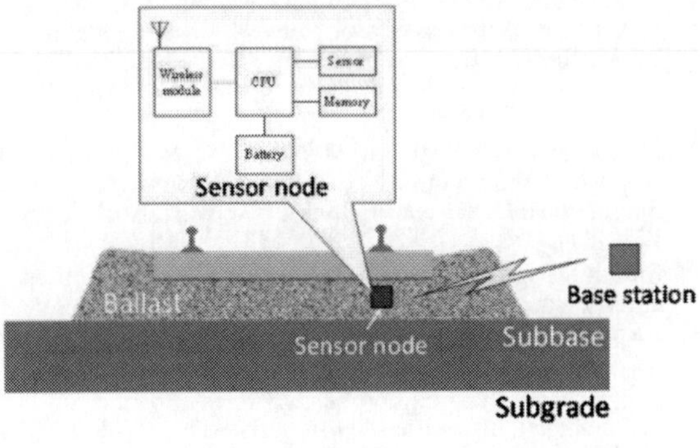

Figure 6. Buried wireless sensor node under ballasted layer

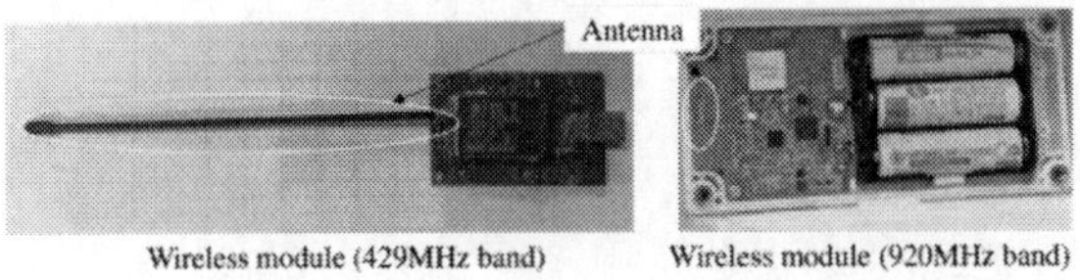

Figure 7. Wireless modules used in the experiment

Figure 8 shows the experimental conditions and Figure 9 shows its scenario. Condition 1 is the state of the transmitters not buried under the ballasted layer, condition 2 is that the ballast is filled by 65mm more than condition 1 and the transmitters are buried under ballasted layer. Then, condition 3 is that the ballast is filled by 60mm more than condition 2 and the transmitters are buried completely under the ballasted layer. We buried wireless modules in a resin-made box under the ballasted layer as transmitters and put wireless modules as receivers at a distance of 5 m from transmitters. We measured the Received Signal Strength Indicator (RSSI) of the receivers.

Figure 10 shows the result of the experiment for using 429 MHz band wireless module, and Figure 11 shows it for using the 920 MHz band wireless module. They show loss of each condition based on the RSSI of the condition 1. Their loss does not exceed 3 dB, so we cannot find an influence of the ballast to propagation characteristics under our experiment's conditions. The possible reason for this is that there were many gaps in the ballasted layer. Then, it is possible to get different results, depending on the positional relation between stones of ballast and antenna. Therefore, the

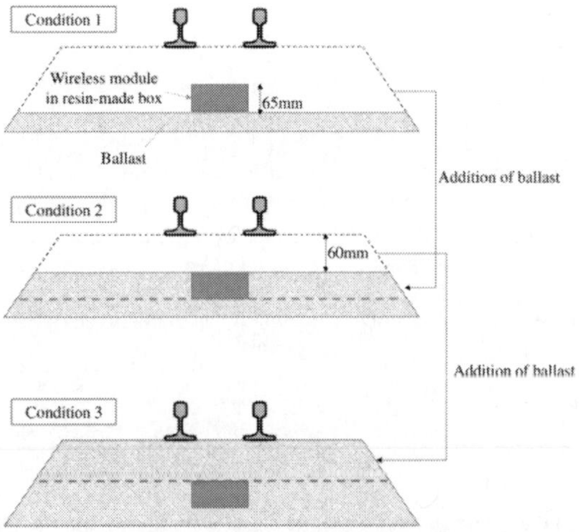

Figure 8. Experiment conditions

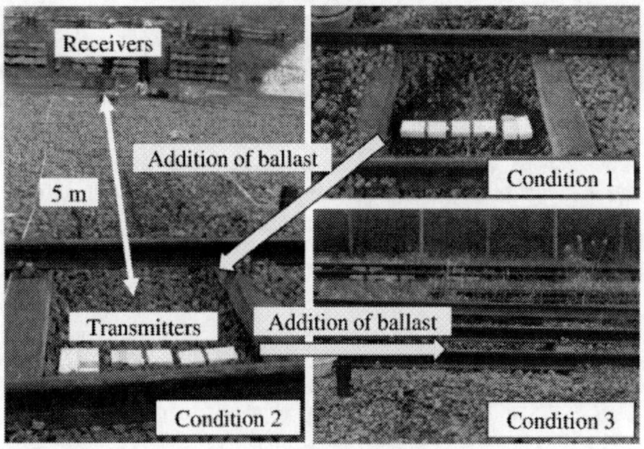

Figure 9. Experiment scenario

loss of RSSI might be affected by ballast fluctuations due to maintenance and train passing, etc.

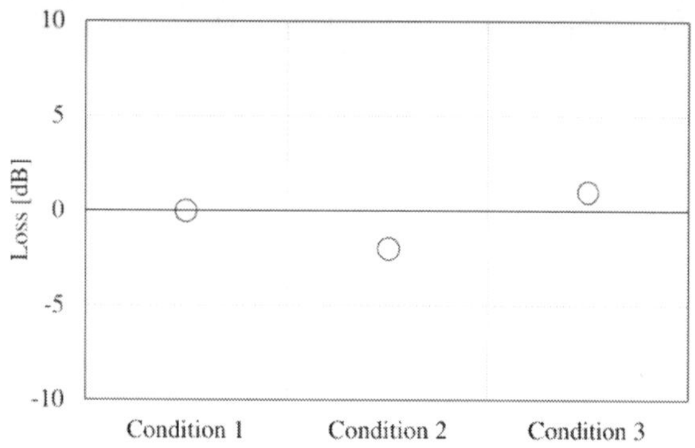

Figure 10. An experiment result for using 429 MHz band wireless module

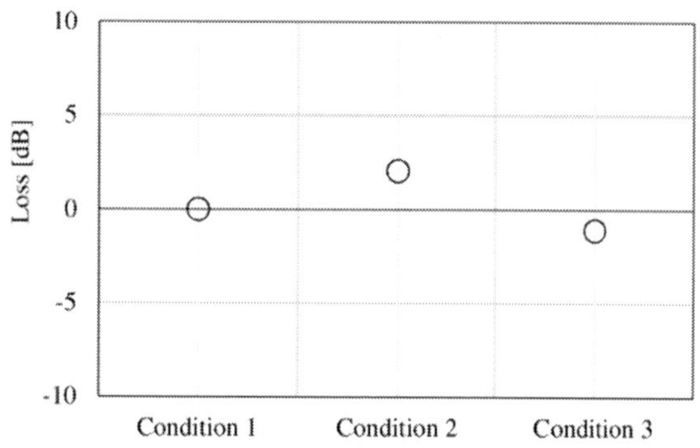

Figure 11. An experiment result for using 920 MHz band wireless module

V. CONCLUSION

This paper proposed the sensor node buried under ballasted layer for the condition monitoring of tracks. To confirm the wireless transmission from the sensor node buried under the ballasted layer, we examined the communication test using wireless devices whose frequency is 429 MHz bandwidth and 920 MHz bandwidth. From the result of the tests, it was confirmed that the amount of attenuation was within 3 dB. Therefore, it can be said that the wireless transmission can be used for communication of the sensor node buried under ballasted layer. However, a dense ballast could cause blockage of the radio propagation path inside that ballast, so further verifications are required under different ballast conditions. We are going to make the prototype and to verify our proposed system at the field considering actual use. In addition, it needs to be examined a method of correcting the acceleration data, because its axis gets shift with long-term use. In practical use, reliability and weatherability of sensors themselves are

REFERENCES

[1] T. Suzuki, M. Ishida, K. Abe, and K. Koro, "Measurement on Dynamic Behaviour of Track near Rail Joints and Prediction of Track Settlement," Quarterly Report of RTRI, vol. 46, no. 2, pp. 124-129, Aug. 2005, doi:10.2219/rtriqr.46.124.

[2] A. Kono, M. Suzuki, and F. Urakawa, "Evaluation of Reducing Effect of USP on Ballasted Track Vibration based on Loading Frequencies," RTRI Report, vol. 32, no. 6, pp. 29-34, Jun. 2018, ISSN: 0914-2990 (in Japanese).

[3] T. Nakamura, Y. Momoya, K. Muramoto, and K. Ito, "Development of Railway Roadbed Improvement Method for Existing Lines by Reusing Deteriorated Ballast," Quarterly Report of RTRI, vol. 55, no. 1, pp. 46-50, Mar. 2014, doi:10.2219/rtriqr.55.46.

[4] A. Aikawa, "Techniques to Measure Effects of Passing Trains on Dynamic Pressure Applied to Sleeper Bottoms and Dynamic Behavior of Ballast Stones," Quarterly Report of RTRI, vol. 50, no. 2, pp. 102-109, Jun. 2009, doi:10.2219/rtriqr.50.102.

[5] V. Bolle and S.K. Banoth, "Review on Railway Bridge & Track Condition Monitoring System," International Research Journal of Engineering and Technology, vol. 3, no. 8, pp. 1092-1095, Aug. 2016, ISSN: 2395-0056.

[6] C. Ngamkhanong, S. Kaewunruen, and B. J. A. Costa, "State-of-the-Art Review of Railway Track Resilience Monitoring," Infrastructures, vol. 3, no. 1, Jan. 2018, doi:10.3390/infrastructures3010003.

[7] E. S. Aw, "Novel Monitoring System to Diagnose Rail Track Foundation Problems," Master's Thesis, Massachusetts Institute of Technology, 2004.

[8] E. Aboelela, W. Edberg, C. Papakonstantinou, and V. Vokkarane, "Wireless Sensor Network Based Model for Secure Railway Operations," IEEE International Perfomance Computing and Communications, pp. 623-628, Apr. 2006, doi:10.1109/.2006.1629461.

[9] N. Iwasawa, T. Kawamura, M. Nozue, S. Ryuo, and N. Iwaki, "Design of Wire Sensor Network in the Railway," International Conference on Sensor Networks, vol. 1, pp. 122-127, Jan. 2018, doi:10.5220/0006638101220127.

[10] Circuit Design, Inc., http://www.circuitdesign.jp/jp/products/products2/mu2/index1.asp [retrieved: Sep., 2019]

[11] Rohm Semiconductor, https://www.rohm.co.jp/products/wireless-communication/specified-low-power-radio-modules/bp35a1-product [retrieved: Sep., 2019]

Performance Measuring Test Results of 920MHz Band Wireless Sensor Network in Buried Condition

Nariya Iwaki
Signalling and Transport Information Technology Division
Railway Technical Research Institute
Tokyo, Japan (Currently JR-Central Consultants Company)
e-mail: n-iwaki@jrcc.co.jp

Nagateru Iwasawa and Satoko Ryuo
Signalling and Transport Information Technology Division
Railway Technical Research Institute
Tokyo, Japan
e-mail: iwasawa.nagateru.81@rtri.or.jp

Abstract— **Increasing number of aging structures and damage caused by natural disasters are major issues in railways. It is difficult to instantly detect the deterioration and damage of structures in normal inspection cycles, hence, studies of the condition monitoring system for railway facilities have been developed to grasp these conditions frequently. Most of condition monitoring systems for railway structures in recent years consist of Wireless Sensor Networks (WSN). To design a WSN, it is necessary to grasp the characteristics of the frequency for the railway environment. In our research, the 920 MHz band of radio wave frequency, which was released as Industry Science and Medical (ISM) band since 2012 in Japan, was focused. Also, as an example of condition monitoring for railway structures, the WSN for railway embankment was selected. We considered the case where the sensor was buried underground and the case of rain as factors affecting wireless transmission and confirmed that the signal strength of 920 MHz radio waves were attenuated in these cases.**

Keywords- Wireless Sensor Network; 920MHz; Railway; Buried Condition.

I. INTRODUCTION

Railways in Japan are excellent transport infrastructure with mass, high speed, safety features, therefore, it plays an important role in passenger and freight transport [1]. However, the number of aging structures is increasing since many of the railway structures were built before the 1970s. Furthermore, railway structures have been severely damaged due to many natural disasters in recent years [2]. Hence, it is required to properly maintain railway structures. On the other hand, in Japan, the aging of workers and the decline of the working population have become serious issues. Under these circumstances, it is an urgent issue to efficiently maintain the increasing aging structures and to take disaster prevention.

At present, maintenance of railway structures is carried out by inspection and soundness evaluation every 2 years, and repair or replacement is performed as necessary [1]. However, a lot of manpower is required in normal inspection since a visual inspection is performed. Hence, it is desirable to develop a method that can efficiently maintain and manage many structures. Additionally, there is a growing need for technology that can quickly grasp the situation in the field when a natural disaster occurs. One of the methods for realizing these requirements is condition monitoring using a WSN. Figure 1 shows an example of WSN [3]. There are various choices for the frequency band of radio waves used for WSN. Among them, the 920 MHz band which is newly released in Japan as an ISM band since 2012, is especially attracting attention. Therefore, research and development of WSN using the 920MHz band has been

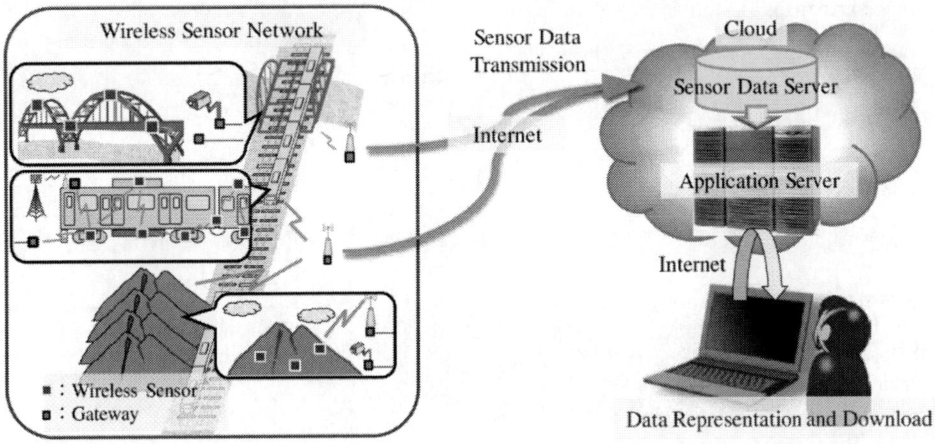

Figure 1. An example of the condition monitoring system using the WSN (adapted from [3])

actively conducted in recent years [3]-[8].

The 920 MHz band can be used without a license when the transmission power is 20mW or less, which corresponds to the 860 MHz band in Europe. Compared with the 429 MHz band which has been used conventionally for a WSN, the 920 MHz band has a high transmission rate and can perform large-scale multi-hop transmission. Similarly, compared with the 2.45 GHz band, it has a longer transmission distance and radio waves are easily diffracted. Therefore, it is expected to be one of the effective frequency bands for use in a railway environment which is spread linearly and has a large number of various facilities [4].

However, in order to receive the desired data stably with WSN in the railway, it is necessary to design an appropriate WSN in consideration of the various railway-specific environment [5][6]. In general WSN design, the transmitter is installed at a high position to improve the radio wave propagation environment [7][8]. On the other hand, in railways, the safe operation of trains is the top priority, so transmitters can't be installed in free places. For example, when constructing a WSN for facilities on the railway slope or near track, if the transmitter is installed at a high position, it may fall and interfere with train operation when a disaster occurs. Therefore, we must design the WSN assuming the transmitter is installed in a low position or buried in the ground.

Japanese railway structures have a high rate of embankment and cutting, and natural disasters can severely damage railway slopes. Therefore, in this study, we selected embankment monitoring as an example of a WSN for railway structures.

To build a WSN that monitors the condition of embankment, we first conducted a transmission characteristic test of the 920 MHz band with the transmitter buried in the ground. Next, based on the test results, we constructed a WSN in the railway test embankment and conducted a performance measuring test for about 1 month.

The rest of the present paper is organized as follows: Section 2 introduces related works about a WSN for slope monitoring and a transmission characteristic test for the 920MHz band. Section 3 describes the transmission characteristic test where the transmitter is buried in the ground. Section 4 describes the performance measuring test of WSN, and Section 5 describes the conclusion and future work.

II. Related Work

When constructing a WSN on the embankment, it is conceivable to early detection the slope failure by measuring the soil moisture content and the inclination angle in the embankment. As a similar existing research, there is research on sensor networks aimed at detecting slope failure [9][10]. Existing research considers data loss rate and sensor measurement values, but does not consider attenuation characteristics by the Received Signal Strength Indicator (RSSI). Also, as existing research that measured the RSSI, there is research that considers the effects of vegetation [11]. Existing research is evaluating the effects of vegetation growth on radio wave propagation based on RSSI measurement values. By measuring RSSI, it is possible to quantitatively grasp the attenuation characteristics of radio waves. In the WSN on the railway embankment that we are aiming for, not only the effects of vegetation but also the possibility of transmitting data with a transmitter buried in the ground. In addition, it may be affected by rainfall due to the outdoor environment. Therefore, in order to receive the desired data stably, it is very important to quantitatively grasp the attenuation characteristics due to the buried condition and rainfall, and improve the accuracy of WSN design.

III. Transmission Characteristic Test In Buried Condition

We conducted a test to confirm to the transmission characteristic of the 920MHz band radio wave in buried condition. This section describes the test methods and results and discussion.

A. *Test Method [5]*

In this test, we used the transmitter of Wireless Smart Utility Network (Wi-SUN), which is one of the 920 MHz band radio communication standards (Table I) [12]. Wi-SUN uses IEEE 802.15.4g, which is an extension of IEEE 802.15.4 used in the Zigbee physical layer, and because it

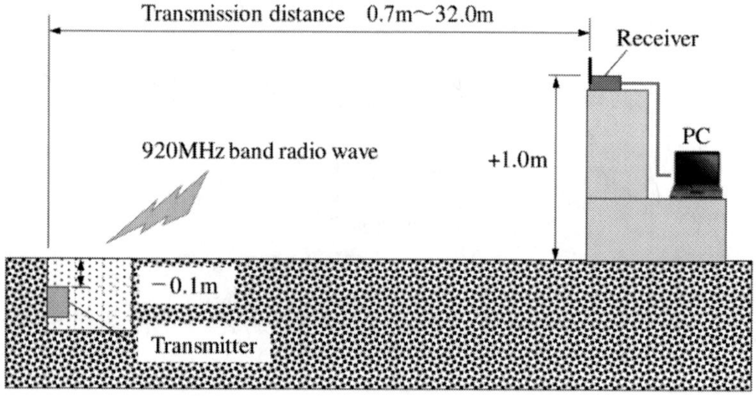

Figure 2. Test Configuration (adapted from [5])

TABLE I. Transmitter Specifications

Radio Communication Standard	Wi-SUN
Modulation Method	2GFSK
Transmission Rate	100kbps
Transmission Power	20mW

can transmit IPv6 packets, it is suitable for storing data in the cloud via a network such as Wi-Fi [4].

Figure 2 and Table II show the test configuration and test conditions. As shown in Figure 2, the transmitter was buried 0.1m below the ground and the receiver was installed 1.0m above the ground surface. First, we measured the RSSI where the transmitter was a normal condition (not buried condition). Then, we buried the transmitter in the ground and measured RSSI again. Also, dry soil was used when burying the transmitter to exclude the influence of moisture originally contained in the added soil. Evaluation of the test results was performed by comparing the RSSI in the normal condition and the buried condition. Also, when the transmission distance was 0.7m, we measured RSSI by changing the soil depth (0.05m, 0.1m, 0.15m). WSN is required to be able to easily perform maintenance such as battery replacement. For that reason, it is not realistic to buried a transmitter deep underground. Therefore, the soil depth was set on the assumption that maintenance is easy.

B. *Results and Discussion [5]*

Figure 3(a)(b) shows the test result. In Figure 3(a), the red dots are the RSSI in the normal condition, and the blue triangles are the RSSI in the buried condition, and the green squares are the Loss (difference between normal condition and buried condition). Each RSSI value is an average value of 100 transmission data. As shows Figure 3, when the transmitter is buried, it can be confirmed that radio waves are attenuated by about 20 dB regardless of the transmission distance. From the above results, we propose to consider a margin of at least about 20 dB when designing WSN with the transmitter buried 0.1m below the ground.

As shown in Figure 3(b), in this test, there was no difference in Loss when the soil depth was 0.05m and 0.1m, but when the soil depth was 0.15m, the Loss was increased by about 3dB. The loss is based on the buried condition of 0.7m transmission distance and 0.1m soil depth.

IV. Performance Measuring Test Of WSN In Buried Condition

We conducted a test to confirm to the performance of the 920MHz band WSN in buried condition. This section describes the test methods and results and discussion.

A. *Test Method*

We constructed a WSN in the test embankment based on the above test results. In railway slope condition monitoring, the sensors must be installed at various positions depending on the shape of the slope. For this reason, in this test, the sensor placement was determined assuming the condition monitoring for the railway slope. Figure 4 shows the transmitter architecture and the construction status of WSN.

As shown in Figure 4, a chip antenna was used as the transmitter antenna, and the transmitter is powered utilizing a rechargeable battery. Also, regarding the construction status of WSN, a total of seven transmitters were installed, where four transmitters were buried 0.1m below the ground, and three transmitters were installed 1.2m above the ground. On the other hand, the receiver was installed on the second floor of the laboratory (4.5m above the ground).

TABLE II. TEST CONDITIONS (ADAPTED FROM [5])

Transmitter Height (m)	-0.1
Receiver Height (m)	1.0
Transmission Distance (m)	0.7, 1.0, 2.0, 4.0, 8.0, 16.0, 32.0

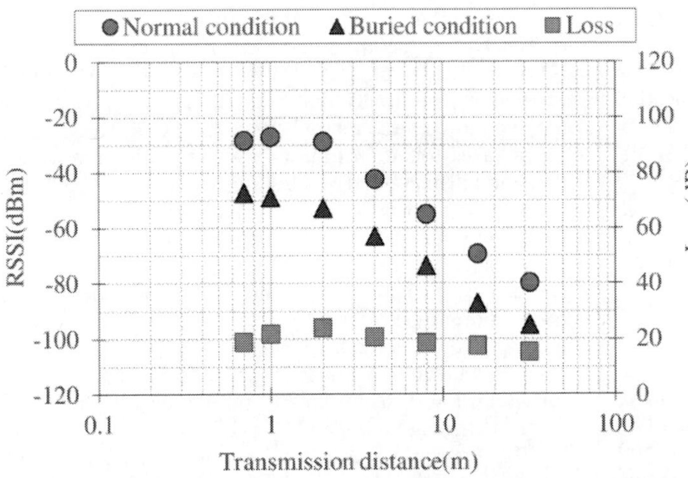

(a) Comparison of normal condition and buried condition (adapted from [5])

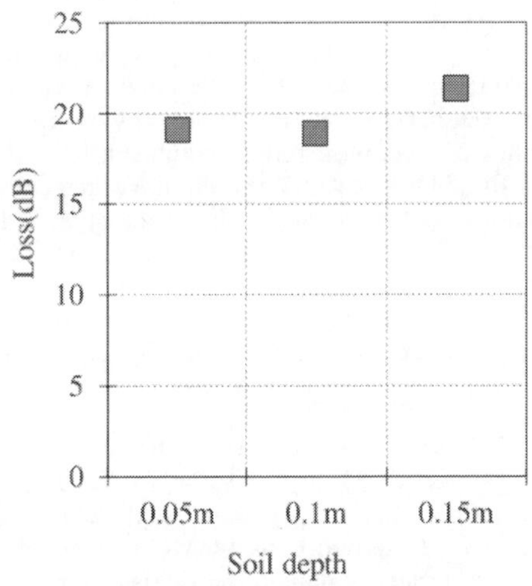

(b) Comparison when changing the soil depth (Transmission distance 0.7m)

Figure 3. Comparion of RSSI in buried condition

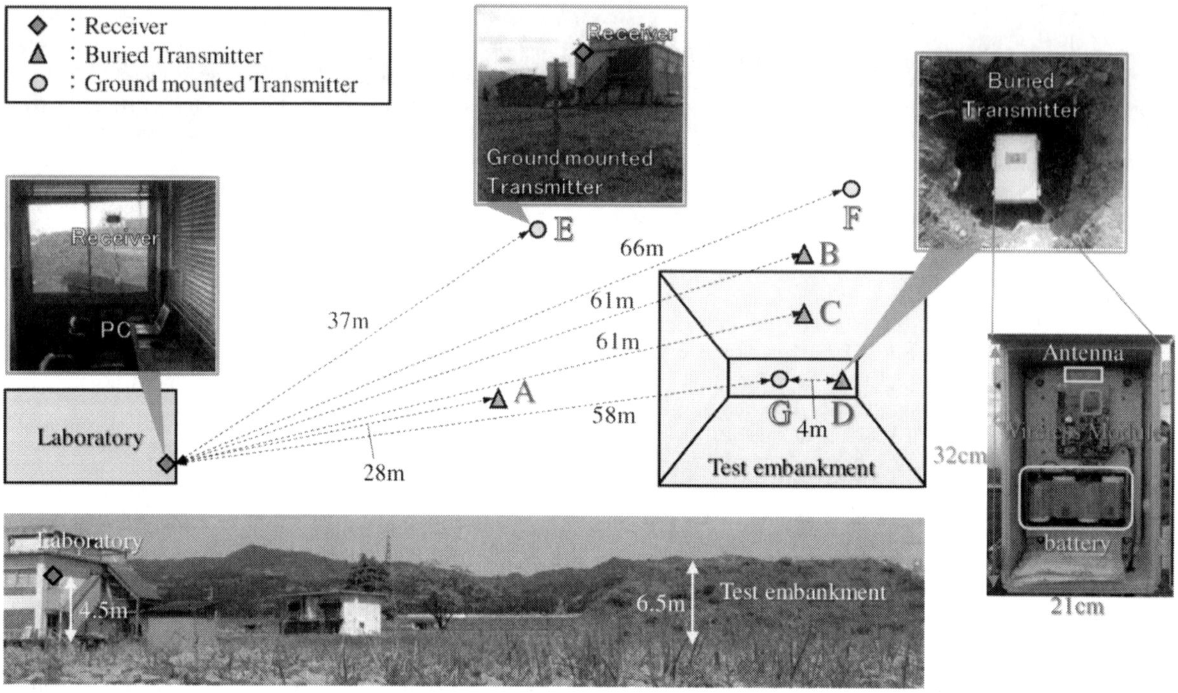

Figure 4. Construction status of WSN and transmitter archtecture (adapted from [5])

TABLE III. MEASUREMENT ITEMS AND THE MEASUREMENT/TRANSMISSION INTERVALS

Measurement Items	RSSI
	Transmission path data
	Weather data(Rainfall, Temperature)
Measurement / Transmission Interval	10 minutes

Table III shows measurement items and transmission intervals. In this test, the transmitters were improved so that transmission path data could be acquired along. If the buried transmitter can't transmit directly to the receiver, the WSN is designed to switch transmission paths and transmit data to the receiver using multi-hop transmission through the ground mounted transmitter. Then, the test for about 1 month was conducted at a data transmission interval of 10-minutes. Also, the weather data was measured by wired communication with a weather observation equipment.

In addition, in this test, the measurement interval is 10-minutes, but we consider that a measurement interval of 1 hour to 1 day is sufficient for continuous condition monitoring in a production environment [13]. When the interval of measurement and transmission is 1 hour, the battery lifetime is assumed to be about half a year.

B. Results and Discussion

This section shows the results of change over time of transmitter RSSI and 10-minutes rainfall. Also, among transmitters that are large attenuated the RSSI due to rainfall, the result of buried transmitter C are shown in Figure 5(a) and the ground mounted transmitter E are shown in Figure 5(b). Although the RSSI attenuation was some difference, similar results were obtained with other transmitters. Additionally, the color of each dot in a figure represents the communication destination, and the green dot shows communicated with the transmitter E and the red dot shows communicated with the receiver. Thereby, the transmission path of each transmitter can be grasped.

Firstly, we describe the attenuation characteristics of radio waves in rainfall. As shown in Figure 5(a), the buried transmitter confirmed that the RSSI was attenuated in conjunction with the rainfall. Furthermore, it was confirmed that it takes a certain time to recover to the normal value after the attenuation. The existing research [6] showed that the 920 MHz band radio waves became more attenuated according to the increase of moisture content of the snow on the transmission path. Therefore, it can be considered that the increase in soil moisture due to rainfall attenuates the RSSI, and influences radio wave propagation until drainage is completed. On the other hand, as shown in Figure 5(b), the ground mounted transmitter shows little fluctuation in RSSI during this test. It seems that the influence of rainfall directly on RSSI attenuation is small.

Also, regarding buried transmitter C, the relationship between rainfall and loss is shown in Figure 6 for the period in which continuous rainfall is observed. The target period is

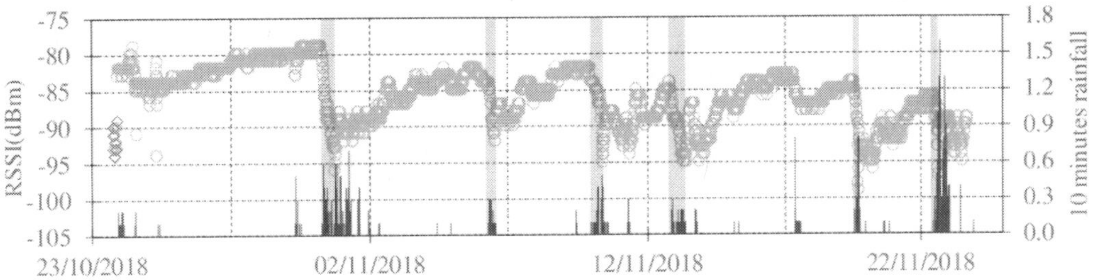

(a) Buried transmitter C

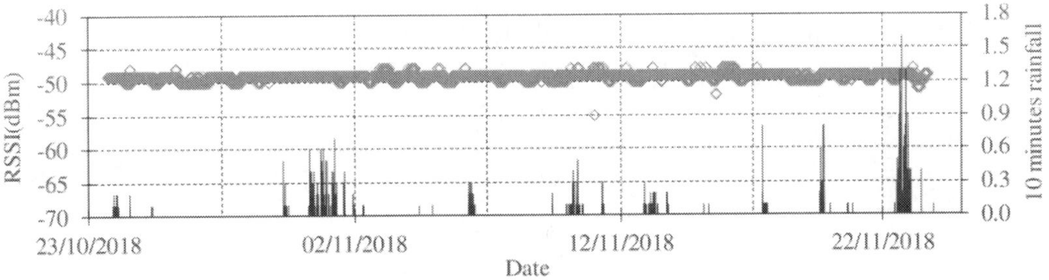

(b) Ground mounted transmitter E

Figure 5. Change over time of RSSI and 10 minutes rainfall

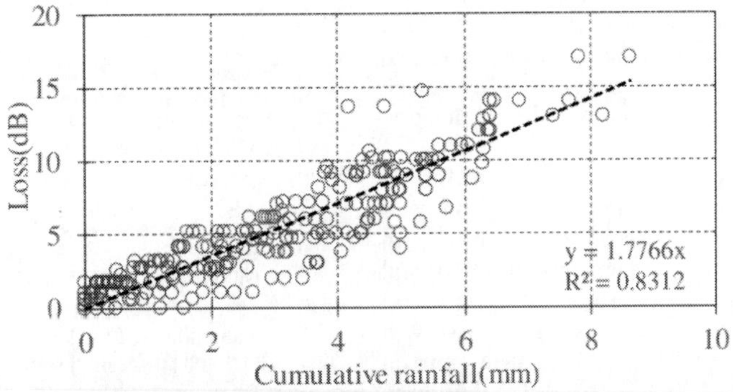

Figure 6. Relationship between Cumulative rainfall and Loss

the portion highlighted in red in Figure 5(a). Here, rainfall is a cumulative value from the observation of rainfall to the point where RSSI has most attenuated, and the loss is a difference between the average value of RSSI before rainfall observation (2 hours) and the RSSI during the rainfall observation. As shown in Figure 6, the loss increases in proportion to the cumulative rainfall, and in this test, a loss of up to 17 dB is confirmed at about 9 mm of cumulative rainfall.

Next, we describe the transmission path. As shown in Figure 5(a), the communication destination is switched from the receiver to the transmitter E at the beginning of the test. Figure 7 shows the result of extracting 6 hours before and after path switching. As shown in Figure 7, the transmission path is switched at the timing of rainfall. Furthermore, when data was directly transmitted to the receiver, the RSSI was -90dBm or less, but after path switching, the RSSI improved by about 10dB. Therefore, we estimate that the path has been switched to the transmitter with a better propagation environment, triggered by the deterioration of the radio wave propagation environment due to rainfall. Additionally, as the results, it has been confirmed that multi-hop transmission is possible in the buried condition. Table IV shows the data arrival rate to the receiver from each transmitter. As shown in Table IV, in the buried transmitters, data loss occurred in 3 out of 4 transmitters. As mentioned above, we estimate that one of the main factors is that the radio wave propagation environment is deteriorated due to rainfall and the RSSI is attenuated.

V. Conclusion and Future Work

In this study, we carried out a transmission characteristic test of 920 MHz band in a buried condition and a performance measuring test of WSN on the test embankment. As the results, in the transmission characteristic test, it is confirmed that there is an attenuation of about 20 dB regardless of the transmission distance when the transmitter is buried in the soil about 0.1m. Furthermore, in the performance measuring test, it is confirmed that multi-hop transmission with switched transmission path is possible

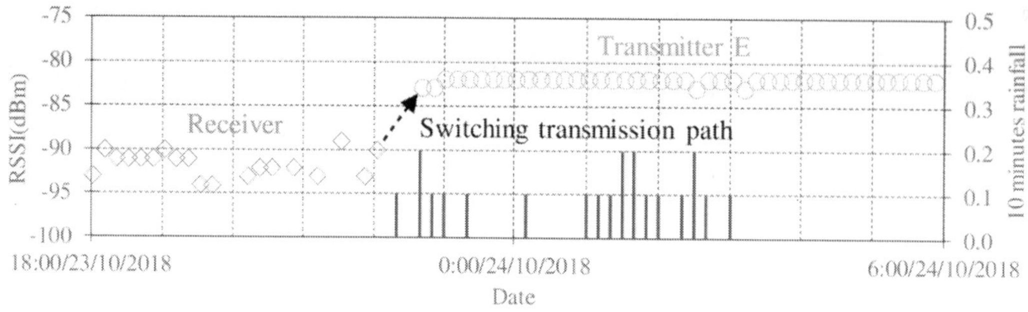

Figure 7. Test result at the switching transmission path

TABLE IV. DATA ARRIVAL RATE

	Installation Method of Transmitter	Number of Transmitted Data	Number of Received Data	Data Arrival Rate
A	Buried 0.1m below the ground	4460	4460	100%
B		4457	4374	98%
C		4458	4411	99%
D		4455	3834	86%
F	Installed 1.2m above the ground	4458	4454	100%
G		4456	4455	100%

even when direct transmission of data to the receiver becomes difficult. On the other hand, when the soil on the propagation path contains moisture due to continuous rainfall, it has been confirmed that the attenuation is so large, and data loss occurs. Consequently, we regard that WSN design in a buried environment needs to consider the attenuation due to burial and rainfall.

In the future, we are going to continue testing to further improve the WSN design in the railway environment. Furthermore, we are also going to confirm the long term performance of WSN and the relationship between soil moisture content and loss. In addition, since the place where the test was conducted this time is a snowfall area, we will also examine the effects of snow depth and melted snow on radio wave propagation in the 920 MHz band. In addition to the embankment where this test was conducted, the railway has many facilities with severe transmitter installation conditions. This result is expected to be used as basic knowledge for constructing a large-scale 920 MHz band WSN in the railway environment in the future.

REFERENCES

[1] T. Mizuno, "Approach to maintenance of Railway structure," Public works management journal, vol.451, pp.74-79, Dec. 2015.

[2] Ministry of Land,Infrastructure,Transport and Tourism, "Disaster prevention and mitigation measures for Railways," Policy review results, p.7, Mar. 2019.

[3] N. Iwasawa, T. Kawamura., M. Nozue, S. Ryuo, and N. Iwaki, "Desigh of Wireless Sensor Network in the Railway," The 7th International Conference on Sensor Networks (SENSORNETS 2018), pp.122-127, Jan. 2018, doi: 10.5220/0006638101220127

[4] M. Nozue, et al., "Application of Wi-SUN Sensor Network for Railway Monitoring," RTRI REPORT, vol.32, no.5, pp.17-22, May 2018.

[5] N. Iwaki, N. Iwasawa, and D. Yamaguchi, "Construction of 920MHz band Wireless sensor network in buried condition," The 2019 Annual Meeting the Institute of Electrical Enginners of Japan(Hokkaido 2019)IEEJ, pp.432-433, Mar. 2019.

[6] N. Iwasawa, S. Ryuo, T. Kawamura, K. Kawasaki, and M. Nozue, "Transmission Performance evaluation of Wi-SUN Wireless Sensor Network During Snowing," In 23rd J-RAIL(Tokyo 2016)IEEJ, pp.53-54, Dec. 2016.

[7] H. Fukutomi, Y. Shumuta, "Sensor Networks Wireless Communication for Condition monitorring of Fossil Fuel Power Systems -Part1:Prototyping of 920 MHz Multihop Wireless Sensor Networks-", CRIEPI Research Report, Q16003, pp.1-7, Apr. 2017.

[8] T. Moribe, H. Okada, K. Kobayashi, and M. Katayama, "Evaluation of 920 MHz Radio Wave Propagation Characteteristics for Wireless Sensor Networks in a Farm," Agricultural Information Research, vol.26, no.1, pp.1-10, 2017, doi:10.3173/air.26.1

[9] H. Suzuki, et al., "Construction of a sensor network to forecast landside disasters using an Ad-Hoc network and EC sensors," The 2nd Information and Communication Systems for Safe and Secure Life(Nigata 2012)IEICE, pp.3-9, 2012.

[10] T. Uchimura, et al., "Precaution and early warning of surface failure of slopes using tilt sensors," Soils and Foundations, vol.55, Issue 5, pp.1086-1099, Oct. 2015, doi:10.1016/j.sandf.2015.09.010

[11] M. Hara, H. Shimasaki, Y. Kado, and M. Ichida, "Effect of vegetation growth on radio wave propagation in 920-MHz band," IEICE Transactions on communications, vol.E99-B, issue 1, pp.81-86, 2016, doi:10.1587/transcom.2015ISP0021

[12] H. Harada, "Wi-SUN, an international wireless communication standard that supports the IoT era," ITU Journal, vol.47, no.2, pp.3-8, Feb. 2017.

[13] Y. Ikekawa, et al., "Monitoring of an active slope by wireless sensor network," The 38th Proceedings of the symposium on rock mechanics, pp.39-44, Jan. 2009.

Genetic Algorithm For LoRa Transmission Parameter Selection

Aghiles Djoudi[1,2], Rafik Zitouni[2], Nawel Zangar[1] and Laurent George[1]

[1]LIGM/ESIEE Paris, 5 boulevard Descartes, Champs-sur-Marne, France
[2]ECE Research Lab Paris, 37 Quai de Grenelle, 75015 Paris, France
Email: {aghiles.djoudi, nawel.zangar, laurent.george}@esiee.fr, rafik.zitouni@ece.fr

***Abstract*—The exponential growth of Internet of things (IoT) applications in both industry and academic research raises many questions in wireless sensor networks. Heterogeneous networks of IoT devices strongly depend on the ability of IoT devices to adapt their data transmission parameters to each application requirement. One of the most important problem of the emerging IoT networks is the limitation in terms of energy consumption and computation capability. These limitations could be addressed by using the edge computing to unload IoT devices from additional computation tasks. Our work is motivated by the idea of matching each transmission configuration with a reward and cost values to satisfy applications constraints. Our goal is to make IoT devices able to select the optimal configuration and send their data to the gateway with the QoS required by IoT applications. In this work, we use LoRa network to evaluate the efficiency of our algorithm. Determining the best configuration among 6720 LaRa transmission settings is challenging. The difficulty is mainly due to the lack of tools that could take all applications requirements into account to select the best settings. To address this problem, we use a genetic algorithm in an edge computing to select the transmission parameters needed by the application. Each LoRa configuration represents a feature that needs to be selected to match better the QoS criteria. Particularly, we analyze the impact of selecting one configuration in 3 kinds of applications: text, voice and image transmission by modeling a new adaptive data rate selection process.**

***Keywords*—Genetic algorithm; Fuzzy logic; LoRaWAN; Adaptive Data Rate (ADR).**

I. Introduction

The need of Low Power Wide Area Networks ($LPWAN$) increased significantly these five last years. The main factor is that IoT devices require low power consumption to transmit data in a wide area. LoRa, Sigfox and Narrowband IoT ($NB - IoT$) are the most known technologies that satisfy these requirements. Applications like smart building and smart environment are one of hundreds use cases that need to be deployed with such technologies. Unlike Sigfox and NB-IoT, LoRa is more open for academic research because the specification that governs it is relatively open. The transmission could be configured with 4 parameters: Spreading Factor (SF), Transmission Power (Tx), Coding Rate (CR) and Bandwidth (BW), to achieve better performance.

The main LPWAN research directions are about link optimization, adaptability and large scale networks to support massive number of devices. The selection of an appropriate transmission parameter for IoT networks typically depends on the nature of the application. In this paper, we investigate the performance of heterogeneous networks (i.e., when each IoT device selects its LoRa transmission parameters according to its link budget and the application requirements). For that purpose, we have developed a LoRa transmission adaptation mechanism. Both ns-3 simulator and the Low cost LoRa Gateway [1] are used to validate our approach. The computation tasks of the selection process will run on the Gateway device (Raspberry-pi) and the required settings will be sent to nodes for the next transmission.

This paper is organized as follows. Section II elucidates summary of related works. In Section III, we propose our approach to solve LoRa parameter selection problem. Our experiments is presented in Section IV. Section V concludes this paper.

II. Related work

Transmission parameter configuration mechanisms, such as Adaptive Data Rate (ADR) scheme [2] need to be developed to fit each application requirement in terms of power consumption, delay and packet delivery ratio. Solutions running on LoRa node should be less complex to match computation limitation of IoT devices as required in LoRaWAN specification. However, LoRa network server could run complex management mechanism, which can be developed to improve network performance. In this paper, we focus on the server-side mechanisms.

The basic ADR scheme [2] provided by LoRaWAN predicts channel conditions using the maximum received Signal Noise Rate (SNR) in the last 20 packets. The basic ADR scheme is sufficient when the variance of the channel is low, it reduces the interference compared with the static data rate [3][4]. However, their simplicity causes many potential drawbacks. First, the diversity of LoRa Gateway models that measures SNR make the measurement inaccurate as a result of hardware calibration and interfering transmissions. Second, selecting the maximum SNR each 20 packets received could be a very long period in many IoT applications that require less uplink transmission. Third, transmission parameters adjustment considers only the link of a single node. If many LoRa nodes are connected to the near gateway, all nodes connected to this one will use the fastest data rate. In this case, the number of

LoRa nodes using the same data rate will increase and the probability of collisions also increases dramatically.

For example, the authors in [4] slightly modify the basic ADR scheme by replacing the maximum SNR with the average function. In this paper, we focus on building a framework that help IoT devices to adapt their transmission parameters to the application requirements in a server side.

III. Proposed Framework

The selection process scheme illustrated in Figure 1 can be described following these five steps:

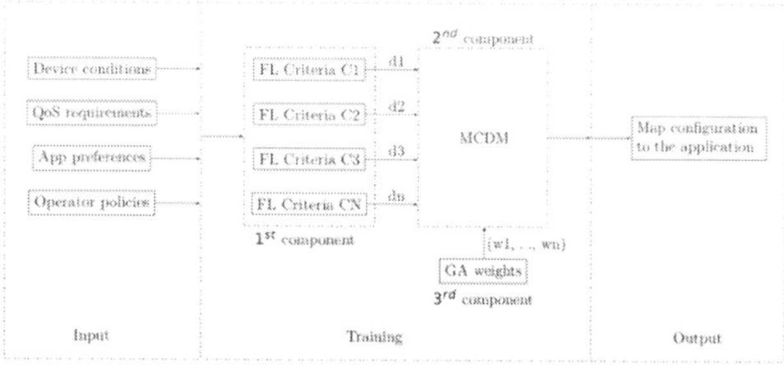

Figure 1. The proposed scheme for LoRa transmission parameters selection based on GA, FL and Multi-Criteria Decision Making $MCDM$.

1) According to the Semtech SX1276 LoRa transceiver [5], there are 6720 possible settings (s_1, ... , s_{6720}) and the framework has to select the most optimal one or to rank them according to their relevance.
2) The first step of the selection process depends on multiple criteria up to i (c_1, ... , c_i). Different type of criteria can be measured from different sources to cover the maximum point of views, as an example, the network server requirements, the applications requirements and the devices conditions.
3) The Fuzzy Logic (FL) based subsystem gives an initial score for each configuration that reflects its relevance. The different sets of scores (d_1, ... , d_i) are sent to the $MCDM$ in the 5th step.
4) At the same time, the GA [6] assigns a suitable weight (w_1, ..., w_i) for each initial selection decision, this selection is made according to the objective function that is required by the application.
5) Using the initial scores coming from the 3rd step and the weights using the 4th step, the multi criteria decision making $MCDM$ will select the most relevant settings and rank them according to their reward.

IV. Experiments

For our experiments we use both real environment (Figure 2) and ns-3 simulator with SX1276 LoRa module. However, to test the scalability of genetic algorithm with numerous IoT devices in a real environment, we use FIT IoT-LAB platform among other platforms presented in [7]. This choice is motivated by the number of devices supported by this platform (up to 2000 nodes).

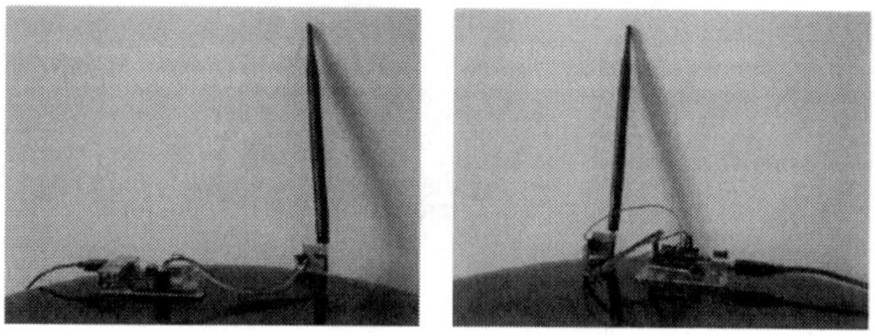

(a) Gateway (Raspberry-pi). (b) Sensor node (Arduino).

Figure 2. Gateway & Sensor node.

Figure 2a presents the LoRa gateway that we build using a low cost LoRa gateway [1] on a Raspberry-pi. Figure 2b presents one of the two Arduino boards equipped with an antenna that cover both 868 and 433 MHz band with a SX1276 LoRa Transceiver.

Due to the energy constraints of LoRa nodes of class A that we use, our framework will send commands through the FCtrl fields to ask nodes to adapt their transmission behavior to the new application or the new environment conditions.

V. Discussion

Our main contribution was to build 3 applications that requires 3 different levels of QoS, such as text, sound and image transmission. We used a low cost LoRa gateway on a Raspberry-pi with 2 Arduino boards equipped with 2 LoRa Transceivers based on the Semtech SX1276 specification. The main challenge addressed in this work was to explore the application of genetic algorithm in LoRa transmission parameter selection. To measure the accuracy of applying genetic algorithm in an edge computing we expect to compare our approach with other adaptive data rate solutions.

References

[1] Pham. (). Low Cost LoRa Gateway, [Online]. Available: https://github.com/CongducPham/LowCostLoRaGw (visited on 08/30/2019).

[2] L. Alliance. (). LoraWAN Specification, [Online]. Available: https://lora-alliance.org/resource-hub/lorawanr-specification-v103 (visited on 08/30/2019).

[3] M. C. Bor, U. Roedig, T. Voigt, and J. M. Alonso, " Do LoRa Low-Power Wide-Area Networks Scale? ", in *Proceedings of the 19th ACM International Conference on Modeling, Analysis and Simulation of Wireless and Mobile Systems - MSWiM '16*, 00223, Malta, Malta: ACM Press, 2016, pp. 59–67.

[4] M. Slabicki, G. Premsankar, and M. D. Francesco, " Adaptive Configuration of Lora Networks for Dense IoT Deployments ", *NOMS 2018 - 2018 IEEE/IFIP Network Operations and Management Symposium*, pp. 1–9, 2018, 00025.

[5] Semtech. (). Semtech LoRa Technology Overview, [Online]. Available: https://www.semtech.com/lora (visited on 09/01/2019).

[6] M. Alkhawlani and A. Ayesh, " Access Network Selection Based on Fuzzy Logic and Genetic Algorithms ", *Advances in Artificial Intelligence*, vol. 2008, pp. 1–12, 2008, 00089.

[7] A.-S. Tonneau, N. Mitton, and J. Vandaele, " How to Choose an Experimentation Platform for Wireless Sensor Networks? A Survey on Static and Mobile Wireless Sensor Network Experimentation Facilities ", *Ad Hoc Networks*, vol. 30, pp. 115–127, Jul. 2015, 00046.

Rating Convergence Measurement in Trust-based Multi-Stakeholder Consensus Decision-Making

Lina Alfantoukh

King Faisal Specialist Hospital &
Research Center, Riyadh, Saudi Arabia
Email: lynaA@kfshrc.edu.sa

Abdullah Alzeer

King Saud University
Riyadh, Saudi Arabia
Email: aalzeer@ksu.edu.sa

Abstract—**In collective decision-making where several participants involved to agree on one selection, reaching the consensus among them is important but it is challenging when the participants have conflicting interests. Therefore, the influence that is based on the trust from one participant to another could be useful to make the others shift their interests to be similar to others. Shifting interest can be long term or short term depending on participants behaviors. In our decision-making framework, there are different rounds where participants interact by ratings. Each round creates a rating matrix. In this paper, we study the rating convergence by analyzing the rating matrix changes by measuring its perturbations in each round and find the effect of these changes on reaching the consensus when using a trust and without it. We built a simulation that generates several decision scenarios. Our result showed that the changes in the rating matrix under the trust improve reaching the consensus in term of decreasing the required number of round and increasing the consensus value. Moreover, our result showed that changing interest in a long term performs better than short term in term of number or rounds reduction.**

Keywords–Trust; Decision-Making; Multi-Stakeholder; Matrix perturbations.

I. Introduction

In the decision-making process where several stakeholders involved, we need a mechanism to reach an agreement specifically when the stakeholders have conflicting interests. In general, the humans' nature gives them the tendency to decide rationally by selecting the decision that gives them the maximum satisfaction according to the Rational Choice Theory [1]. However, in reality, people might have different interest. Therefore, relying on rationality makes reaching a consensus decision to be challenging [2]. As a result, the stakeholders could use the influence on each other using the assumption of the Social Influence Theory [3] to make their interest similar and in turn reach the consensus. In our existing trusted-based decision-making framework [4], the trust of the stakeholder is used to influence the others. The higher the trust the higher the reputation of the stakeholder. As a result, any stakeholder with a high reputation could influence the others in term of recommending decisions or even changing their interests [5]. Changing the interest can be short term or long term [2]. In this work, the short-term change of interest is done locally during the negotiation in each round but does not affect the future choices. The long-term change of interest is done in a way that affects the stakeholder current and future choices.

In multi-stakeholder consensus decision-making, there is a network of stakeholders who might or might not influence one another. They meet, propose solutions and modify them in several rounds to reach a solution that suits everyone. During these rounds, the stakeholders rate each other to declare their opinions regarding the proposed solutions and these ratings can later be translated to trust. As a result, due to the involvement of humans who interact during the negotiation, trust among them comes into the picture. Trust provides many benefits, such as extra information through the impression the stakeholders develop of each other over time in a particular context, which helps to reach the consensus [6]. Also, trust indicates the interests similarity among stakeholders. As a result, the stakeholders' reputations can be obtained from the trust. The more ratings, the better because they increase the amount of information available about the stakeholders. The longer the history, the better because it increases the chances of having more ratings. The fact of having the stakeholders come from different backgrounds, hold different expertise and not to mention the conflicting objectives makes the consensus decision-making to be challenging.

In this paper, we aim to study the rating convergence of our proposed decision-making framework [4] by studying the rating matrix perturbation. The consensus is achieved when either all the stakeholders propose the same solution or they all give the maximum rating to one solution. The trust is an influencer factor that lead the stakeholders to adjust their selections based on the trustworthy stakeholders guides. Such influences may affect the rating behavior, as well as changing their initial interests they have in a way to be similar to the highly trusted stakeholders.

This paper is organized as follows. In Section II, we list the existing related works. Then, we show our trust model and the generic decision-making framework in Sections III and IV. In Section V, we address rating convergence measurement. After that, we explain the experimental setup and results in sections VI and VII. Finally, in Section VIII, we conclude the paper.

II. Related Work

Interactions among stakeholders when they make a collective decision is important since they negotiate while they are seeking for a solution to choose. In decision-making framework that uses machines to moderate the stakeholder negotiations, the interaction could be rating or even written comment to express the others opinion regarding the individuals choices and preferences [7]–[9]. Such notion of preferences occurs in decision-making field [2]. The individuals' preferences can be changed over the time due to the changes in the interests.

Those interests change can be a result of the influence by the others [6], the choices made before or even other factors that are based on the individuals situation at the time of making selection. Several studies showed that the individual interest and preferences are changing [5] [6] [10]–[15] and these study are different in term of the causes that lead changing the preferences. In [12], they predicted the changes in preferences based on the feedback of the negotiation process. Hansson [13] presented the dominant theories of belief change that may be called input-assimilating models. They expressed how the subject's belief state is transformed upon assimilation of an input. In addition to the different factors that change the individuals' preferences, the choices proposed while making a decision may affect the preferences or in other word, it shapes them [15]. Babajide and et al. [6] explained the change in the initial preference of an individual to match the others choices, either through coercion from others or selection by the individual team member. Preferences changes can be short or long term [2] [5] [16] [17]. Short term preferences affect the current choices while negotiating but the long term one affects the choices in the future. In social psychology field where they study the peoples' behavior, there are different theories that predict the preferences changes. For example, dissonance theory [10] [18] [19] motivates individuals to change their preferences to match their prior decision that can be a result of a selection they made in the past based on influence.

III. Trust

In reference to Alfantoukh and et al. [4], trust is a result of meeting expectations in a particular context. Therefore, there is no universal definition of trust because it is context-dependent [20]. We may represent trust as the level of an individual's agreement with a proposed solution due to the interests associated with it. We model trust by using the solution ratings during the agreement. Trust can be classified as local trust and global trust. Global trust is modeled by using all the historical interactions between any two individuals, which creates the stakeholders' reputations that can be used as a weight to influence other decisions. The local trust consists of current negotiation interactions between any stakeholders and it is used for updating the global trust. We have proposed a trust system based on the measurement theory [21]–[30]. This trust system has three stages: trust modeling, trust management, and decision making. The quantification of trust has been taken care of in the trust modeling and management phases. In our trust system, we define two metrics, impression and confidence, as continuous values in [0, 1]. The impression m shows the stakeholder's usefulness by evaluating his/her decision. Every two stakeholders have several interactions at different times, which lead to a distribution of their impressions of each other $M = \{m_1, m_2, \ldots, m_k\}$. The impression value is the mean of the distributions (1). The other metric, confidence c, shows the degree of certainty about the judgments. The confidence of the judgment is obtained by knowing how far away from the real impression the stakeholder can be (2), where r is equivalent to the square root of the standard error.

$$m = \frac{(\sum_{i=1}^{i=k} m_i)}{k} \tag{1}$$

$$c = 1 - 2 * r \tag{2}$$

IV. Multi-stakeholder Decision-Making Model Based on Trust and Risk

We have designed a generic framework for multi-stakeholder decision making based on trust and risk that produces a decision agreed upon by the participants [4]. In this framework, the stakeholders negotiate with each other by 5-star rating to declare their agreement regarding the other solutions. The process starts with the stakeholder proposing their solutions that have corresponding interest value is calculated by the utility function. This utility function is context-dependent. The trust relationship among stakeholders construct the network of them. Those trust values form the reputation of the stakeholders. The trust is computed by our existing trust system [4] [21]–[29] that is based on measurement theory. Next, the stakeholders rate each other to declare their opinions of the proposed solutions. Then, the Group Decision making Model (GDM) entity aggregates those ratings. After that, the aggregated rating values of the solutions are ranked descendingly. The consensus level is obtained by the aggregated rating values. Therefore, the top value should have a value higher than or equal to a threshold value to indicate that consensus is achieved. Otherwise, a new round will start.

A. Rating

If we assume that the rating system is 5-star rating and stakeholder a rates stakeholder b, then the rating will depend on how far the a's interest of its own decision from the interest he gets from what b proposed. If b's decision give more interest to a than what a's proposed then the rating is the maximum, 5 stars. Otherwise, we consider the differences between the interest of decision proposed by a and the interest of decision proposed by b. The larger the difference the lower the rating and vice versa. Therefore, to compute the star rating associated with the difference, it requires to transform the difference value range ($diff$) to 5-star value range. $diff$ range is [0,1] and the start range is [0,5]. However, since the larger difference means lower rating, we need to find the transformation function, $f(diff)$, from [1,0] to [0,5], meaning to find value $rate$ in [0,5] associated with value $diff$ in [1,0]. If we assume the function to be linear, we may use the affine transformation function to find the rating from the differences. Using the affine transformation function, we can calculate the rating using (3)

$$f(diff) = 5 * (1 - diff) \tag{3}$$

B. Aggregation

The outcome of the rating's phase is the rating matrix. Suppose that there is a set of stakeholders, S, a set of decisions, D, and a set of corresponding trust values for each stakeholder. The stakeholders rate each other as represented in matrix R. In this matrix, the element r_{ij} represents the rating from stakeholder i to stakeholder j regarding j's proposed solution. Each stakeholder has an assigned trust value represented in the vector T. The sum of the trust values is W. The rating weighted average operator is RWA and computed by using R, T and (4). Here, the trust T is used to weigh the ratings. The outcome is a vector of consensus degrees corresponding to the proposed solutions. The selected decision is the decision with the maximum consensus degree, which is later compared to consensus threshold to check the consensus achievement.

$$T = \begin{bmatrix} T_1 & T_2 & T_3 \end{bmatrix}$$

$$W = \sum_{n=1}^{3} T_n$$

$$R = \begin{bmatrix} 1 & r_{12} & r_{13} \\ r_{21} & 1 & r_{23} \\ r_{31} & r_{32} & 1 \end{bmatrix}$$

$$RWA = \frac{1}{W} * T * R \quad (4)$$

V. Rating Convergence Measurement

As we indicated before, our framework generates rating matrices during the negotiation, the more the ratings the larger the magnitude of the matrices. Matrix norm can be used to measure the rating matrices magnitude and then use it to find the perturbations. For example, the Frobenius norm [31] can be used for calculating the ratings matrix norm by computing the square root of the sum of the absolute squares of each rating in the matrix. Suppose, the rating matrix is M and has elements r_{ij}, which each r_{ij} represents the rating from stakeholder r_i to the decision proposed by r_j and n is the number of decision makers, the Frobenius norm is computed by (5)

$$\| M \|_F = \sqrt{\sum_i^n \sum_j^n | r_{ij} |^2} \quad (5)$$

The matrix norm shows how big the matrix is. Therefore, if the ratings become higher in every round then the matrix norm becomes larger than the previous round. Larger norms is an indicator of the ratings convergence to the consensus degree level. Our interpretation is that trust is an important factor to influence the stakeholders which leads to increase the matrix norm. To find the matrix perturbations, we use the difference of norms between the current round and the previous one. Supposed that there are three stakeholders s_1, s_2 and s_3 and three consensus degree values c_1, c_2 and c_3 stored in consensus vector, **c** respectively. The rating matrix R stores all the rating for one round.

$$R = \begin{bmatrix} r_{11} & r_{12} & r_{13} \\ r_{21} & r_{22} & r_{23} \\ r_{31} & r_{32} & r_{33} \end{bmatrix}$$

Let's assume there is a vector,**x**, of x_1,x_2 and x_3 which has a solution in the following linear system:

$$r_{11}x_1 + r_{21}x_2 + r_{31}x_3 = c_1$$
$$r_{12}x_1 + r_{22}x_2 + r_{32}x_3 = c_2$$
$$r_{13}x_1 + r_{23}x_2 + r_{33}x_3 = c_3$$

We can write the linear system above as:

$$R\mathbf{x} = \mathbf{c} \quad (6)$$

Suppose that after one round, changes occurred, Δ. We write the rating matrix , R$\prime$ as:

$$R\prime = \begin{bmatrix} r_{11} + \Delta_{11} & r_{12} + \Delta_{12} & r_{13} + \Delta_{13} \\ r_{21} + \Delta_{21} & r_{22} + \Delta_{22} & r_{23} + \Delta_{23} \\ r_{31} + \Delta_{31} & r_{32} + \Delta_{32} & r_{33} + \Delta_{33} \end{bmatrix}$$

There is is a vector, **y**, of y_1,y_2 and y_3 such that

$$\mathbf{y} = \mathbf{x} + \Delta \quad (7)$$

TABLE I. List of the parameters used in the simulation with their corresponding values.

Parameter	*Description*	*Value*
$NoSH$	Number of StakeHolders	15
$numbStakehoder$	Number of StakeHolders per project	5
$globalNoD$	Total number of decisions to propose	100
noS	Total number of samples	5
$pCount$	Number of Projects generated per sample	200
$roundCount$	Maximum Number of rounds per project	10
T	Trust Value range	[0,1]
$Interest$	Interest Value range	[0,1]
$consThreshold$	Minimum Consensus Degree	1.0

Also, each rating from i to j is changed such that

$$r_{ij}\prime = r_{ij} + \Delta_{ij} \quad (8)$$

This victor has a solution in the following linear system:

$$r_{11}\prime y_1 + r_{21}\prime y_2 + r_{31}\prime y_3 = c_1 + \Delta_1$$
$$r_{12}\prime y_1 + r_{22}\prime y_2 + r_{32}\prime y_3 = c_2 + \Delta_2$$
$$r_{13}\prime y_1 + r_{23}\prime y_2 + r_{33}\prime y_3 = c_3 + \Delta_3$$

We can write the linear system above as:

$$(R + \Delta)\mathbf{y} = \mathbf{c} + \mathbf{\Delta} \quad (9)$$

To compute the perturbation, we find the difference between **x** and **y** (6) and (9) using matrix (5) and vector (10) norms.

$$| v |_2 = \sqrt{\sum_i^n | v_i |^2} \quad (10)$$

In the result section, we will present whether there is a correlation or not between the amount of perpetuation and the number of rounds to reach the consensus.

VI. Experiment

1) Experiment objective: The aim of the experiment is to study the ratings changes when several stakeholders want to make a decision and study the effect of the trust on those rating changes. Such an effect can be examined through the number of required rounds, the consensus degree average in each round, and the consensus achievements. We have designed and implemented a simulation to generate decision-making scenarios. We used a Netbeans framework with java language to build the simulation software. We created a database using derby and then linked it to the java program to store the data.

2) Experiment setup: In this experiment, we selected five users for each case of the interest overlap. So, for full overlap interests, we assigned IDs from 1 to 5 to stakeholder, for no overlap interests, we assigned IDs from 6 to 10 and finally for semi overlap, we assigned IDs from 11 to 15. Then, for each user, we stored the interest vales which is the rating he/she gives. For each interest overlap scenario, we created five samples and each sample has 200 selection project. Also, these projects were generated one time with trust and one without. Therefore, the total projects generated for each samples were 1200 projects. Additionally, we generated these projects under two assumptions: one with long term interest and the other is short term. Table I shows the parameter setup.

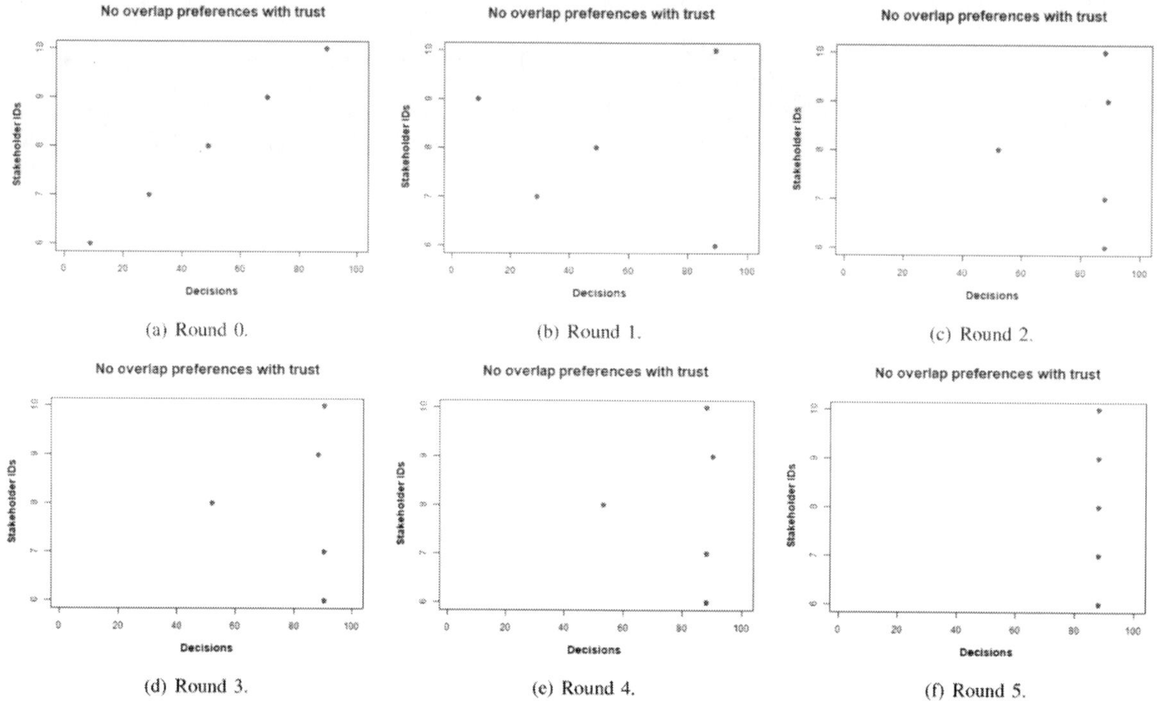

Figure 1. Stakeholders selections movement during the negotiation for no overlap case with trust

VII. Results

In this section, we show the result of the decision making simulation. In this light, we present the stakeholders selections movement during the negotiation for one of the generated project of the no overlap case. Our evaluation criteria are changes of the rating norm, the consensus degree convergence, number of rounds and the correlation between the rating matrix perturbation and the number of rounds.

Figure 1 shows the stakeholders decisions movement for a project that took 5 rounds to reach the consensus. In round 0 (Figure 1(a)), all the stakeholders proposed different decisions. In round 1 (Figure 1(b)), stakeholder 6 changed his decision to be similar to stakeholder 10. In round 2 (Figure 1(c)), stakeholders 7 and 9 selected decisions closer to 6 and 10. In round 3 (Figure 1(d)), stakeholder 9 selected a new decisions closer to 6,7 and 10. Round 4 (Figure 1(e)) is similar to round 3. In round 5 (Figure 1(f)), stakeholder 8 changed his decision to be similar to the rest. Therefore, the consensus was achieved. Table II shows the percentage of the projects that reached consensus. Our result showed that applying the trust helped on increasing the consensus achievement. Moreover, the long term preferences performed better than short term. Similarly with the number of rounds (Table III). Table IV shows the rating matrix norm values and the consensus degree for the same project. The rating norm and the consensus kept increasing.

Figure 2 presents the changes in the rating matrix norm during negotiations. When considering trust, 82% of the interactions had the norm increased, 2% no change and 16% was decrease. However, without trust, the norm never increased neither decreased and it remained unchanged. Figure 3 presents the number of rounds for each project with trust for short-term preference 3(a) and long-term preference 3(b). It can be noticed that the number of round for no overlap and semi overlap never decreased without trust. However, the rounds can be decreased with trust and it is more decreasing for long-term preference compared with short-term preferences. The matrix perturbation has an effect on the number of round as there is a moderate negative correlation, -0.45. So, when the average

TABLE II. Percentage of the projects that reached consensus for long term and short term preferences.

(a) With Trust

Preferences	*Overlap*	*No overlap*	*Semi overlap*
Short term	100%	98%	92%
Long term	100%	99%	99%

(b) Without Trust

Preferences	*Overlap*	*No overlap*	*Semi overlap*
Short term	100%	0%	0%
Long term	100%	0%	0%

TABLE III. Average round of the projects that reached consensus for long term and short term preference.

(a) With Trust

Preferences	*Overlap*	*No overlap*	*Semi overlap*
Short term	1	5	5
Long term	1	1	1

(b) Without Trust

Preferences	*Overlap*	*No overlap*	*Semi overlap*
Short term	100	10	10
Long term	1	10	10

TABLE IV. RATING MATRIX NORM VALUES AND THE CONSENSUS DEGREE FOR ONE PROJECT.

Round Number	*Rating Norm*	*Consensus Degree*
1	3.098386677	0.81
2	3.666060556	0.88
3	3.794733192	0.89
4	3.752332608	0.92
5	4.507771068	1

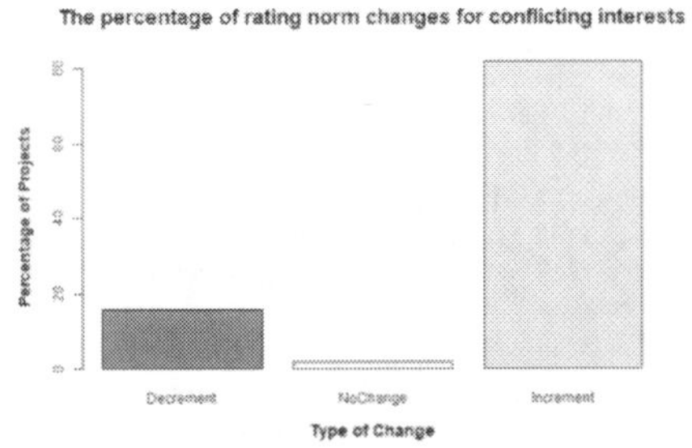

(a) With Trust

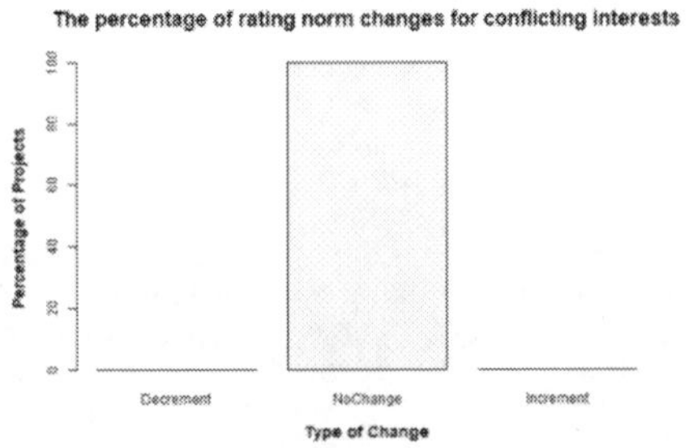

(b) Without

Figure 2. Rating matrix norm changes for no overlap case with trust and without

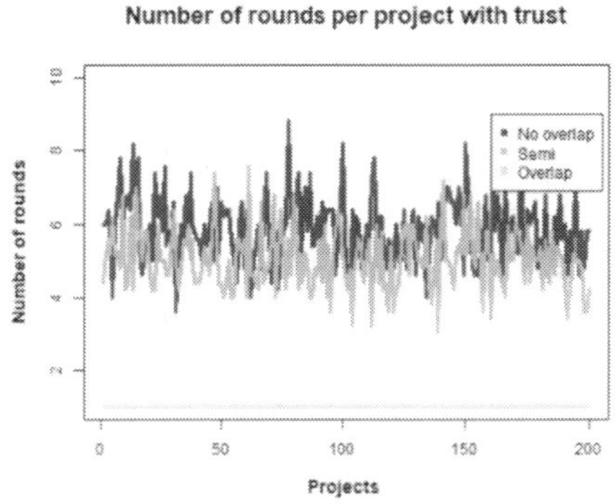

(a) With trust for short-term

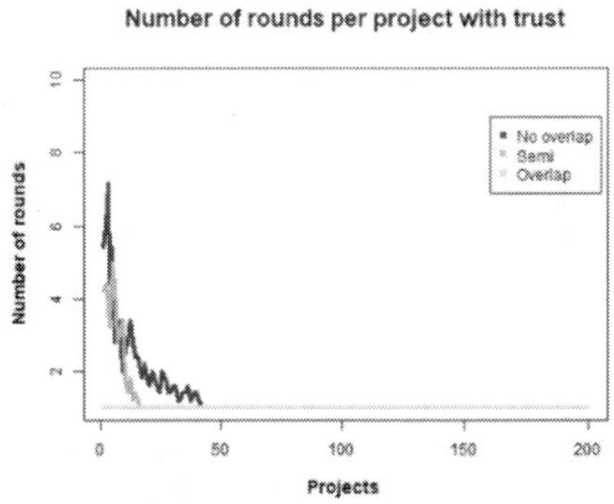

(b) With trust for long-term

Figure 3. Number of rounds in each project for all the three overlap cases

perturbation is high then the number of rounds is decreasing. From the results, we found that:

- Trust helps the stakeholders to reach the consensus when conflicting interest exists by the influence from the highly trusted participants.
- Trust increases the rating matrix norm in most of the cases. Increase the norm means increasing the rating which leads to increase the consensus degree.
- Trust helps changing the preferences whether long-term or short term. Changing the preference in the long run helps to decrease the number of rounds later,
- Trust helps decreasing the number of project rounds except few cases, such as when a trusted participant has his decision liked by the others and then he changes his opinion frequently for the coming rounds.
- Trust helps to increase the rating changes which leads to increase the rating norm and the matrix perturbation.

VIII. CONCLUSION AND FUTURE WORK

In collective decision-making where several participants involved to agree on one selection, reaching the consensus among them is important but it is challenging when the participants have conflicting interests. The influence among them can help to eliminate this challenge. Such an influence can be obtained from trust of one participant to another. The trust is useful in changing the participants preferences whether it is a long or short term depending on participants behaviors. In this study, we apply our decision making framework that is based on trust for investigating the rating convergence during negotiation. We used the matrix norm as a measurement for obtaining the magnitude of the rating matrices and then find the perturbation accordingly. The larger the magnitude the more chances to reach the consensus. Our result showed that the changes in the rating matrix under the trust improve reaching the consensus in term of decreasing the required number of round and increasing the consensus value. Also, our result showed that changing interest in a long term performs better than short term in term of number or rounds reduction. Moreover, we found that there is a negative moderate correlation between the matrix perturbation and the number of round needed to reach consensus. For future work, we will validate the rating convergence measurement in a real application.

ACKNOWLEDGMENT

The authors would like to thank King Faisal Specialist Hospital and Research Centre for the financial support and thank Prof. Arjan Durresi, Prof. Mohammad Al Hasan, Prof. Snehasis Mukhopadhyay and Prof. Mihran Tuceryan for their academic advice.

REFERENCES

[1] J. Levin and P. Milgrom, "Introduction to choice theory," 2004 [retrieved: 10, 2019]. [Online]. Available: https://web.stanford.edu/ jdlevin/Econ%20202/Choice%20Theory.pdf

[2] J. V. Benthem and F. Liu, "Dynamic logic of preference upgrade," Journal of Applied Non-Classical Logics, vol. 17, 2005 [retrieved: 10, 2019], pp. 157–182.

[3] H. Kelman, "Compliance, identification, and internalization: Three processes of attitude change," Journal of Conflict Resolution, vol. 2, no. 1, 1958 [retrieved: 10, 2019], pp. 51–60.

[4] L. Alfantoukh, Y. Ruan, and A. Durresi, "Multi-stakeholder consensus decision-making framework based on trust: A generic framework," in 2018 IEEE 4th International Conference on Collaboration and Internet Computing (CIC), Oct 2018 [retrieved: 10, 2019], pp. 472–479.

[5] S. Ghosh and F. R. Velázquez-Quesada, "Agreeing to agree: Reaching unanimity via preference dynamics based on reliable agents," in Proceedings of the 2015 International Conference on Autonomous Agents and Multiagent Systems, ser. AAMAS '15. Richland, SC: International Foundation for Autonomous Agents and Multiagent Systems, 2015 [retrieved: 10, 2019], pp. 1491–1499. [Online]. Available: http://dl.acm.org/citation.cfm?id=2772879.2773342

[6] O. Babajide, H. S. Roxanne, and P. Katia, "Seeing is believing (or at least changing your mind): The influence of visibility and task complexity on preference changes in computer-supported team decision making," Journal of the Association for Information Science and Technology, vol. 67, no. 9, pp. 2090–2104. [Online]. Available: https://onlinelibrary.wiley.com/doi/abs/10.1002/asi.23555

[7] D. Denker and H. Gewald, "Influential factors for patients' online ratings of general practitioners," in 2017 International Conference on Research and Innovation in Information Systems (ICRIIS), July 2017 [retrieved: 10, 2019], pp. 1–6.

[8] S. L. Sohr-Preston, S. S. Boswell, and K. McCaleb, "Professor gender, age, and hotness in influencing college students' generation and interpretation of professor ratings," Higher Learning Research Communication, vol. 6, no. 3, 2016 [retrieved: 10, 2019], pp. 1– 23. [Online]. Available: https://eric.ed.gov/contentdelivery/servlet/ERICServlet?accno=EJ1132744

[9] Z. Zhang, Q. Ye, R. Law, and Y. Li, "The impact of e-word-of-mouth on the online popularity of restaurants: A comparison of consumer reviews and editor reviews," International Journal of Hospitality Management, vol. 29, no. 4, 2010 [retrieved: 10, 2019], pp. 694 – 700. [Online]. Available: http://www.sciencedirect.com/science/article/pii/S0278431910000198

[10] J. R. Curhan, M. A. Neale, and L. Ross, "Dynamic valuation: Preference changes in the context of face-to-face negotiation," Journal of Experimental Social Psychology, vol. 40, no. 2, 2004 [retrieved: 10, 2019], pp. 142 – 151. [Online]. Available: http://www.sciencedirect.com/science/article/pii/S0022103104000022

[11] D. A. Kaufman, "Negative externalities and welfare improving preference changes," Environmental and Resource Economics, vol. 6, no. 1, Jul 1995 [retrieved: 10, 2019], pp. 53–71. [Online]. Available: https://doi.org/10.1007/BF00691411

[12] N. Hariri, B. Mobasher, and R. Burke, "Adapting to user preference changes in interactive recommendation," Proceedings of the Twenty-Fourth International Joint Conference on Artificial Intelligence, 2015 [retrieved: 10, 2019], pp. 4268–4274. [Online]. Available: https://www.ijcai.org/Proceedings/15/Papers/607.pdf

[13] S. O. Hansson, "Changes in preference," Theory and Decision, vol. 38, no. 1, Jan 1995 [retrieved: 10, 2019], pp. 1–28. [Online]. Available: https://doi.org/10.1007/BF01083166

[14] K. Bakir, D. Donko, and H. Supic, "Temporal dynamics of changes in group user's preferences in recommender systems," in 2015 38th International Convention on Information and Communication Technology, Electronics and Microelectronics (MIPRO), May 2015 [retrieved: 10, 2019], pp. 1262–1266.

[15] T. Sharot, C. M. Velasquez, and R. J. Dolan, "Do decisions shape preference?: Evidence from blind choice," Psychological Science, vol. 21, no. 9, 2010 [retrieved: 10, 2019], pp. 1231–1235, pMID: 20679522. [Online]. Available: https://doi.org/10.1177/0956797610379235

[16] K. Taylor and X. Li, "Interactive multiobjective optimisation: Preference changes and algorithm responsiveness," in Proceedings of the Genetic and Evolutionary Computation Conference, ser. GECCO '18. New York, NY, USA: ACM, 2018 [retrieved: 10, 2019], pp. 761–768. [Online]. Available: http://doi.acm.org/10.1145/3205455.3205624

[17] M. Fedrizzi, M. Fedrizzi, R. A. M. Pereira, and A. Zorat, "A dynamical model for reaching consensus in group decision making," in Proceedings of the 1995 ACM Symposium on Applied Computing, ser. SAC '95. New York, NY, USA: ACM, 1995 [retrieved: 10, 2019], pp. 493–496. [Online]. Available: http://doi.acm.org/10.1145/315891.316074

[18] S. Lindenberg, "Preference versus constraints: A commentary on von weizsäckers 'the influence of property rights on tastes'," Zeitschrift für die gesamte Staatswissenschaft / Journal of Institutional and Theoretical Economics, vol. 140, no. 1, 1984 [retrieved: 10, 2019], pp. 96–103. [Online]. Available: http://www.jstor.org/stable/40750678

[19] K. Izuma, M. Matsumoto, K. Murayama, K. Samejima, N. Sadato, and K. Matsumoto, "Neural correlates of cognitive dissonance and choice-induced preference change," Proceedings of the National Academy of Sciences, vol. 107, no. 51, 2010 [retrieved: 10, 2019], pp. 22014–22019. [Online]. Available: http://www.pnas.org/content/107/51/22014

[20] D. Cvrček and K. Moody, Combining Trust and Risk to Reduce the Cost of Attacks. Berlin, Heidelberg: Springer Berlin Heidelberg, 2005 [retrieved: 10, 2019], pp. 372–383. [Online]. Available: http://dx.doi.org/10.1007/11429760_26

[21] Y. Ruan, L. Alfantoukh, A. Fang, and A. Durresi, "Exploring trust propagation behaviors in online communities," in 2014 17th International Conference on Network-Based Information Systems, Sept 2014 [retrieved: 10, 2019], pp. 361–367.

[22] Y. Ruan and A. Durresi, "A survey of trust management systems for online social communities - trust modeling, trust inference and attacks," Know.-Based Syst., vol. 106, no. C, Aug. 2016 [retrieved: 10, 2019], pp. 150–163. [Online]. Available: http://dx.doi.org/10.1016/j.knosys.2016.05.042

[23] Y. Ruan, L. Alfantoukh, and A. Durresi, "Exploring stock market using twitter trust network," in 2015 IEEE 29th International Conference on Advanced Information Networking and Applications, March 2015 [retrieved: 10, 2019], pp. 428–433.

[24] Y. Ruan, A. Durresi, and L. Alfantoukh, "Trust management framework for internet of things," in 2016 IEEE 30th International Conference on Advanced Information Networking and Applications (AINA), March 2016 [retrieved: 10, 2019], pp. 1013–1019.

[25] Y. Ruan and A. Durresi, "A trust management framework for cloud computing platforms," in 2017 IEEE 31st International Conference on Advanced Information Networking and Applications (AINA), March 2017 [retrieved: 10, 2019], pp. 1146–1153.

[26] P. Zhang, A. Durresi, Y. Ruan, and M. Durresi, "Trust based security mechanisms for social networks," in 2012 Seventh International Conference on Broadband, Wireless Computing, Communication and Applications, Nov 2012 [retrieved: 10, 2019], pp. 264–270.

[27] P. Chomphoosang, Y. Ruan, A. Durresi, M. Durresi, and L. Barolli, "Trust management of health care information in social networks," in 2013 Seventh International Conference on Complex, Intelligent, and Software Intensive Systems, July 2013 [retrieved: 10, 2019], pp. 228–235.

[28] Y. Ruan, P. Zhang, L. Alfantoukh, and A. Durresi, "Measurement theory-based trust management framework for online social communities," ACM Trans. Internet Technol., vol. 17, no. 2, Mar. 2017 [retrieved: 10, 2019], pp. 16:1–16:24. [Online]. Available: http://doi.acm.org/10.1145/3015771

[29] Y. Ruan, A. Durresi, and L. Alfantoukh, "Using twitter trust network for stock market analysis," Knowledge-Based Systems, vol. 145, 2018 [retrieved: 10, 2019], pp. 207 – 218. [Online]. Available: http://www.sciencedirect.com/science/article/pii/S0950705118300248

[30] A. Lina, R. Yefeng, and D. Arjan, "Trust-based multi-stakeholder decision making in water allocation system," in dvances on Broad-Band Wireless Computing, Communication and Applications. BWCCA 2017, vol. 12, November 2017 [retrieved: 10, 2019], pp. 314–327.

[31] G. W. Stewart, "Perturbation theory for the singular value decomposition," Technical Reports from UMIACS, 1998 [retrieved: 10, 2019].

A Survey in Multi-stakeholder Decision-Making based on Trust and Risk

Lina Alfantoukh

King Faisal Specialist Hospital &
Research Center, Riyadh, Saudi Arabia
Email: lynaA@kfshrc.edu.sa

Maha Aleid

King Faisal Specialist Hospital &
Research Center, Riyadh, Saudi Arabia
Email: mahaeid@kfshrc.edu.sa

Abstract—**Decision-making is expected to be encountered in many aspects of people's lives and is involved in fields such as economy, business, health care, and education. There are also different methods of making a decision, as well as various factors that affect making such decisions. Decision-making, therefore, depends on the context. It can be individual or group level. Group decisions are more challenging than individual decisions because of the existence of conflicting objectives among the participants or stakeholders. Group decisions may require negotiation, which involve the stakeholders' influences on each other. Such influences could be acquired from the trust among them. Therefore, trust is used as a criterion for making group decisions. Usually, the decisions come with consequences even if it is short term or long term; therefore, it is important to put those consequences into consideration before making any selections. Such consequences can be addressed by perceived risk. The main contribution of this paper is that it applies trust and risk as decision criteria in the field of multi-stakeholder decision-making. Additionally, we study multi-stakeholder decision-making processes and models based on our analysis of existing works. We found the consensus process and GDM1 model are mostly applied in the existing schemes.**

Keywords–Trust; Risk; Decision-Making; Multi-stakeholder.

I. INTRODUCTION

In real life, people encounter different situations, ranging from critical to noncritical, that entail making a selection among several options. Therefore, there have to be some techniques or methods that help people with the selection process. Trust and risk are criteria used for decision-making because of the uncertainty of consequences involved in these situations. Jøsang and et al. [1] stated that "Risk and trust are two tools for making decisions in an uncertain environment."

In multi-stakeholder decision-making, a group of people proposes an action or solution. From a psychological perspective, each individual in the group builds an impression toward others based on his or her selection or experience. As a result, we can imagine a network of participants who represent nodes and the links between them are the feelings they build for each other. This impression can be translated to trust. In this situation, each person proposes a solution that is feasible to him- or herself regardless of the effect it may have on others. Therefore, the multi-stakeholder decision-making model should help reach a solution that benefits everyone and prevents damage to the network of participants.

Numerous works on decision-making use different factors depending on the field and even the applications within the fields. Those factors can be used to model trust. Therefore, trust influences decision-making [2]. Moreover, every decision comes with consequences and, as a result, makes risk another important criterion in decision-making. The use and application of trust and risk as the two criteria in decision-making are beneficial.

Trust can be a result of the decision maker's expertise or experiences, as well as the interaction between the decision maker and other entities (e.g., humans and machines) [3]. Risk can be the result of estimating the potential damage or loss that may occur following the outcome of the decision [2]. Furthermore, when two entities interact with each other, such interactions, which can influence decision-making, can be risky [4]. It is necessary to survey multi-stakeholder decision-making schemes to determine how to use trust value and risk value when making decisions. Various trust systems have been proposed, such as [5]–[15], including our framework [16]–[26].

The main contributions in this paper are:

- Study the relationship between trust and risk.
- Study multi stakeholder decision-making process and models.
- Survey multi stakeholder decision-making schemes based on trust and risk.
- Analyze the challenges of existing multi stakeholder decision-making schemes.

There are several challenges associated with multi-stakeholder decision-making. For example, the participants may come from various backgrounds and have different expertise. Also, the participants may have partial views about the problem domain, as well as have conflicting objectives. Regarding the use of trust and risk in a decision, several challenges, such as risk quantification and, more specifically, rare events or those that have never occurred, arise as well. Another challenge can emerge from knowing how to apply trust and risk as decision criteria.

To the best of our knowledge, this is the first survey of multi-stakeholder decision-making using trust and risk. The outcomes of this survey include classifying the processes of multi-stakeholder decision-making and knowing the trust and risk models that were used for making decisions.

This paper is organized as follows: In Section II, we investigate different definitions of trust and risk, then we introduce the possible relationships between them by analyzing existing related works. Next, in Section III, we discuss trust and risk in multi-stakeholder decision-making by presenting existing multi-stakeholder decision-making schemes. In Section IV, we conclude the paper.

II. Trust and Risk

In this section, we discuss trust and risk concepts by listing some definitions and the relationship between them.

A. Trust

There is no exact universal definition for it according to Daniel et al. [27]. Grandison and Sloman [28] indicated that many researchers use the definition of trust in a very specific form relating to topics, such as authentication, or the ability to pay for purchases. Townend and et al. [29] defined trust as the level of reliance placed on an entity based on experience of a particular context. Pereira and et al. [30] viewed the trust concept as the degree of confidence given to an entity. Neama et al. [31] considered trust as an assurance among participants while engaging in online auctions. Many researchers defined trust as a subjective probability that leads an individual to believe that another person will behave as expected [32] and as a particular level of subjective probability in which an agent assesses one or more agents to perform a specific action [33] [34].

B. Risk

Similar to trust, risk depends on the context as well. However, several works interpret risk as the probability of a negative event occurring. When taking risk into consideration, it is important to identify then evaluate it. The evaluation can be qualitative or quantitative. Flinn and et al. [35] defined risk as finding the balance between the likely cost and the possible reward. The cost is based on the likelihood of harm and its magnitude, which can be hard to asses. Jarvenpaa and et al. [36] defined risk perception as the "trustor's belief about likelihoods of gains and losses." Yet Dwaikat and Parisi-Presicce [37] defined risk as the probability of exploitation of vulnerabilities in terms of software. Liu and et al. [38] mentioned the ISO/IEC TR 133351 definition of risk, which is related to the likelihood of exploiting vulnerabilities. Risk was also defined as the likelihood of an unwanted event and its consequence according to some studies [29] [32].

C. Relationship Between Trust and Risk

It is necessary to understand the relationship between trust and risk to know how to use them for decision-making. According to our analysis of previous works, many types of relationships were identified.

1) Risk influences trust: In this relationship, risk may influence trust calculation [39],trust definition [1] and trust relationships [40].Also, some works [28] [36] [41] showed that trust is associated with lower perceived risk.

2) Trust influences risk: In this relationship, trust may influence risk calculation [4], risk assessment [42], risk mitigation [43], risk relationship [44], and risk management [45].

3) Complements to each other: Trust and risk can be viewed as complements to each other. Daniel and Ken [27] demonstrated that most systems consider trust and risk as complementary or ignore them. In our opinion, having such a relationship might lead to the use of one of them as a factor for decision-making because the other one is its complement.

4) No relationship: It is also possible that there is no connection between trust and risk. For example, trust can be considered as a property of principles but risk as a property of a process [27]. Kim and et al. [46] showed that it is common to treat trust and risk as different concepts. In our opinion, this is practical if we deal with trust as a property of an entity that can make decisions and uses risk as a property of the decision itself.

III. Using Trust and Risk in Multi-stakeholder Decision-Making

Decision-making is not limited only to an individual's decision. Some scenarios involve more than one person to make a decision. In these cases, it is called multi-stakeholders or Group Decision-Making (GDM) [47]. One member involved in a group no longer makes the final decision without the involvement of other members. In social settings, different approaches, such as taking the average of all the participant responses or taking the majority decision as final, have been proposed. Arrow's impossibility theorem is used in the field of GDM. According to Herrmann [48], "When we consider the group decision-making problem (with more than two choices), it is clear that it would be nice to have a 'fair' procedure that combined the individuals' preferences about the alternatives (expressed as rankings) into a statement about the group's preferences about the alternatives while preserving the autonomy of each individual."

A. Multi-stakeholder decision-making process

The involvement of multiple participants when making a decision makes it essential to construct a process that takes each individual selection into consideration to reach a final decision. There are different types of multi-stakeholder decision-making processes. However, based on our analysis of the existing works, we found that the three common processes are consensus, ranking, and voting(Table I).

Voting, for example, is considered a simple method because it involves making a decision based on the majority vote. However, its limitation comes from treating all participants equally even though they are different in terms of expertise. Also, the outcome of voting may be unsatisfactory for the members whose decisions received less votes [8]. Consensus, however, does have the advantage of reaching a solution that is agreed by everyone [7]. Thus, the decision makers need to negotiate several rounds, and in each round, they must modify their proposed solutions to be decided by other participants. However, this has its limitation as the participants cannot influence others, which could lead to an infinite number of rounds. The ranking process is used in several multi-stakeholder decision-making model by ranking the suggestions of each participant [9]. This has the advantage of knowing the degree of group convergence, which is useful in selecting the solution that receives the higher ranking. However, its limitation is the difficulty of ranking a large number of decisions. Also, it is possible that each participant will rank the solutions but will give his or her own the highest ranking.

In terms of using trust on those processes, it has been applied in a different way like obtaining the advices from the trusted individuals or weighting each alternative with the trust of the individual. Tundjungsari and et al. [5] used trust for the consensus process and showed that the consensus decision is

TABLE I. LIST OF COMMON MULTI-STAKEHOLDER DECISION-MAKING PROCESS WITH THE ASSOCIATED CHALLENGES.

Process	*Description*	*Challenges*
Voting	Take the majority's opinion	The outcome is winning or not wining.Treat participants equally
Consensus	Consider the group decision instead of selecting one	The outcome is hard to reach if there is conflict
Ranking	Show the degree in which the group preferences converge	Difficulty to rank the large number of decisions

reached when decision makers adjust their preferences, such as the importance of the decision criteria, which can be obtained from the advice of other trusted participants. For the voting process, Rodriguez [8] aggregated single votes to a single collective decision and used trust to weight the influences of the decision makers in decision-making. Capuano and et al. [9] proposed a multi-stakeholder decision-making model to rank the preferences. However, in some cases, the decision makers may not have enough information about some alternatives to accurately rank them. Therefore, the decision maker's opinion about such alternatives is influenced by other experts he or she trusts.

B. *Multi-stakeholder Decision-Making Models*

According to French and et al. [49], there are five classes of GDM models. The first model, GDM1, assumes that the decision makers propose then aggregate their individual solutions, rank them based on their utilities, and finally select the highest ranked solution. In the second model, GDM2, the decision makers propose their individual solutions and use them as preferences when voting. In the third model, GDM3, there is a supra-decision maker that manages the decision-making process among the decision makers. The fourth model, GDM4, finds group utility to reach a consensus. In the fifth model, DGM5, the decision makers use the bargaining theory. There is no model better than the others because each model is useful in specific applications. For example, GDM1 is useful for applications that take individual preferences into account, GDM2 for applications that use voting as a decision-making process, GDM3 for applications where there is a hierarchy among participants, GDM4 for applications that take group preferences for the consensus process into account, and GDM5 for applications that deal with resource allocations.

C. *Trust in Multi-stakeholder Decision-Making*

Trust in multi-stakeholder decision-making is crucial [6] because it is a valuable group component and is essential in the collaboration process. It becomes, however, a further complicated or more dependent parameter when an expert may be uncertain, have incomplete information, or cannot access information. Experts have to use their domain expertise to arrive at a decision. An expert may give his or her subjective preferences, but they may not be agreed to by other team members. In such situations, experts have to collaborate, exchange information, and arrive at a consensus. Jian Wu and Francisco Chiclana [50] stated that the trust can indicate the actual reputation between experts Consequently, it should be taken into account as a credible source to be used in deriving aggregation weights for individual experts. As a matter of a fact, trust can be used in the decision-making process to weight the influence of different decision makers [8].

Several schemes for multi-stakeholder decision-making vary in terms of the trust model, as well as the GDM model and process. In addition, each of the schemes comes with limitations. For example, some schemes [5] [6] [10] [12]–[14] do not allow the stakeholder to modify the decision outcome because there is a fixed set of decisions to select from. Such fixed outcomes limit the stakeholder's ability to propose a new outcome. Some schemes [8] [9] apply preferences ordering. A large number of preferences is challenging to the stakeholder to order. In addition, each stakeholder might rank his or her own preference higher if he or she is the one proposing the decision outcome. Some schemes [7] [15] do not use historical interactions; they may lead to missing extra information that might help the stakeholder when proposing solutions and selecting the final decision. Some schemes [7] [11] limit trust to specific stakeholders, which leads to limited information in the problem domain (Figure 1).

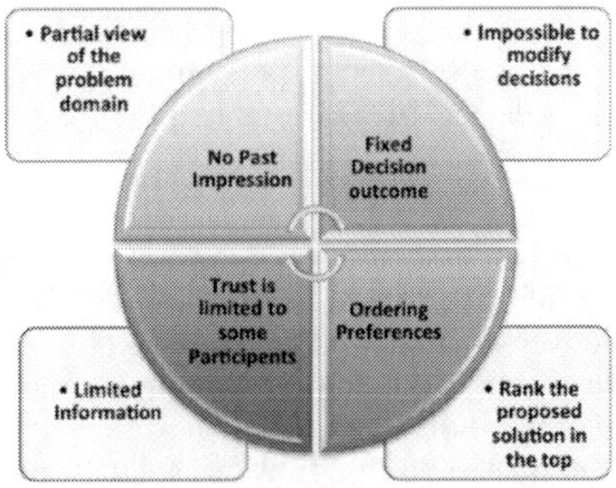

Figure 1. Limitations of Existing Multi-stakeholder Decision-making Schemes

Table II shows the existing multi-stakeholder decision-making schemes with the corresponding trust model, GDM process and model, limitations, and applications.

1) Tundjungsari, Istiyanto, et al.: Tundjungsari, Istiyanto, et al. [5] proposed a multistakeholder decision-making model for urban planning in rural areas by combining a trust model proposed by Abdul-rahman and Hailes [51] and the GDM3 model that assigns a supra-decision maker to manage the consensus process. This scheme is useful for applications that require assigning different roles to decision makers based on trust.

2) Indiramma and Anandakumar: The authors proposed a multistakeholder decision-making model for soil erosion applications [6]. In their scheme, they showed a multi-agent-based collaborative decision-making framework for distributed environments. Trust is strengthened by familiarity and similarity beliefs and evaluated during collaboration. The proposed decision model starts by collecting the decision maker's decisions and allows each agent to discuss any decisions, criteria, and conflicts. The trust values are then computed and aggregated, and each agent rates those trust values. The highest trusted decision is selected as the final decision.

3) Alonso, Perez, et al.: The authors proposed a multistakeholder decision-making model for applications that involve

TABLE II. MULTISTAKEHOLDER DECISION-MAKING SCHEMES WITH THE CORRESPONDING TRUST MODEL, GROUP DECISION-MAKING PROCESS, GROUP DECISION-MAKING MODEL, THE LIMITATION AND THE APPLICATION

Scheme	*Trust Model*	*GDM Process*	*GDM Model*	*Limitation*	*Application*
[5] Tundjungsari, Istiyanto, et al.	Direct interaction between participants	Consensus	GDM3	Fixed Decision outcomes	Urban planning
[6] Indiramma and Anandakumar	Direct experience/social interaction	Consensus	GDM1	Fixed Decision outcomes	Soil erosion
[7] Alonso, Perez, et al.	Opinions of all the experts involved in the process	Consensus	GDM2	No past impression and the trust is limited to some participants	Online and web systems
[8] Rodriguez	Similarity and expertise	Voting	GDM1 & 2	Ordering Preferences	Social decision support system
[9] Capuano, Chiclana, et al.	The history of past actions and behavior	Ranking	GDM1	Ordering Preferences	Incomplete information
[10] Lau, Singh and Tan Scheme	Agent tendency of accepting other agent to join	Voting	GDM2	Fixed Decision outcomes	Multi-agents system
[11] Sanchez-Anguix, Julian, et al.	Full knowledge about the information	Voting	GDM3	Trust is limited to some participants	Bilateral alternating protocol in electronic systems
[12] Wu, Chiclana, et al.	Social Network Analysis with incomplete linguistic information.	Consensus	GDM1	Fixed Decision outcomes	Incomplete Linguistic Information Context
[14] Wu, Chiclana, et al.	Social Network Analysis	Consensus	GDM1	Fixed Decision outcomes	Cloud service suppliers
[13] Liu, Liang, et al.	Opinions of the experts	Consensus	GDM1	Fixed Decision outcomes	Cloud services selection
[15] Park, Cho, et al.	Expertise for each criterion	Consensus	GDM1	Fixed Decision outcomes and no past impression	Supplier selection

large numbers of decision makers [7]. In their scheme, there are two groups: the selected expert and the nonselected expert groups. The nonselected expert group provides the utility toward the selected ones to establish the trust network.

4) Rodriguez: The author proposed a multistakeholder decision-making model for social decision support system applications [8]. In this scheme, the author proposed a process consisting of three serial stages; individual solution ranking,collective solution ranking and solution selection from collective solution ranking. Trust reflects the similarity and expertise of the individuals and is used to weight the influence of decision makers in the decision-making process.

5) Capuano, Chiclana, et al.: The authors proposed a multistakeholder decision-making model for applications that have incomplete information [9]. In their scheme, they proposed a model that adopts fuzzy rankings to collect experts' preferences on available alternatives and trust statements on other experts. Sometimes, experts cannot express an opinion on any of the available alternatives, leading to incomplete information. Therefore, to estimate the missing preferences, the Social Influence Network (SIN) addresses the experts' influences. Then, the aggregation process is applied, followed by selection of the best alternative.

6) Lau, Singh and Tan Scheme: The authors proposed a multistakeholder decision-making model for coalition formation applications in multiagent system environments [10]. In their scheme, they proposed a Weighted Voting Mechanism (WVM) that allows agents to join existing coalitions. There are two types of votes: agreement and disagreement. The trust element is the main criterion for deciding the weight in the voting session. The trust ration can be low, medium, or high.

7) Sanchez-Anguix, Julian, et al.: The authors proposed a multistakeholder decision-making model for a bilateral alternating protocol in electronic systems [11]. In their scheme, they proposed a mediated negotiation model for agent-based teams that negotiate with an opponent. This negotiation model defines the communication protocol with the opponent and the decisions of the negotiation team. Trust only applies to the group meditator because he manages the negotiation process and counts the votes from the team members.

8) Wu, Chiclana, et al.: The authors proposed a multistakeholder decision-making model for incomplete linguistic information contexts [12]. They proposed a trust propagation method to derive trust from incomplete connected trust networks. The decision-making model consists of computing trust degrees; estimating unknown preference values; determining the consensus index, consensus identification, recommendation, and feedback; and establishing a selection process. Similarly, they proposed a decision-making model [14] that is different from one [12] that employs dual trust (trust, distrust) and nonlinguistic assessments.

9) Liu, Liang et al.: The authors proposed a multistakeholder decision-making model for cloud service suppliers [13]. The proposed decision-making model consists of four stages: "(1) Constructing the interval-valued trust decision making space; (2) Determining the consensus degree at three levels; (3) Visual consensus identification, trust induced recommendation and rationality analysis; and (4) Selection Process.". This model has the advantage of having a fewer number of rounds by using the harmony degree in addition to the consensus degree.

10Park, Cho, et al.: The authors proposed a multistakeholder decision-making model for supplier selection [15]. The proposed scheme uses the stakeholder trustworthiness as an influencing factor on the final decision. The decision-making process uses weighted scoring system, where the trustworthiness are used for the weights. Moreover, decision alternatives ranking is applied in this decision-making scheme.

D. Risk in Multi-stakeholder Decision Making

Due to the consequences that might occur following the decision, using such consequences as decision criteria could be practical to decision makers. Table III summarizes the existing GDM model with the corresponding risk model and process.

TABLE III. MULTI-STAKEHOLDER DECISION-MAKING SCHEME WITH THE ASSOCIATED RISK MODEL AND THE DECISION PROCESS

Scheme	Description	Risk Model	GDM Process
[52] Li, Kendall, et al.	Group decision making process that allow agents to express their utilities or evaluations over different alternatives	Based on evidence support logic and expected utility theory	Voting
[53] Pham,Tran, et al.	Dynamic group decision making which aggregates expert preferences and sensibilities, quantified by Self-Organizing Map (SOM) in order to select appropriate alternatives	Human Reasoning = fuzzy rules, quantitative knowledge and reasoning evidence	N/A
[54] Wibowo and Deng	Risk-oriented group decision making for modeling the inherent risk in the multi-criteria group decision making process	Subjective assessments	Ranking

IV. CONCLUSION AND FUTURE WORK

Decision-making is deeply interwoven in people's lives and is saturated in almost every field. It also incorporates various methods and factors that can affect the outcome of a decision. Collaborative decisions may involve negotiation, which requires creating some level of trust among the participants. Usually, decisions come with consequences. The main contribution of this paper is analyzing the existing schemes of multi-stakeholder decision-making based on trust and risk. This paper also explores the concepts of trust and risk and categorizes the relationship between them to investigate how to adopt them when designing a decision model. Moreover, we investigate some decision-making processes such as voting, consensus, ranking, and GDM models. We found the consensus process and GDM1 model are mostly applied in the existing schemes. For future work, we will build a multi-stakeholder decision-making framework that is applicable to every context and uses trust and risk as factors.

REFERENCES

[1] A. Jøsang and S. L. Presti, Analysing the Relationship between Risk and Trust. Berlin, Heidelberg: Springer Berlin Heidelberg, 2004 [retrieved: 10, 2019], pp. 135–145. [Online]. Available: http://dx.doi.org/10.1007/978-3-540-24747-0_11

[2] B. Alcalde, E. Dubois, S. Mauw, N. Mayer, and S. Radomirović, "Towards a decision model based on trust and security risk management," in Proceedings of the Seventh Australasian Conference on Information Security - Volume 98, ser. AISC '09. Darlinghurst, Australia, Australia: Australian Computer Society, Inc., 2009 [retrieved: 10, 2019], pp. 61–70. [Online]. Available: http://dl.acm.org/citation.cfm?id=1862758.1862768

[3] Y. Li, M. Zhao, H. Sun, and Z. Chen, "A trust and risk framework to enhance reliable interaction in e-commerce," in 2008 IEEE International Conference on e-Business Engineering, Oct 2008 [retrieved: 10, 2019], pp. 475–480.

[4] C. Zuo, J. Zhou, and H. Feng, "A security policy based on bi-evaluations of trust and risk in p2p systems," in 2010 2nd International Conference on Education Technology and Computer, vol. 5, June 2010 [retrieved: 10, 2019], pp. V5-304–V5-309.

[5] V. Tundjungsari, J. E. Istiyanto, E. Winarko, and R. Wardoyo, "A reputation based trust model to seek judgment in participatory group decision making," in 2010 International Conference on Distributed Frameworks for Multimedia Applications, Aug 2010 [retrieved: 10, 2019], pp. 1–7.

[6] M. Indiramma and K. R. Anandakumar, "Collaborative decision making framework for multi-agent system," in 2008 International Conference on Computer and Communication Engineering, May 2008 [retrieved: 10, 2019], pp. 1140–1146.

[7] S. Alonso, I. J. Perez, F. J. Cabrerizo, and E. Herrera-Viedma, "A fuzzy group decision making model for large groups of individuals," in 2009 IEEE International Conference on Fuzzy Systems, Aug 2009 [retrieved: 10, 2019], pp. 643–648.

[8] M. A. Rodriguez, "Social decision making with multi-relational networks and grammar-based particle swarms," in System Sciences, 2007. HICSS 2007. 40th Annual Hawaii International Conference on, Jan 2007 [retrieved: 10, 2019], pp. 39–39.

[9] N. Capuano, F. Chiclana, H. Fujita, E. Herrera-Viedma, and V. Loia, "Fuzzy group decision making with incomplete information guided by social influence," IEEE Transactions on Fuzzy Systems, vol. PP, no. 99, 2017 [retrieved: 10, 2019], pp. 1–1.

[10] B. P. L. Lau, A. K. Singh, and T. P. L. Tan, "Weighted voting game based algorithm for joining a microscopic coalition," in 2013 IEEE International Conference of IEEE Region 10 (TENCON 2013), Oct 2013 [retrieved: 10, 2019], pp. 1–4.

[11] V. Sanchez-Anguix, V. Julian, V. Botti, and A. Garcia-Fornes, "Reaching unanimous agreements within agent-based negotiation teams with linear and monotonic utility functions," IEEE Transactions on Systems, Man, and Cybernetics, Part B (Cybernetics), vol. 42, no. 3, June 2012 [retrieved: 10, 2019], pp. 778–792.

[12] J. Wu, F. Chiclana, and E. Herrera-Viedma, "Trust based consensus model for social network in an incomplete linguistic information context," Applied Soft Computing, vol. 35, no. Supplement C, 2015 [retrieved: 10, 2019], pp. 827 – 839. [Online]. Available: http://www.sciencedirect.com/science/article/pii/S1568494615001246

[13] Y. Liu, C. Liang, F. Chiclana, and J. Wu, "A trust induced recommendation mechanism for reaching consensus in group decision making," Knowledge-Based Systems, vol. 119, no. Supplement C, 2017 [retrieved: 10, 2019], pp. 221 – 231. [Online]. Available: http://www.sciencedirect.com/science/article/pii/S0950705116305172

[14] J. Wu, F. Chiclana, H. Fujita, and E. Herrera-Viedma, "A visual interaction consensus model for social network group decision making with trust propagation," Knowledge-Based Systems, vol. 122, no. Supplement C, 2017 [retrieved: 10, 2019], pp. 39 – 50. [Online]. Available: http://www.sciencedirect.com/science/article/pii/S0950705117300436

[15] P. Kijung, C. Jay, and O. K. Gül E, "A dynamic multi-person decision making method to reflect interpersonal trust," in Proceedings of the 2014 Industrial and Systems Engineering Research Conference, 2014 [retrieved: 10, 2019].

[16] Y. Ruan, L. Alfantoukh, A. Fang, and A. Durresi, "Exploring trust propagation behaviors in online communities," in 2014 17th International Conference on Network-Based Information Systems, Sept 2014 [retrieved: 10, 2019], pp. 361–367.

[17] Y. Ruan and A. Durresi, "A survey of trust management systems for online social communities - trust modeling, trust inference and attacks," Know.-Based Syst., vol. 106, no. C, Aug. 2016 [retrieved: 10, 2019], pp. 150–163. [Online]. Available: http://dx.doi.org/10.1016/j.knosys.2016.05.042

[18] Y. Ruan, L. Alfantoukh, and A. Durresi, "Exploring stock market using twitter trust network," in 2015 IEEE 29th International Conference on Advanced Information Networking and Applications, March 2015 [retrieved: 10, 2019], pp. 428–433.

[19] Y. Ruan, A. Durresi, and L. Alfantoukh, "Trust management framework for internet of things," in 2016 IEEE 30th International Conference on Advanced Information Networking and Applications (AINA), March 2016 [retrieved: 10, 2019], pp. 1013–1019.

[20] Y. Ruan and A. Durresi, "A trust management framework for cloud computing platforms," in 2017 IEEE 31st International Conference on Advanced Information Networking and Applications (AINA), March 2017 [retrieved: 10, 2019], pp. 1146–1153.

[21] P. Zhang, A. Durresi, Y. Ruan, and M. Durresi, "Trust based security mechanisms for social networks," in 2012 Seventh International Conference on Broadband, Wireless Computing, Communication and Applications, Nov 2012, pp. 264–270.

[22] P. Chomphoosang, Y. Ruan, A. Durresi, M. Durresi, and L. Barolli, "Trust management of health care information in social networks," in 2013 Seventh International Conference on Complex, Intelligent, and Software Intensive Systems, July 2013 [retrieved: 10, 2019], pp. 228–235.

[23] Y. Ruan, P. Zhang, L. Alfantoukh, and A. Durresi, "Measurement theory-based trust management framework for online social communities," ACM Trans. Internet Technol., vol. 17, no. 2, Mar. 2017 [retrieved: 10, 2019], pp. 16:1–16:24. [Online]. Available: http://doi.acm.org/10.1145/3015771

[24] Y. Ruan, A. Durresi, and L. Alfantoukh, "Using twitter trust network for stock market analysis," Knowledge-Based Systems, vol. 145, 2018 [retrieved: 10, 2019], pp. 207 – 218. [Online]. Available: http://www.sciencedirect.com/science/article/pii/S0950705118300248

[25] A. Lina, R. Yefeng, and D. Arjan, "Trust-based multi-stakeholder decision making in water allocation system," in dvances on Broad-Band Wireless Computing, Communication and Applications. BWCCA 2017, vol. 12, November 2017 [retrieved: 10, 2019], pp. 314–327.

[26] L. Alfantoukh, Y. Ruan, and A. Durresi, "Multi-stakeholder consensus decision-making framework based on trust: A generic framework," in 2018 IEEE 4th International Conference on Collaboration and Internet Computing (CIC), Oct 2018 [retrieved: 10, 2019], pp. 472–479.

[27] D. Cvrček and K. Moody, Combining Trust and Risk to Reduce the Cost of Attacks. Berlin, Heidelberg: Springer Berlin Heidelberg, 2005 [retrieved: 10, 2019], pp. 372–383. [Online]. Available: http://dx.doi.org/10.1007/11429760_26

[28] T. Grandison and M. Sloman, "A survey of trust in internet applications," IEEE Communications Surveys Tutorials, vol. 3, no. 4, Fourth 2000 [retrieved: 10, 2019], pp. 2–16.

[29] P. Townend, V. Viduto, D. Webster, K. Djemame, L. Lau, V. Dimitrova, J. Xu, S. Fores, C. Dibsdale, J. Austin, J. McAvoy, and S. Hobson, "Risk assessment and trust in services computing: Applications and experience," in 2013 IEEE International Conference on Services Computing, June 2013 [retrieved: 10, 2019], pp. 392–399.

[30] A. Pereira, N. Rodrigues, J. Barbosa, and P. Leitao, "Trust and risk management towards resilient large-scale cyber-physical systems," in 2013 IEEE International Symposium on Industrial Electronics, May 2013 [retrieved: 10, 2019], pp. 1–6.

[31] G. Neama, R. Alaskar, and M. Alkandari, "Privacy, security, risk, and trust concerns in e-commerce," in Proceedings of the 17th International Conference on Distributed Computing and Networking, ser. ICDCN '16. New York, NY, USA: ACM, 2016 [retrieved: 10, 2019], pp. 46:1–46:6. [Online]. Available: http://doi.acm.org/10.1145/2833312.2850445

[32] C. Burnett, L. Chen, P. Edwards, and T. J. Norman, "Traac: Trust and risk aware access control," in 2014 Twelfth Annual International Conference on Privacy, Security and Trust, July 2014 [retrieved: 10, 2019], pp. 371–378.

[33] M. S. Lund, B. Solhaug, and K. Stolen, "Evolution in relation to risk and trust management," Computer, vol. 43, no. 5, May 2010 [retrieved: 10, 2019], pp. 49–55.

[34] A. Abdul-Rahman and S. Hailes, "Supporting trust in virtual communities," in Proceedings of the 33rd Annual Hawaii International Conference on System Sciences, Jan 2000 [retrieved: 10, 2019], pp. 9 pp. vol.1–.

[35] S. Flinn and S. Stoyles, "Omnivore: Risk management through bidirectional transparency," in Proceedings of the 2004 Workshop on New Security Paradigms, ser. NSPW '04. New York, NY, USA: ACM, 2004 [retrieved: 10, 2019], pp. 97–105. [Online]. Available: http://doi.acm.org/10.1145/1065907.1066043

[36] S. L. Jarvenpaa, N. Tractinsky, and M. Vitale, "Consumer trust in an internet store," Information Technology and Management, vol. 1, no. 1, 2000 [retrieved: 10, 2019], pp. 45–71. [Online]. Available: http://dx.doi.org/10.1023/A:1019104520776

[37] Z. Dwaikat and F. Parisi-Presicce, "Risky trust: Risk-based analysis of software systems," SIGSOFT Softw. Eng. Notes, vol. 30, no. 4, May 2005 [retrieved: 10, 2019], pp. 1–7. [Online]. Available: http://doi.acm.org/10.1145/1082983.1083206

[38] F. Liu, J. Wang, H. Bai, and H. Sun, "Access control model based on trust and risk evaluation in idmaas," in 2015 12th International Conference on Information Technology - New Generations, April 2015 [retrieved: 10, 2019], pp. 179–184.

[39] D. K. W. Chiu, H. fung Leung, and K. man Lam, "Making personalized recommendations to customers in a service-oriented economy: a quantitative model based on reputation and risk attitude," in ICEC, 2005 [retrieved: 10, 2019].

[40] J.-H. Cho, K. Chan, and S. Adali, "A survey on trust modeling," ACM Comput. Surv., vol. 48, no. 2, Oct. 2015 [retrieved: 10, 2019], pp. 28:1–28:40. [Online]. Available: http://doi.acm.org/10.1145/2815595

[41] P. C. Sun, Y. L. Liu, and J. J. Luo, "Perceived risk and trust in online group buying context," in 2010 3rd International Conference on Information Management, Innovation Management and Industrial Engineering, vol. 3, Nov 2010 [retrieved: 10, 2019], pp. 660–663.

[42] F. Caldeira, T. Schaberreiter, E. Monteiro, J. Aubert, P. Simoes, and D. Khadraoui, "Trust based interdependency weighting for on-line risk monitoring in interdependent critical infrastructures," in 2011 6th International Conference on Risks and Security of Internet and Systems (CRiSIS), Sept 2011 [retrieved: 10, 2019], pp. 1–7.

[43] A. Khosravani, B. Nicholson, and T. Wood-Harper, "A case study analysis of risk, trust and control in cloud computing," in 2013 Science and Information Conference, Oct 2013 [retrieved: 10, 2019], pp. 879–887.

[44] Y. Wang and F. r. Lin, "Trust and risk evaluation of transactions with different amounts in peer-to-peer e-commerce environments," in 2006 IEEE International Conference on e-Business Engineering (ICEBE'06), Oct 2006 [retrieved: 10, 2019], pp. 102–109.

[45] B. McInnis, D. Cosley, C. Nam, and G. Leshed, "Taking a hit: Designing around rejection, mistrust, risk, and workers' experiences in amazon mechanical turk," in Proceedings of the 2016 CHI Conference on Human Factors in Computing Systems, ser. CHI '16. New York, NY, USA: ACM, 2016 [retrieved: 10, 2019], pp. 2271–2282. [Online]. Available: http://doi.acm.org/10.1145/2858036.2858539

[46] D. J. Kim, D. L. Ferrin, and H. R. Rao, "A trust-based consumer decision-making model in electronic commerce: The role of trust, perceived risk, and their antecedents," Decision Support Systems, vol. 44, no. 2, 2008 [retrieved: 10, 2019], pp. 544 – 564. [Online]. Available: http://www.sciencedirect.com/science/article/pii/S0167923607001005

[47] I. Palomaresa, L. Martíneza, and F. Herrera, "Mentor: A graphical monitoring tool of preferences evolution in large-scale group decision making," Knowledge-Based Systems, vol. 58, 2014 [retrieved: 10, 2019], pp. 66 – 74, intelligent Decision Support Making Tools and Techniques: {IDSMT}. [Online]. Available: http://www.sciencedirect.com/science/article/pii/S0950705113002050

[48] J. W. Herrmann, Group Decision Making. Hoboken, New Jersey: John Wiley and Sons, 2015 [retrieved: 10, 2019], p. 95.

[49] S. French, D. R. Insua, and F. Ruggeri, "e-participation and decision analysis," Decision Analysis, vol. 4, no. 4, 2007 [retrieved: 10, 2019], pp. 211–226. [Online]. Available: https://doi.org/10.1287/deca.1070.0098

[50] J. Wu and F. Chiclana, "A social network analysis trust-consensus based approach to group decision-making problems with interval-valued fuzzy reciprocal preference relations," Knowledge-Based Systems, vol. 59, 2014 [retrieved: 10, 2019], pp. 97 – 107. [Online]. Available: http://www.sciencedirect.com/science/article/pii/S0950705114000343

[51] A. Abdul-Rahman and S. Hailes, "A distributed trust model," in Proceedings of the 1997 Workshop on New Security Paradigms, ser. NSPW '97. New York, NY, USA: ACM, 1997 [retrieved: 10, 2019], pp. 48–60. [Online]. Available: http://doi.acm.org/10.1145/283699.283739

[52] J. Li, G. Kendall, S. Pollard, E. Soane, G. Davies, and R. Bai, "A decision support approach for group decision making under risk and uncertainty," in 2010 International Conference on Logistics Systems and Intelligent Management (ICLSIM), vol. 3, Jan 2010 [retrieved: 10, 2019], pp. 1856–1860.

[53] H. V. Pham, K. D. Tran, T. Cao, E. Cooper, and K. Kamei, "A new approach using dynamic group decision making for selection of multiple alternatives under risk and uncertainty," in 2011 Third International Conference on Knowledge and Systems Engineering, Oct 2011 [retrieved: 10, 2019], pp. 176–180.

[54] S. Wibowo and H. Deng, "Risk-oriented group decision making in multi-criteria analysis," in 2010 IEEE/ACIS 9th International Conference on Computer and Information Science, Aug 2010 [retrieved: 10, 2019], pp. 9–14.

Blockchain-based Decentralized KYC (Know-Your-Customer)

Syed Azhar Hussain
University of Nicosia
Nicosia, Cyprus
qadria[at]gmail[dot]com

Zeeshan-ul-hassan Usmani
University of Nicosia
Nicosia, Cyprus
zusmani78[at]gmail[dot]com

Abstract— **Know Your Customer (aka KYC) is the regulatory and compliance obligation for the conventional banking and financial system to capture customer information before onboarding and providing any financial services. In banks, KYC is embedded into the account opening forms, which mandate customers to provide accurate information and ideally update as soon as any change occurs in the KYC data. Similarly, other financial institutions such as stocks, Mutual Funds, Insurance companies, etc. also require KYC information from prospective customers. Primarily KYC helps financial institutions to prevent identity thefts, money laundering, terrorist financing, and profiling and eliminating the runaway creditors. Conventional banking and financial institutions spend a substantial part of customer acquisition costs of operating residents and isolated KYC databases and try to keep them updated and accurate. The overall cost of managing the silo KYC per customer increases because of a lack of transparencies, poor control, mistrust, and data duplication. Blockchain technology offers a solution to establish trust and transparency and provide a secure and publicly verifiable KYC. This paper presents a unique trust management platform based on self-sovereign and decentralizes Know-Your-Customer (DKYC) model to enhance customer privacy through consent-based access, featuring regulator governance and helping banks to use trusted and accurate customer data while reducing the customer acquisition costs.**

Keywords-Blockchain application; self-sovereign identity; trust system; know your customer (KYC); customer privacy.

I. INTRODUCTION

Blockchain is an emerging technology, a trust protocol, envisioned by Satoshi Nakamoto [1] with an extraordinary digital currency use case. In just a short span of 10 years, blockchain technology has disrupted every industry to establish trust and transparency through immutable provenance. The financial sector is facing many challenges, especially higher transaction costs [2] in trustless environments and eventually, all cost burdens shifted to end-customers. Additionally, banks pay huge sums to prevent fraud, but data breaches, leaks, and hacks [3] are fairly prevalent. This paper specifically examines the most important use case of financial sector i.e., "Know Your Customer" KYC (Figure 1), and addresses the key challenges it faces such as a high cost of managing the KYC per customer, increasing the unbanked customers [4], verification time, audit error and most importantly, the isolated centralized databases which do not talk to each other. This paper proposes a novel DKYC model, which is going to disrupt the current KYC implementations through distributed ledger technology and offers benefits such as lower transaction costs, with higher provenance, immutability, and transparency in transactions.

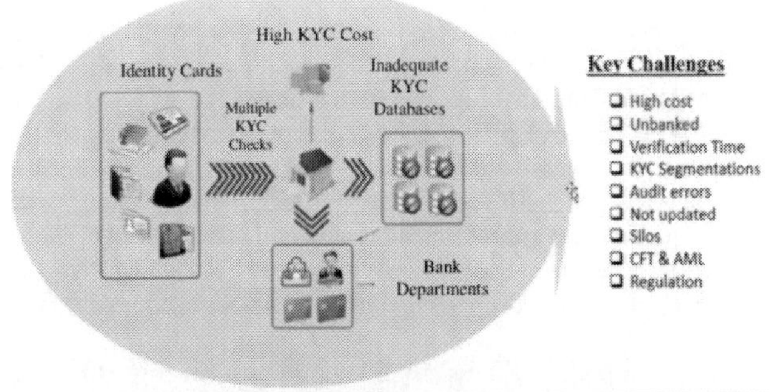

Figure 1. Know your customer

This paper is structured as follows; Sections I, II and III discuss the KYC challenges related to processes, implementations and regulatory implications in the financial sector. Sections IV and V explain our proposed model of distributed KYC (DKYC) solution. Section VI briefly highlights the viable incentive mechanisms, and Section VII summarizes the paper with key topics open for further study.

II. BACKGROUND ANALYSIS

In today's glo1bal economy, we live in a world where the users are in full control of their identity and are the sole authorizer to whom they may share their information. Know-Your-Customer has become pivotal in the digital world and large financial institutions need to identify ways to trust foreign banks and have more transparency into recipients' profile. Most financial institutions are sticking to the conventional procedures of KYC [4] which are inefficient and convey an unpleasant consumer interaction with the long and arduous process that KYC entails. Also, because of the involvement of many parties in the traditional KYC processes, it becomes prone to flaws and human errors and is very inefficient. Following are the key market dynamics and barriers of the KYC processes [5]:

- Despite dramatic increases in headcount and spend, KYC resource remains the greatest challenge to financial institutions

- The largest financial institutions ($10billion+ turnover) have seen average spend on KYC-related procedures increase from $142m in 2016 to $150m in 2017
- The number of financial institutions employees working on KYC adherence has rocketed from an average of 68 in 2016 to 307 in 2017
- Despite the rise in headcount, a third (34%) of financial institutions report that a lack of resources remains the biggest challenge in conducting KYC and customer because of diligence processes
- Financial institutions claim that on average it takes 26 days to onboard a new client, up from 24 days in our 2016 survey. However, corporate customers claim that on average it takes 32 days
- Financial institutions expect onboarding times to rise again by 12% in the next year

Many of the barriers can be eased with the adoption of state-of-the-art technology that can revolutionize this process both for the institution and the user. By using distributed ledger-based KYC [6], which can be shared by multiple banks, we are looking at a game-changing, innovative process that will reduce the burden of many processes and also provide more transparency and visibility let alone an enhanced user-friendly environment for KYC. We make identity verification secure and accessible on-demand.

Example KYC implementations using blockchain technology:

TABLE I. KYC IMPLEMENTATIONS

Company	Description
Argos Solution [7]	Argos provides KYC form submission and screening for errors and fraud cases. It also provides checkups on the customer lists with our AML global watch lists and targeted profile investigation and risk leveling. AML report publishing and Whitelist finalization. HQ in South Korea.
KYC-Chain [8]	A B2B managed workflow application that enables organizations to manage their KYC processes for individuals and corporates. It provides a solution to streamline the onboarding process for the customer. Review and process incoming KYC applications by streamlining workflow and automating the screening and verification process. HQ in Hong Kong.
Tradle [9]	KYC on blockchain provider. Aims to build a global trust provisioning network to give retail, wealth, SME and institutional customers of financial institutions access to capital and risk allocation. Uses pre-integrated vendor products such as biometrics, ID scanning, sanctions, and PEPs checkers. HQ in New York.
KYC Legal [10]	Provides blockchain KYC document verification through a mobile application, and verification of identity and documents with a KYC LEGAL agent. After verification into the blockchain, the user can use the stored data to verify identification for multi-purposes. The application is available for iOS and Android mobile devices. Provides B2B and B2C services. Offices in Berlin, San Francisco, and Moscow.
Confirm [11]	The company's platform uses algorithms and big data analysis to provide data on blockchain transactions and parties. It provides an AML Platform that offers anti-money laundering (AML) products for companies and financial institutions operating in the cryptocurrency ecosystem. Provides an end-to-end know your customer solution covering entities' activity in the crypto ecosystem. HQ in London, UK.

III. Regulatory Frameworks

In this paper, have taken up the regulatory part to shed some light on how regulatory challenges affect the growth of DKYC based blockchain model. It is important to compare the traditional framework [2] with the perceived updated one across jurisdictions and the ways by which it makes compliance to allow decentralized growth. This will help us to form an adjustable framework that complies with all existing compliance models and can be changed regarding the jurisdiction in question.

A. Customer Case Studies

Because of the decentralized nature of our platform, it is difficult to formulate a common and adjustable framework, as different individuals and entities from different parts of the world will need separate frameworks for establishing KYC compliant infrastructure. An individual from the Eurozone in need of a GDPR compliant KYC/AML[12] framework cannot pass the legal hurdles with the local authorities when provided with an AML/CFT II framework established by the U.S. Regulatory Framework Act. Thus, there is a need for simplification of complexities of frameworks, as the traditional KYC model discourages knowledge transfer from one to another, limiting the exchange of value, information and ideas.

B. Frameworks

Most countries follow a similar KYC/AML framework [13], all taking its roots from either the European or the American standard of compliance. Most organizations have an inefficient system of asking for KYC/AML [6] documents separately, each time a new customer comes in. This model is flawed and inefficient as the same person might have to submit the same documents again and again with different entities throughout their lifetime, and inefficient on the business side and it brings in extra costs. By forming a common framework by which both sides can do away with this repetitive process, millions, if not billions can be saved in operating costs around the globe. 2015 saw a continued rise in regulatory frameworks developed by governing bodies [14] with a key focus area for management, finance, registration, and authentication. Know Your Customer (KYC) and anti-money laundering regulations are becoming important to help businesses protect themselves from identity theft, money laundering and financing terrorism. Incidents like the one above, are all too common and the costs of complying with KYC's anti-corruption due diligence procedures are high.

According to the International Monetary Fund [15], incidents involving money laundering, compliance violations of KYC regulations, and other breaches are estimated to cost between two and five percent of the world's gross domestic product. The compliance with the regulatory frameworks (as illustrated in Figure 2) such as AML/CFT, Basel III, MiFID II, PSD2, GDPR is imperative for any KYC solution both at state and/or country level.

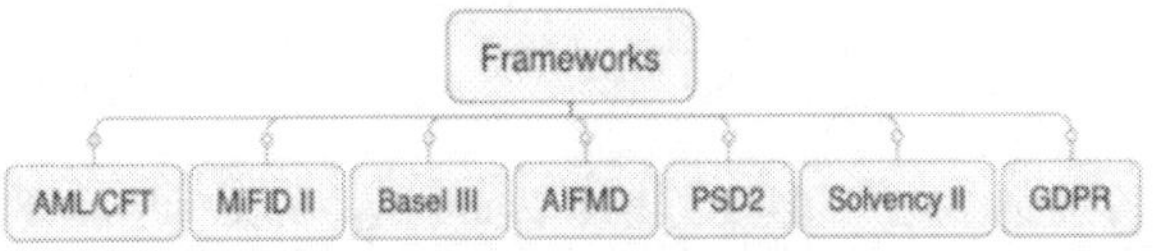

Figure 2. Regulatory Frameworks

The frameworks differ from area to area, depending on the perceived needs of the authorities to discourage unethical and unlawful practices. There are innumerable challenges when coming up with a common framework that is adjustable depending on the area and situation. Therefore, it is of utmost importance to show a robust KYC/AML framework with enough privacy, management, and oversight that ultimately understands and mitigates non-compliance and AML risks.

C. Other Compliance Costs

A financial institution spends on an average of about $50 million a year on KYC related expenses [16], with larger institutions going as high as $150 million dollars. Our aim is to propose a DKYC model to cut these costs that are associated with the tedious process of traditional KYC. The major cost that DKYC might incur is the registration with Governments of various countries. Each country has its own KYC norms that need undivided attention to detail as the subtle difference can lead to scrupulous outcomes. A research team will be necessary to go through the details of each country one by one to be thorough in all respects.

IV. DKYC Model

KYC forms (as depicted in Figure 3) are complex and contain lots of information related to the customer including Name, Birth Dates, Addresses, Income, etc. And as most of the information is dynamic in nature, the update process is very tedious and complex. In our study we have examined the data requirements of KYC, to understand the structured relationships and how it can be captured and reshaped through the DKYC model. There will be two different major segmentations, which hold and serve the Individuals KYC and Business KYC, and subsequently, both segments have different treatments.

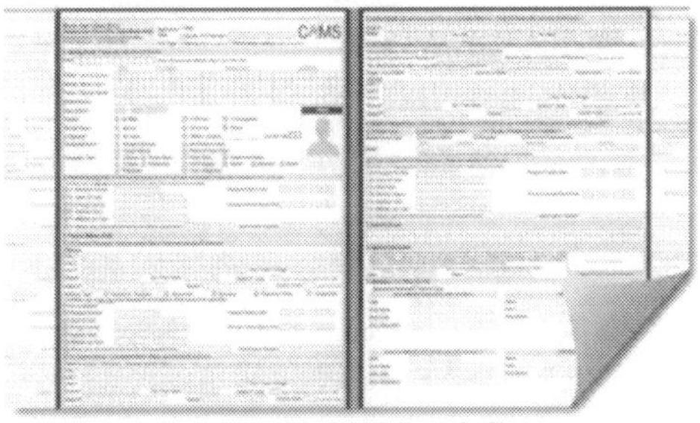

Figure 3. KYC Sample Form

Traditional KYC is based on the Pull mechanism where the customer information captured while onboarding the customer. DKYC supports both the Push (customer sending information to the service provider) and the Pull models (bank or service provider seeking an update on customer profile) with customer consent on what, where and whom he/she would like to share the information.

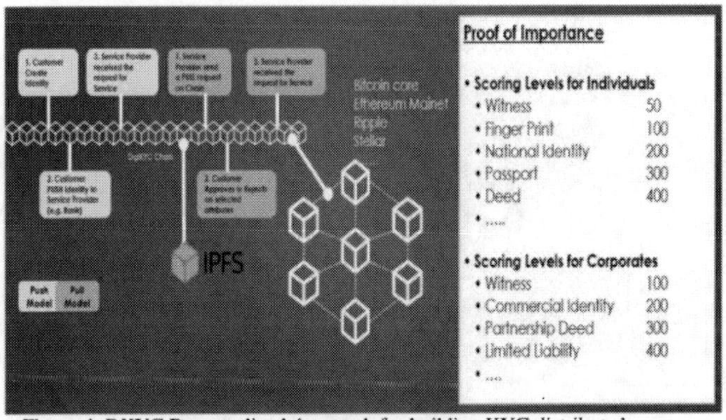

Figure 4. DKYC Decentralized Approach for building KYC distributed network

As illustrated in Figure 4, the typical scenario starts when a customer creates his/her identity on the chain and likes to push his/her information to the service provider for example to create a bank account. Bank will validate the request through the chain and start the customer onboarding. DKYC will be a public blockchain where anyone without geographical restriction joins the identity platform. We will apply Proof of Importance consensus algorithm to establish a scoring mechanism where existing conventional identities establishments e.g. Civilian Identities, Regulators, National Security Numbers, other private sector identities stores can also participate and part of the network to set the scoring. For example, from an Individuals segment, anyone can join the network by having the basic form of proof is "peer witnesses", however, the score is 50.

If the customer provides his fingerprint (which is unique in the world), his/her score in the DKYC chain will increase to 100. Similarly, if the customer provides the National Identity proof than his/her score will increase to 200. And A similar mechanism applies to a business establishment where the score will increase based on the maturity of their proof of importance starting from peer witnesses to commercial identity, etc.

Now the service providers when they would like to pull identity of an Individual or Business, they will send the request and after the consent from the Individual/Business, the selected information will be shared with the service provider to complete his/her business transactions (e.g. creating an account). In our model, scoring sensitivity would be selected by the Service Provider (e.g. banks, stocks, etc.) depending on the Service to Offer. For example, bank open accounts with score 50 and lend when the score is greater than 150. In this way everyone either small or big and regardless of their income they can be part of the network and present the proof of identity.

V. SOLUTION ARCHITECTURE

As per the segmentation, there would be two different end-users of this DKYC Model one for retail/consumer referred to as DKYC Individual and another one for Business referred to as DKYC Business. On the DKYC public chain, every Individual or Business identities represented by the unique address which will be used in the chain for the business processes interactions and workflows.

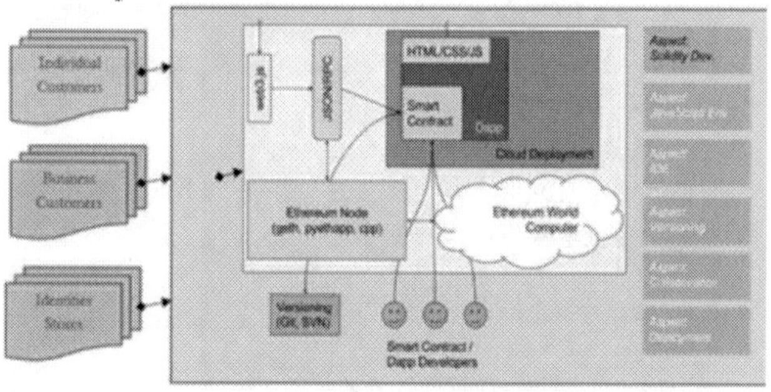

Figure 5. DKYC Solution Architecture

Proposed technology stack includes a hard-fork of the current Ethereum mainnet (development architecture illustrated in Figure 5) and adds customizations such as replacing the gas fee with the transaction-based fee which will be based on the transaction and paid by the requestor, with specific smart contracts to cover following high level use cases (listed in Table II). However, at the application layer, we will keep our development frameworks like the Ethereum development architecture (illustrated in Figure 5) where the community may use the existing platforms for dApp design, integrations, and developments. In a typical workflow, a customer will create his identity first time and pay the transaction fee for peer witnessing nodes, when the customer adds his/her fingerprint or national identity or passport, he or she will pay the verification node of civilian oracles node (onetime) and the record will be part of blockchain database. Moving forward for any network transaction the approving node will receive the benefits of service. Following are the list of Key Use Cases:

TABLE II. USE CASES

No.	Use Cases Name (Transactions Types)	Requestor
1	Customer Onboarding Use Case	Customer
2	Business Onboarding Use Case	Business
3	Verification Use Case	Any Entity
4	Risk Notifications Use Case	Customer or Business
5	Annual Profile Review Use Case	Customer or Business
6	Retire Record Use Case	Customer or Business
7	Activate Record Use Case	Customer or Business
8	Customer Consent Use Case	Customer or Business

VI. INCENTIVE MODELS

We have explored multiple incentivized business models, where CAPEX would be covered through seed funding or ICO. However, OPEX is incentivized by node subscriptions, network usage fee or extrinsic token-based fees. Figure 6 explains the key CAPEX and OPEX based models, which will be selected as per the applicable law in the jurisdiction. At the beginning of the project, CAPEX fundraising shall be done through Seed or ICO, whereas in OPEX several business model options are available such as collecting fees from nodes subscription, or charging a fee based on network usage and lastly we can also explore the applicability of fungible tokens.

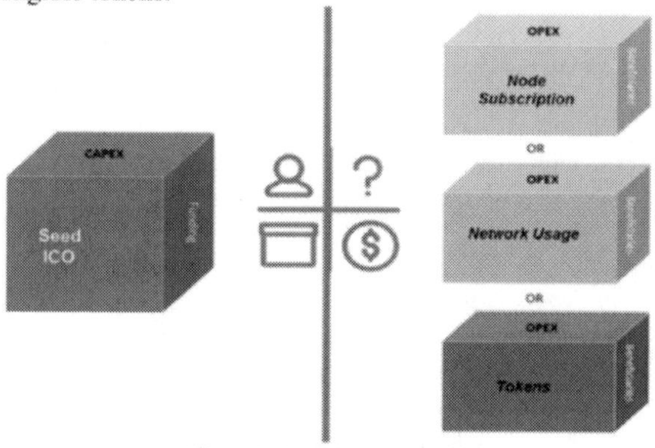

Figure 6. Incentive Approaches

VII. CONCLUSION

In our exploratory approach, we have tried to identify the core problems that current traditional KYCs databases are facing and how advances of blockchain could revolutionize the whole identity ecosystem (in trustless digital world) and bring the privacy control back to the end-users or end-customers where they will leverage the DKYC as decentralize, transparent, and trust-based know your customer. The open areas for research are; to address challenges such as fraud protection using artificial intelligence, creating the devices' identity, dApps application models, on-chain/off-chain oracles, performance and the blueprint for decentralized score-based KYC.

REFERENCES

[1] S. Nakamoto, "Bitcoin: A Peer-to-Peer Electronic Cash System."

[2] KELVIN DICKENSON, "The Future of KYC – How Banks Are Adapting to Regulatory Complexity," Opus.com, 2018. [Online]. Available: https://www.opus.com/future-of-kyc/. [Accessed: 02-Sep-2019].

[3] LILY HAY NEWMAN, "How Hackers Pulled Off a $20 Million Mexican Bank Heist | WIRED," Wired.com, 2019. [Online]. Available: https://www.wired.com/story/mexico-bank-hack/. [Accessed: 02-Sep-2019].

[4] AFI, "KYC Innovations, Financial Inclusion and Integrity," no. March, pp. 1–103, 2019.

[5] Refinitiv, "KYC compliance: the rising challenge for financial institutions," p. 33, 2019.

[6] J. Parra Moyano and O. Ross, "KYC Optimization Using Distributed Ledger Technology," Bus. Inf. Syst. Eng., vol. 59, no. 6, pp. 411–423, 2017.

[7] "Product | Argos Solutions," Argos Solutions, 2019. [Online]. Available: https://argos-solutions.io/product/. [Accessed: 02-Sep-2019].

[8] KYC-Chain, "What is Know Your Customer (KYC) and how does it affect your business? - KYC-Chain," KYC-Chain, 2019. [Online]. Available: https://kyc-chain.com/what-is-know-your-customer-kyc-and-how-does-it-affect-your-business/. [Accessed: 02-Sep-2019].

[9] Tradle.io, "Tradle. Trust provisioning on blockchain.," Tradle.io, 2019. [Online]. Available: https://tradle.io/. [Accessed: 02-Sep-2019].

[10] KYC.Legal, "KYC - Blockchain user verification," KYC.legal, 2019. [Online]. Available: https://kyc.legal/faq-en. [Accessed: 02-Sep-2019].

[11] Coinfirm, "Coinfirm Reports," coinfirm, 2019. [Online]. Available: https://www.coinfirm.com/resources/coinfirm-reports. [Accessed: 02-Sep-2019].

[12] SUMSUB.COM, "5 Most Important AML Compliance Laws You Need In 2019 | SumSub.com," SUMSUB.com, 2019. [Online]. Available: https://sumsub.com/blog/aml-compliance-laws/. [Accessed: 02-Sep-2019].

[13] D. Mulligan, "Know Your Customer Regulations and the International Banking System: Towards a General Self-Regulatory Regime," Fordham Int. Law J., vol. 22, no. 5, pp. 2324-, 1998.

[14] International Telecommunications Union, Digital financial services: Regulating for financial inclusion - an ICT perspective. 2016, 2016.

[15] FATF, "Money Laundering - Financial Action Task Force (FATF)," FATF, 2019. [Online]. Available: https://www.fatf-gafi.org/faq/moneylaundering/. [Accessed: 02-Sep-2019].

[16] John Callahan, "Council Post: Know Your Customer (KYC) Will Be A Great Thing When It Works," Forbes, 2018. [Online]. Available: https://www.forbes.com/sites/forbestechcouncil/2018/07/10/know-your-customer-kyc-will-be-a-great-thing-when-it-works/#47624be48dbb. [Accessed: 02-Sep-2019].